37 CD-BZE-6607

EDUCATION, POLITICS, AND BILINGUALISM IN TEXAS

José E. Vega

UNIVERSITY
PRESS OF
AMERICA

Copyright © 1983 by
University Press of America, Inc."
P.O. Box 19101, Washington, D.C. 20036

All rights reserved

Printed in the United States of America

Library of Congress Cataloging in Publication Data

Vega, Jose E.
  Education, politics, and bilingualism in Texas.

  Bibliography: p.
  1. Education, Bilingual--Law and legislation--Texas.
2. Education, Bilingual--Government policy--Texas.
I. Title.
KFT1595.3.V33 1983   344.764'0791   82-23734
ISBN 0-8191-2985-2   347.6404791
ISBN 0-8191-2986-0 (pbk.)

Dedicado
a
Mis Padres

Hispanic students are a rapidly growing presence in American public schools and are the dominant minority group already in a number of states. This study, of the most important Hispanic educational reform movement of the 1970's in the state which has traditionally been the most discriminatory toward Mexican-American children, substantially expands our knowledge of the political struggles that helped to shape the classroom experiences of hundreds of thousands of minority children who have not had their full measure of success in public education.

Advocates of bilingual education were struggling to address two very difficult problems--the well documented inequality of education for Mexican-merican children and the special problems of large numbers of children who simply could not understand what was going on in English language classrooms. In Texas, according to comparative statistics measuring many dimensions of discrimination, inequality was the most severe in the Southwest. The state government was firmly in the control of conservatives. Bilingual advocates were often seen to be challenging very important norms dealing the superiority of the national language and of American culture, and the need for the public schools to apply these norms to all. It was, to say the least, an unlikely setting for a successful reform movement within state government.

Adding to the difficulties was the fact that the reform which was proposed was essentially untested. Although the problems of Mexican-American education in Texas had been discussed for decades by Mexican-American organizations, scholars, the U.S. Civil Rights

Commission, and others, the solution--bilingual education--had only emerged as a serious proposal in the late sixties and early seventies. In fact, Texas Mexican-American organizations had historically fought separate "Mexican rooms" for Spanish-speaking children. There was very little research showing that bilingual education would, in fact, solve the problems associated with Mexican-American educational achievement when these issues were presented to the state legislature. The leaders of this movement had not only to convince Texas leaders to accept far-reaching educational changes, but also had to accept the value of the changes on faith.

Vega's analysis is not only a fascinating and important contribution on policy making for a very important minority community, but also adds significantly to the study of state education policy making. Although all scholars in education policy know that the state and local agencies are the dominant sources of funds and policy for public eduction, there is far more attention given to federal policy. What happens in Austin, Sacramento and a handful of other state capitals will be of decisive importance to the future of Mexican-American education. A particularly interesting aspect of this study is Vega's treatment of the complex relationship between the federal courts and the state government in the evolution of state legislation. The obvious importance of this work should encourage parallel research in other states.

Gary Orfield
Professor of Political Science,
Public Policy, and Education
THE UNIVERSITY OF CHICAGO

TABLE OF CONTENTS

Table of Contents (continued)

x

CHAPTER I

INTRODUCTION

Politics, education and policy-making are all inextricably interconnected aspects of human behavior (Abernathy and Coombe, 1965). The explicit and matter-of-fact assertion of this statement, however, does not necessarily represent an accurate portrait of reality or a consensus of opinion among professional educators, legislators and citizens regarding the actual role which politics plays in the determination of local, state and national educational policy-making. The notion that politics and education were mutually exclusive processes had generally been the widely shared, though unspoken, cardinal of faith of both educators and scholars from the 1890's until the sixth decade of the twentieth century. The dichotomization of politics and education and the myth that evolved regarding the inviolate nature of education was not accidental nor has it been the product of some rational thought process. The myth and its subsequent effects on our present educational system can be traced to the turbulent economic, social and institutional forces which significantly altered the educational structure and policy-making patterns in the nation's large, industrial urban centers at the end of the nineteenth century (Iannaccone and Lutz, 1970).

The concentration of manufacturing enterprises in the core of cities and the simultaneous development of a capitalistic economy contributed to the rapid growth of some of the largest urban centers in the United States between 1800 and 1920. Increased economic prosperity during this period gave birth to and nurtured a burgeoning new class of business elite imbued with the practices and values of scientific management which had been introduced and espoused by Frederick W. Taylor. The rapid social and ethnic differentiation in the cities resulting from the increased immigration of southern and eastern Europeans, the exploitation of these groups by industrial conglomerates, the corruption and inefficient system of city government and the fear that the basic democratic ideology and Protestant character of American society was about to disappear, contributed to the first phase of what became known as the Progressive Movement, 1900 to 1914 (Hofstadter, 1955; Callahan, 1962).

According to Hays (1964), this period of reform was largely the initiative of upper class, advanced professional and large business groups who wanted to take formal political power from the lower and middle class groups in the city in order to advance their own ethical, moral and business views on public policy. Guided by the principles of scientific management, which placed heavy emphasis on the maximization of human productivity, the reformist mentality contributed to a highly centralized form of

1

government with limited popular representation, placing the decision-making process in the hands of allegedly impartial, highly dedicated and expert administrators.

Banfield and Wilson, in contrast, described the Reform Movement as being largely inspired by an Anglo-Saxon Protestant ethos which viewed public service as a proper place for demonstrating political integrity and selfless interest in serving the public. This meant that only the best qualified men would decide policy and its implementation would be the job of experts, such as superintendents, who would be left free to manage highly centralized organizations. Interference in public affairs for private of other vested interests would not be tolerated for fear that they would compromise the public good (Banfield, 1963).

It became evident to these "administrative progressives" that education needed to be sheltered from "politics" and its noxious consequences. Impressed with the new advances which business conglomerates had achieved in adopting efficient management standards, educators readily assumed that similar standards were applicable to education. As a result education decision-making became centralized in boards of education whose members were viewed as miniature factories, where children were seen as raw materials, teachers as laborers, and the principal and superintendent as managers. Emphasis was placed on cost per pupil ratios, accurate record keeping, and the adoption of measurable standards (Callahan, 1962; Tyack, 1974).

The belief that educational governance and policy-making were two distinct functions persisted until the late 1950's. In 1959, Thomas H. Eliot urged that the "taboo" which had been placed on politics and public school governance by educator and scholar "be exorcised, for the future of public education" (Eliot, 1959). Eliot convincingly argued that public schools were established by elected officials, that they constituted a part of government and that, therefore, they were an area which could be profitably studied by political scientists. He suggested that educators, school board members and legislators were all engaged in making governmental decisions as well as actively participating in covert and explicit kinds of activities which were designed to gain and keep the power to make authoritative educational decisions. In essence, politics was very much a part of the educational structure and therefore very much a subject for research and analysis (Eliot, 1959).

The analysis of education as a political process largely came from the perspective insights of political scientists such as David Easton and Thomas H. Eliot in the late 1950's. Easton analyzed the school as an agent of political socialization (Easton, 1957). Eliot followed by specifically delineating the need for research in public school politics at the local, state and federal level (Eliot, 1959). In spite of the long and scholarly tradition which had preceded this renewed interest in education as a political process, very little was written about it prior to the early 1960's.

Several reasons are given for this dearth of interest and research in the politics of education. Eliot has suggested that the governance of schools was not considered a worthwhile enterprise among political scientists. In addition, politics as well as political scientists were considered anathema by most professional educators. The negative attitude, he proposes, might have come from the gratuitous suggestions to educators by political scientists that school systems merge with other local governing units such as cities and towns, and that the heads of state departments of education be appointed by the governor rather than being in the hands of a semi-independent board (Eliot, 1959). Masters, on the other hand, has argued that educators in important positions deliberately perpetuated the myth in order to discourage any serious inquiry into their political behavior (In Iannaccone and Lutz, 1970).

V.O. Key (1961) suggested that the decentralized structure of education in the United States detracted attention to its potential significance. Moreover, Easton felt that the way political science was conceptualized as a discipline, in addition to its special concern with the study of power and normative political theory, were also important factors (Easton, 1957). Other observers have attributed the neglect in the politics of education to the low status of education, the non-controversial nature of education, the preoccupation of political scientists with other forms of politics and finally, to the notion developed during the Reform period that politics be taken out of education.

Development of the politics of education as a field for research and teaching is believed to have begun shortly after the Second World War. Legislators at all levels, pressured by steadily increasing public demands, began to question the unlimited and constantly increasing budgetary demands of educators without the accompanying evidence to justify the requests. Secondly, increased federal and state intervention in education made an abundant amount of otherwise unavailable data accessible to the interested researcher. This unexpected event, in turn, encouraged research into new areas which had previously not been studied (Kirst and Mosher, 1969).

Other social and political events which occurred during the 1960's contributed to and accelerated the interest in politics, education and policy-making as an area worthy of serious study.

It is suggested by Harman (1974) that the greatest impetus for research in this area came from educational administration scholars, who, increasingly attracted to the role of politics in society, had become more cognizant of the interrelatedness of different social and political institutions.

In 1959, Eliot recommended that studies be undertaken on the "pressures on the legislatures and their responses." He prognosticated that the future role of state legislatures on educational issues would probably escalate, making profound changes on the course of educational policy. He suggested that useful findings could be obtained from comparative studies on states. The works of Stephen K. Bailey, et al. (1962), Nicholas Masters, et al. (1964), and Michael Usdan, et al. (1963) were early responses to Eliot's suggestion.

Since 1965 considerable attention has been given to studying the effects of increased federal involvement in education (Berke and Kirst, 1972). Other studies have focused on the enactment process (Meranto, 1967). The influence of linguistic and cultural minorities on the educational policy-making at the federal level in the mid 1960's is another aspect of the politics and education matrix which has until recently gained more interest among educators (Sanchez, 1973; Schneider, 1976). In this present study attention has focused on the phenomenon of ethnic group politics and its effects on state educational curriculum policy-making.

Statement of the Problem

Introduction

Federal support for general and specific educational reforms, such as bilingual education, increased considerably during the 1960's and 1970's. Moreover, state governments have increasingly assumed a greater role in educational leadership, support and control of such programs (Mosher and Wagoner, 1978). Since the enactment of the Bilingual Education Act of 1968, twenty-six states have passed similar education laws which either permit or mandate the use of bilingual education instruction for public school children with limited English-speaking competence (A Study of State Programs in Bilingual Education, 1977). In spite of this continued interest on behalf of linguistically and culturally different children in many states, little research has linked the process of ethnic group political behavior to educational legislative policy outcomes in the states which have enacted such laws.

4

Why was the first mandatory bilingual education law enacted in Massachusetts and not in Texas? Were the tactics and aims of the various groups who supported this kind of legislation the same or different? How did such things as government structure, attitudes or the political environment in each state influence the organization and strategy of these pressure groups? What was the nature and extent of the federal influence on those states which enacted language education laws? These and other questions dealing with bilingual education interests and policy outcomes have not been examined. The literature of politics and education has given this phenomenon scant attention.

On the other hand, ethnic related politics has been a major theme in political science. In the eastern and northern sections of the United States the persistence of cultural, religious or linguistic similarities has often been the basis for political organization (Handlin, 1944). The character and persistence of ethnicity in American society has most often been measured in terms of election results and benefits (Bailey and Katz, 1969). Since the early 1920's social scientists were convinced that it was only a matter of time before cultural distinctions based on language, religion or some other ethnic associated belief system would disappear (Wirth, 1928). Efforts to explain the causes of Black activism and its impact on other minorities during the 1960's, however, challenged the commonly accepted notions of assimilation and political pluralism in American life (Litt, 1970).

Ethnic group politics has been a distinctive feature of Texas political history since the earliest days of the Republic. It has been noted that although Texans have had "little cause to be obsessed about the Negro," as has been the case in Missippi, they have been concerned about "Mexicans" (Key, 1949, 254). Social and political voluntary associations such as the League of United Latin-American Citizens and American G.I. Forum have often played a major role in articulating the concerns and demands of Mexican-Americans in Texas since the mid 1920's (Garcia, 1973). Among the many social concerns of Mexican-Americans, education has always been a high priority. The need to improve the educational status of the Mexican-American has never been a disputed issue. The differing views regarding the role of language and culture in the public school curriculum, however, have often been the basis for contention among Chicanos and Anglos.

The use of another language other than English as a medium of instruction in elementary public schools was a common practice in Texas dating back to 1926. Yet it was not until 1969, after the persistent efforts of two Mexican-American legislators, that the legislature authorized the use of another language other than

English for instructional purposes. Texas had the greatest number of bilingual programs in the United States prior to 1968, and a considerably long history of bilingual schooling. However, it was not until 1973 that the Texas legislature enacted a mandatory bilingual education law (Zamora, 1977).

The historical evidence suggests that statewide and local politics in Texas has been affected by the ethnic factor. Likewise, ethnic group tactics have been influenced by the political culture of the state. While the ethnic basis for political organizations in northern and eastern states have been temporary, in Texas the ethnic factor has been an historic phenomenon. Finally, the evidence seems to suggest that the most recent state legislative enactments on behalf of Mexican-Americans have been a reflection of the unique political ambiente, as well as an explicit demonstration of the nature and extent of the federal influence.

Purpose of the Study

The purpose of this study was to analyze and describe the genesis and enactment of the Texas Bilingual Education and Training Act of 1973. The study sought to identify the factors that contributed to the passage of this legislation, and to examine the nature and extent of influence which the federal Bilingual Education Act of 1968 may have had on the passage of this state law.

Significance of the Study

The great bulk of the literature on state educational policy-making has dealt with the influence of professional groups and elites on the legislative process and their effects on the level of state funding. Research on the federal influence on state educational innovation has judged the success or failure of federal programs according to pre-conceived federal criteria. Most studies have ignored the phenomenon of ethnic political participation and its effect on state legislative policy outcomes in the field of bilingual education.

Fishman suggested that there was a need to know how the various parties interested in bilingual education legislation went "about trying to get their way: proposing, compromising, bargaining, threatening, influencing, rationalizing, withdrawing or advancing, and their reasons, public or private, for so doing" (Fishman, 1977, 2). The need was all the more pressing because "most of the recent policy decisions concerning U.S. bilingual education have remained largely undocumented in terms of the processes and pressures that transpired in connection with them

..." (Fishman, 1977, 1).

Lacking in the research literature is documentation of the factors which led various state legislatures, in this case, Texas, to redefine the government's role in education, and most particularly in terms of the language of instruction. What prompted Texas legislators to revise old statutes which prohibited the use of any language other than English as a medium of instruction in public schools? What factors account for the acceptance of demands by ethnic group leaders that their language be used as a legitimate medium of instruction in Texas? How were these groups able to obtain funds from the Texas legislature for bilingual programs? These and other questions assisted in determining the kind of research design and the procedures used in this study.

Methodology and Procedures

Research efforts in the politics of education have been disappointing because the area lacks a theoretical framework and a methodology capable of analyzing the vast amount of data which has been collected (Wirt, 1977). Political science and education research have not provided any clear and satisfactory methods for observing "politico-educational" interactive patterns and their analysis in a systematic manner (Kirst and Mosher, 1969). It has been suggested that what is needed is a new theory which would enable social scientists to generate new propositions about causal relations among the many factors in the environment of school politics. The theory would not only account for observable difference, but whether these differences can be adequately explained within the context of an ever-changing political arena (Wirt, 1977).

Furthermore, Wirt suggests that what is needed is "a better specified and defined concept of the patterns of interaction between state and school" (Wirt, 1977, 407). Clarifying the conceptual meanings of "politics" and "education," he contends, would contribute immensely to the future direction which can be taken in the politics of education as a field of study.

The politics of education as a field of study, however, is plagued with the same problems and drawbacks found in other social sciences. The problem stems in part from the penchant of social scientists to apply the same rigorous procedures of scientific experimentation on research in human behavior. Research on human behavior is, however, far more complex to investigate than the physical sciences. Three factors contribute to this complexity in social science research. First, the stimulus to which an individual is exposed is likely to be complex. Second, the way a stimulus is processed will differ from one person to another.

Third, the manner in which any individual is likely to react to any given stimulus is also highly complex (Borg and Gall, 1971). Another problem for social science research is that most of it is essentially ex post facto research. The researcher has no control over the phenomena under observation. Therefore, he must work from the dependent variable back to the independent variable to try to disentangle the myriad variables that may have contributed to the event. Then he must make some meaningful though tentative propositions about what, how and why something occurred (Kerlinger, 1973).

All of the work to date on the politics of education has been done in this ex post facto mode. The knowledge derived from such studies, however, is no less valuable simply because the methods are not exact and the theories fail to offer adequate explanation. It is optimistically suggested that to a great extent the problems encountered in politics of education research are not too different from those experienced by any new social science attempting to isolate and investigate new areas of human behavior. Thus, while every effort should be made to derive a new methodology, high expectations for such a breakthrough should not be entertained too seriously. Such prospects would only have the effect of clouding the possible contributions which education and political science may still be able to make (Harman, 1974).

Thus far, research in the politics of education has utilized the methods and tools of survey research and the case study approach. In 1969, Kirst and Mosher recommended more macro-analysis research be undertaken, because of the low reliability of case studies. They suggested that a combination of the two approaches would probably yield a better picture of educational governance throughout the nation. They lamented the fact that although the need for "the systematic study of change in educational government" was needed, "many of the needed tools for the job" did not exist. The nature of this study, time limitations and the cost factor limited the present research to the historical study approach.

Research Methodology

To gain an in-depth understanding of how the Texas legislature responded to the demands of Mexican-Americans between 1969 and 1973 for bilingual education, an historical approach was employed. An historical study of the Texas legislature was used in order to ascertain how such factors as federal initiatives, ethnic demands for educational reform, or changes in the legislature affected the enactment of bilingual education legislation in Texas.

8

Conceptual Framework

The collection, organization and analysis of the data in this study was generally guided by Easton's general systems approach. Meranto's particular approach in his investigation of the enactment of the Elementary and Secondary Education Act of 1965 was used in this study (Easton, 1957 a, 1965 b; Meranto, 1967).

Meranto's model of legislative actions included two categories of environmental changes: circumstantial conditions and demand articulators. Circumstantial conditions referred to those unexpected changes in the political system which impinged on the policy-making process. Demand articulators identified those actors which directly affected the policy-making process through direct lobbying, letter writing and by votes. The model also called for an examination of those changes which occurred within the legislature itself. Figure 1 illustrates how some of the data obtained was meaningfully arranged.

The conceptual framework adopted for the study elicited four basic questions which served to guide the direction of the study.

1. What was the nature and extent of the federal government's influence as a circumstantial condition on the legislative process concerning bilingual education?

2. How did other circumstantial changes affect the response of the legislature toward new demands for bilingual education?

3. What role did ethnic group leaders and others play as demand articulators in directing the attention of the legislators towards bilingual education?

4. What role did changes in the legislature play in shaping the responses to the demands for bilingual education in the legislative process?

Data Collection

Pertinent primary and secondary historical documents were examined. These documents included the transcript of the proceedings during the regular legislative sessions as they are recorded in the House and Senate Journals. Copies of the House and Senate versions of the bilingual bills which were introduced were reviewed. Transcripts of the official positions and statements of the State Board of Education which were included in the

9

ENVIRONMENTAL CHANGES

A. CIRCUMSTANTIAL CONDITIONS

1. Bilingual Education Act of 1968

2. Office for Civil Rights May 25th Memorandum

3. Sharpstown Scandal

4. 1972 Elections

B. MAJOR DEMAND ARTICULATORS

1. Ethnic Group Influence:
   a) LULAC
   b) American G.I. Forum

2. Education Associations:
   a) TACAE
   b) TASB

3. Texas Education Agency

4. Governor's Office

LEGISLATIVE CHANGES

1. Election of Reform minded Legislature in 1972
   77 House Members
   15 Senators

NEW INPUTS --

2. New Legislative Leadership
   a) Speaker of the House Price Daniel, Jr.
   b) President of Senate William P. Hobby
   c) Governor Dolph Briscoe

NEW INPUTS -- 3. Collaboration of House and Senate Human Resources Committee Chairmen:

Carlos F. Truan: House
Chet Brooks: Senate

NEW OUTPUT-- TEXAS BILINGUAL EDUCATION AND TRAINING ACT OF 1973

Figure 1. Model of State Curriculum Policy-Making

Official Agenda were examined, and the reports which were issued by the Texas Education Agency on the subject of bilingual education were read. Reports by other gobernment agencies, position statements made by professional interest groups and other pertinent documents associated with the passage of the new law were also examined. Secondary sources included some of the state's important newspapers: The Texas Observer (Austin), The Dallas Morning News, Express-News (San Antonio), and The Chronicle (Houston). In addition, articles in national magazines and other newspapers were used for background information.

The major instrument employed for obtaining information about the events which transpired between 1969 and 1973 was the interview. A few of the key figures in the process were identified in some of the public documents which were reviewed in the early stages of the study. Other leading participants were identified by the reputational method. Nominations of participants were made by knowledgeable key actors in the decision-making process.

Participants were initially contacted by mail. The introductory letter was used to explain the purpose of the study and to ask whether the person would be willing to be interviewed. Favorable responses were followed up by telephone calls to determine a convenient place, date, and time in which to conduct the tape-recorded interview.

On several occasions interviews were conducted by telephone with those participants who could not be interviewed in person, because of their work schedules and the extra cost involved in having to meet with these individuals in separate parts of the state. Several of the respondents were interviewed more than once.

Those individuals interviewed included professional educators who were directly involved with lobbying efforts or sought by legislators and state education officials as consultants, legislators and their assistants who sponsored the bilingual bills, spokesmen for different professional lobbying organiztions, and the former and current commissioner of education for the state of Texas. Repeated attempts to talk to former governors Preston Smith and Dolph Briscoe were not successful. However, a telephone interview with one of former Governor Briscoe's administrative assistants was fruitful.

After some of the background information was reviewed and the key participants in the process were identified, questions were developed for the interviews. A semi-standardized interview schedule was used. The schedule allowed the interviewer to ask a number of major questions, while at the same time permitting freedom to probe. The major advantage of this kind of interview schedule was that it permitted a certain amount of uniformity, providing the investigator with a standard with which to cross validate the factual information, recollections, and the different perceptions of the respondents.

The following general questions are typical of those that were asked to all of the interviewees. Some of the questions were adapted from another study on the politics of school finance in the state of Wisconsin. The author of the study employed the same conceptual framework to investigate why and how a particular finance bill was enacted (Geske, 1975).

1. Circumstantial Conditions:

   a. What kinds of political changes in Texas prior to 1973 do you think might have aided in the enactment of the Bilingual Education and Training Act?

   b. What kind of influence, if any, do you think the federal government might have had in the enactment of this language related legislation?

2. Demand Articulators:

   a. How did Texas legislators become aware that bilingual instruction in some of its public schools was the best way to meet the educational needs of many Mexican-American school children?

   b. Can you recall what kind of role the governor played in endorsing and influencing the passage of the bilingual bill during the 63rd Legislature?

3. Legislative Changes:

   a. What legislative factors would you say aided in the passage of the bilingual bill during the 63rd Legislative session in contrast to the two previous legislative sessions?

   b. Can you tell me something about how agreements on particular events were reached?

Limitations

The study was limited by several difficulties. State documentation of legislative proceedings in Texas was limited to House and Senate Journals. The proceedings of public committee hearings were not available in written form. It was only during the "Reform" Legislature in 1973 that attempts were made to tape record House and Senate floor debates and committee hearings. The transcriptions of these tapes, however, were only available by request, and were not free to the public.

The research in most instances heavily relied on the recollections, perceptions and willingness of respondents to divulge accurate information on events which occurred six to ten years ago. For many respondents it was admittedly difficult to remember. For other individuals, the recollections were much more lucid.

Lastly, persons with intentions of conducting similar historical research should be prepared to allow a considerable amount of time to the interviewing schedule. The main problem encountered with this part of the research task was not the wilingness of the individuals to be questioned, but the time that they could devote to such interviews.

Outline of the Study

Chapter II will include a review of some of the literature pertaining to the role of the federal government in education, state educational policy studies, and policy analysis. Attention will be given to the literature on ethnicity and politics in the United States. Lastly, the literature on bilingual education will be discussed.

Chapter III will be a discussion of four major environmental factors which were identified as having played a major role in influencing the enactment of bilingual education legislation by the Texas Legislature between 1968 and 1972.

Chapter IV will describe the historical events which took place during the 61st (1969) and 62nd (1971) Legislative Sessions.

Chapter V will be a description of the factors which contributed to the enactment of the mandatory bilingual education law during the 63rd Legislature in 1973.

Chapter VI presents a summary, analysis and concluding remarks on the events which contributed to the enactment of bilingual education legislation between 1968 and 1973.

Chapter VII will describe and analyze subsequent lobbying attempts by bilingual education advocates to expand and strengthen bilingual education legislation since 1973.

CHAPTER II

REVIEW OF THE LITERATURE

In order to understand the development and nature of state legislative educational policy initiatives on behalf of linguistically and culturally different minorities since the early 1970's, we will review five aspects of the literature which are important for thepurposes of this study: first, the role and influence of the federal government in education; second, studies on the politics of education at the state level; third, recent thoughts on the analysis of public policy-making; fourth, some of the literature pertaining to ethnic group politics; and finally, the relevant literature in bilingual education.

The Federal Government and Education

The federal involvement in education has grown considerably in the past twenty years. Before the passage of the Elementary and Secondary Education Act in 1965, controversial matters such as segregation, government aid to parochial and private schools, and states' rights had been some of the major issues which had prevented increased federal involvement in educational policy-making at the state and local level (Tiedt, 1966).

Since 1785 to the present the role of the federal government has been limited to meeting specific problems on a national scale. In 1917, for example, the Smith-Hughes Vocational Assistance Program was enacted in response to a rapidly expanding industrial economy. Similarly, during the depression of the 1930's the federal government aided local schools by providing a free lunch program for needy school children (Allen, 1950). The federal government has also played a major role in the creation and continued expansion of public land grant colleges and universities as the nation grew from a small contingent of thirteen to fifty states (Babbidge and Rosenzweig, 1962).

In the mid-1950's interest in the nation's security as well as the successful Russian launching of the first satellite contributed to the enactment of the National Defense Education Act of 1958. The Act was intended to increase the nation's pool of scientists and engineers, believed at the time to be desperately low, by encouraging and strengthening instruction and interest in math, science and the study of languages (Sundquist, 1970). In 1963, the federal government's involvement with higher education increased even more with the passage of the Higher Education Academic Facilities Act (Pettit, 1965).

15

Perhaps the most important even in the history of the federal role in education has been the enactment of the Elementary and Secondary Education Act in 1965. Several works dealing with the history and political events of this act have been published (Eidenburg and Morey, 1969; McLaughlin, 1975; Barkin and Hettich, 1968). Meranto's (1967) analysis of the event, however, is particularly insightful. The authro not only explains the political and social forces which led to its successful passage, but he also provides a conceptual framework by which educational innovation can be examined within the American political system. Another very useful volume on the subject deals exclusively with the law's implementation by the United States Office of Education (Baily and Mosher, 1968).

The magnitude of this law is what distinguishes it from previous enactments of national significance. Through ESEA, the lawmakers were interested in fomenting education changes, in eradicating the nation's last vestiges of poverty and in strengthening the capacity of each state to educate its local citizens on the basis of equity. Its lofty purposes were one thing, its implementation and outcome in each state was an entirely different matter (Murphy, 1971).

The role of the federal government in local education efforts has not been achieved without conflict and serious objections. The nature of the issue is deeply rooted in the ideology of the American political system and its traditions. Autonomy and individualism are two highly valued ideals of American democracy. Economic dependence and lack of local control are not so favorably considered (Atkin, 1969). To others the problem is not whether the federal government should be involved in the education of its citizens, bu as to how extensive this involvement should actually be (Milstein, 1970).

Another area which has received attention by educators and political scientists has been studies on the actual impact of federal intervention to equalize the benefits and outcomes of education. The results of such evaluative studies have been mixed and not conclusive, mainly because the focus of analysis has primarily been directed at pupil achievement scores. Such was the case with Title I ESEA funds. Attached to this bill was the provision that appropriate instruments would be developed to evaluate the effectiveness of such programs in "meeting the special educational needs of culturally deprived children" (Wirt and Kirst, 1975, 157). Exclusive concentration on achivement scores by evaluators obscured the other politically salient objectives of Title I. Moreover, their reports rarely affected the voting patterns of Congressmen.

Research on the impact of federal aid to elementary and secondary schools has shown that the money has in fact not equalized the economic disparities between poor and rich school districts, or between states. In addition, the amount of such aid has been considered far too little to even make a tiny dent into the problems that afflected public education (Berke and Kirst, 1972).

The most recent controversy involving the goals and accomplishments of federal aid to local school districts has been the adoption of Title VII (Epstein, 1977). In 1968, Congress passed the Bilingual Education Act as an amendment to ESEA. The law directed that federal funds be spent on the education of non-English-speaking or limited English-speaking public school students. This time the federal government not only addressed itself to the issue of poverty, but it clearly articulated the government's first legislative policy statement on language and education. The act was directed specifically at public school children who, it was alleged, were not benefiting from the full education opportunity because they could not speak or understand English. There were other reasons, e.g., poverty or low self-esteem, but language difficulty was at the very heart of the bill (Schneider, 1976).

It should be noted that prior to the enactment of the Bilingual Education Act of 1968 there had been considerable federal judicial pronouncements on the constitutional rights of citizens, or persons under United States protection, and the use of non-English languages in businesses, and in public and private schools (Meyer v. Nebraska, 1923; Yu Cong Eng v. Trinidad, 1925; Farrington v. Tokushige, 1927; Mo Hock Ke Lock Po v. Stainback, 1944).

Federal involvement in American education dates back to the establishment of the republic. The expansion of the federal role in education is attributable to its response to specific national needs and the reassessment of its role by each generation of Americans. In the 1950's national security increased the federal role in education. During the decade of the sixties increased support for education came in response to economic and civil rights issues.

State Government and Education

According to the federal constitution, public school education is ultimately a state function and the pwer to establish an educational system resides in the legislature of the state. The legislature has the unrestricted right to prescribe the methods of education. The only instance where a state's power

17

over education con be contested is if the legislation goes contrary to state and federal constitutional provisions (Alexander, et. al., 1969). Since the early 1960's the state governments have also increased their support and control of education (Milstein and Jennings, 1973). Several reasons are suggested as having contributed to this trend.

The increased interest of the federal government in education, especially since the enactment of the ESEA of 1965, has encouraged state legislative bodies, through their education departments, to examine problems which had not been previously addressed or had been ignored. In line with the federal initiatives and incentives which were offered, the states began to critically look at the needs and past deficiencies in their educational systems which previously had not been defined nor considered problems. Another factor which contributed to this trend was the increasing unrest and dissatisfaction of the public regarding the educational system. The public included influential private citizens, progressive and highly critical scholars and disenchanted Black and Spanish-speaking minorities in the cities. Court cases (Brown v. Board of Education of Topeka, I and II, 1954 and 1955; Serrano v. Priest, 1970; Lau v. Nichols, 1974; Aspira v. N.Y.C. Board of Education, 1974) also encouraged legislative activity in such areas as finance, desegregation, equity education, the education of the handicapped and the linguistically different. Finally, what made educational innovation possible at the rate that it occurred was the federal dole and revenue surpluses of the early 1970's (James, 1976; Hurwitz, Jr. and Tesconi, Jr., 1972).

Increasing demands for public revenues and a splintering of education interest groups have also contributed to the active role of state government in educational policy-making (Milstein and Jennings, 1973). These trends in state educational policy-making, therefore, have enabled scholars to focus their research interests on several aspects of state politics because the changes occurring from state to state have been quite similar. These similarities, it is suggested, make it possible to compare the political activities of governors, state education commissions, pressure groups, legislatures, or any other aspect of state government to determine how these activities interact to affect the educational structure of the state.

The earliest studies on the politics of education at the level of the state were conducted by Bailey, et al. (1962), Usdan (1963) and Masters, et al. in 1964. These early research efforts concentrated on such things as structure and educational organization, how coalitions were made among the various conflicting interests and on how these interests exerted an influence on state governments. The education policy-making process was of minor concern to Usdan and Bailey. In the Master et al. study, reference was made about the permissible limits of political influence on public school policy which were determined by governors and legislators, but the legislative process per se was not the main interest.

Sometime after the passage of ESEA, Kirst and Iannaccone studied the impact of the politics of federal aid to education in Texas and Massachusetts. They compared the political behavior of the governor, legislature, urban school lobby and the state education agency in each state in an effort to determine to what extent federal aid would alter the local political milieu. They concluded that federal aid did little to bring about significant changes at the local district (Berke and Kirst, 1972).

In 1969, Milstein and Jennings attempted to augment the previous studies on the states by concentrating on the policy-making activities of government officials and the tactics of interest groups to influence these state officials. They also probed to ascertain how effective these external pressures were on the policy-making behavior of legislators (Milstein and Jennings, 1973). The findings of the study were significant in that they pointed to definite interactive patterns and how these forces were likely to change over time. The generalizability of these as well as other findings on state-education politics, however, is a problem which has as yet not been resolved. Although some identical interactive patterns have been isolated, the differences between the states make these few important insights relatively useless for constructing an adequate theory of politics and education among the states. The certainty of change in the politics further complicates studies in the area (Iannaccone, 1967).

Neigher the inherent dynamics of the political process nor the variations among states has prevented or discouraged political scientists and educators from studying the educational-political activities of public officials and private citizens at the local, state and federal levels. It has not dampened the enthusiasm of researchers in this area from encouraging each other to find an adequate methodology and a good theory that could account for change in the political behavior of those persons involved in educational policy-making (Wirt, 1977).

The financing and control of public schooling in the United States has been a function of state government. Increased federal assistance enabled state educational authorities and

19

VRJC LIBRARY

legislators to expand their educational services to more segments of the school population. Similar trends in educational policy-making among the states encouraged political scientists to study the dynamics of politics and education at the state level.

Public Policy-making

Interest in the formation of policy as a suitable area for social science inquiry shortly after World War II coincided with similar interests in the politics of education (Kirst and Mosher, 1969). The area of policy-analysis was assisted by long established planning procedures in government as well as by the development of new decision-making paradigms (Ukeles, 1977).

Policy planning in governmental agencies such as the defense and state departments was a long standing tradition. The increased involvement of the federal government in domestic affairs during the 1960's led to increased investment in research and analysis in order to cope with such things as urban problems, highway construction and the elimination of poverty. The push to solve the ills of American society in a rational and more systematic manner increased the need to have newer and better ways of obtaining adequate and abundant information on which to base policy-making decisions (Ukeles, 1977).

In 1951, Lasswell called for "the development of a science of policy forming and execution" that would shed light on how policy was made as well as providing the necessary intelligence to guide the policy-making process (Ukeles, 1977). Seventeen years later, Dror suggested that there was no need for policy-makers in the twentieth century to be making unwise policies. He confidently believed that systematic, scientific inquiry could be harnessed to reform the policy-making process (Dror, 1968). The effects of this new focus have been significant, but "policy analysis has failed to develop a unique methodology specifically appropriate to public sector policy problems" (Ukeles, 1977, 226).

Lindblom (1968) characterized the policy-making process as being highly complex and non-systematic. For a few purposes, the process could consist of a well ordered sequence of steps designed to make the best choice among many alternatives. This way of looking at policy, however, obscured the political aspects inherent in the process, its apparent disorder and the different policies which actually resulted. He proposed to look at policy-making as a process which had neither an alpha nor an omega. Policies were clearly the result of a myriad number of forces.

In a ten-year study conducted by Bauer, Pool and Dexter (1968) on foreign trade policy-making in Congress, they found that policy-making was not the orderly, rational procedure it was conceived to be by political scientists. Neither problem formulation nor the decisions which were eventually made were the producets of some ordered, deliberate behavior by any of the participants. To the contrary, they found that lobbyist efforts to pressure congressmen were restrained compared to the generally accepted notions of such tactics. Some lobbyists, to their surprise, were just as ignorant as to where they could exert the most useful influence.

The result of the study cast serious doubts on the patently accepted notions of steam-cooker political influence peddling on congressmen, and on the actual effectiveness of special interest groups in articulating their positions. They concluded that public institutions functioned best when they were accepted by a concensus of the society, and when they permitted compromise, adjudication, bargaining and deals. "They operate best when sharp breaks in the customary way of doing things are rare and introduced gradually" (Bauer, Pool and Dexter, 1968, 489). The findings and some of the conclusions of this study may share a close and significant resemblance to the way policy-making occurs at the state legislative level.

Unobtrusive introduction of controversial legislation, such as an education bill specifically related to the education problems of one particular group, may have been a tactic of the supporters of the mandated bilingual education law which was passed in Texas in 1973. It should be noted that the introduction and passage of similar laws in other states met with virtually no opposition from organized groups or politicians. One possible exception to this may have been the enactment of Colorado's bilingual-bicultural education law in 1975 and its reauthorization in 1977 ("Bilingual Battling," 1977).

Public policy-making has been defined as "A purposive course of action followed by an actor or set of actors in dealing with a problem or matter of concern" (Anderson, 1975, 3). The problem with this definition is that it fails to account for the unanticipated policies. It implies that policies spring from some problem pool, are selected and are subsequently dealt with by the affected parties. Studies in human political behavior have not corroborated this ordered pattern.

Mann (1975) accepted a definition of public policy that encompassed "the content of most academic fields, their inter-relationships, and all the real-world behavior they represent" (11). He distinguished policy-problems as being public in nature, consequential, complex, dominated by uncertainty, and lastly, as being characterized by continual goal disagreement.

In 1972, Dye defined the parameters of policy analysis as having several objectives. Policy analysis was primarily concerned with explanation rather than prescription for the causes and impact of public policies. It sought to record reliable research findings of general significance as they developed, and also to test general propositions about the causes and results of public policy. Lastly, it sought to develop general theories about public policy which were reliable and could thereby be applied to different policy areas (Anderson, 1975).

Policy analysis encompasses two aspects: normative and positive policy analysis. Postive policy analysis is essentially involved in the analysis of policy-making with the objective of explaining phenomena. The normative aspect is an activity which seeks to improve the policy-making process as well as the results of such policy-making (Ukeles, 1977). In this study we were primarily concerned with explanation rather than with prescription.

Ethnic Group Politics and Bilingual Education

Politics, ethnicity and education are social phenomena which are just as cogent and interrelated today as they were during the reform period in American history. At the turn of the century, the nation's largest cities had the greatest concentration of immigrants. In almost any major school system immigrants represented more than half the student's population. During this period, the public schools were one of the major vehicles for upward social mobility and cultural accommodation for thousands of Jews, Poles, Italians and others.

In addition, recent historical research on the period 1880 to 1930 also strongly indicates a relation between the success of the newly emerging American public school system and the social aspirations of many immigrants (Smith, 1969). Much of the mobility and adjustments which were made by the immigrants would not have been possible without the legitimate and less than legitimate political behavior of the ward bosses.

Tyack's description of 19th century pluralistic school politics is not only revealing, but reminiscent of present day issues regarding the place and role of language and culture in American public schools.

> Although teaching Polish to pupils
> in immigrant wards might have seemed

an unwise concession to parochial
interests to a bureaucrat, it was
a proud affirmation to parents
from the old country. Mixed together in the political contents
for control were both tangible and
symbolic stakes: direct economic
benefits derives from jobs and
contracts, and intangible but
highly important issues centering
on ethnic and religious differences.
Different groups sought not only
cash but affirmations of their
values and life styles in the
schools (Tyack, 1974, 79-80).
(Italics added)

Traditionally, ethnic group politics has received its major
strength from the local ward or community. Its power for
minorities and politicians alike has come from the direct relationship between votes and jobs (Bailey and Katz, 1969). In
New York City politics, for example, no candidate for mayor would
entertain the thought of alienating the pwerful Jewish vote.
Similarly, Mexican-American ethnic political and social organizations such as American G.I. Forum, League of United Latin-
American Citizens (LULAC), and La Raza Unida Party have made
their presence felt in the social and political development of
Texas.

The character and persistence of ethnic group politics has
been well documented (Glazer and Moynihan, 1970). The study of
ethnicity and political participation in American society is
said to have been hampered by the overwhelming acceptance of
the assimilationist thesis (Wirth, 1928). Efforts to explain
the causes of Black activism and its impact on other ethnic
minorities during the 1960's, however, challenged the commonly
accepted notion of political pluralism and also the theory of
assimilation in American society (Litt, 1970). According to
Milton Gordon, earlier assimilation models had failed to take
into account the distinction between "cultural" and "structural"
assimilation. Cultural assimilation referred to a group's or
person's acquisition of the behavioral norms, sentiments, and
historical memories of a host society. Structural assimilation
referred to the large scale entrance of a minority group into
a host society's clubs, cliques, and major institutions on a
primary group level. The full realization of cultural assimilation by a minority group or person was no guarantee that structural assimilation would also follow (Gordon, 1964).

An analysis of politics and ethnicity, using Gordon's distinctions between cultural and structural assimilation, led Parenti to the conclusion that "...ethnic distinctiveness can still be treated as a factor in social and political pluralism" (Parenti, 1966, 724). Further research on the nature of ethnic group politics in the United States has led to the introduction of a useful concept: "old" and "new" style ethnic politics. The distinctions are based on the group's time of entry into the United States, the origins of the group, and the differing political ethos of the two groups. The "old" ethnics, those who arrived prior to 1880, are characterized as being oriented towards a rewards and benefits system based on elections turn-outs, jobs and bossism (Litt, 1970). The "new ethnic politics differed in that it was based on the group's collective problems and not on discrete personal issues. It sought to involve the community into a broader sense of civic affairs. It also sought to find legitimacy based on moral and legal concepts of minority rights and agency obligations and "not in the personalism of self-sacrifice attached to the patron role and not in the attribution of monolithic influence in partisan politics in the boss role" (Rogler, 1974, 66).

Ethnic group politics is an historical fact of American life. Its persistence has contributed to its treatment in social science research as a useful factor in the analysis of American political behavior.

Bilingual Education

The politics of the bilingual-bicultural education movement in the early 1960's was spearheaded by the emerging Spanish-speaking minority: Mexican Americans from the southwest and Puerto Ricans from New York City (Sanchez, 1973). The political, social and economic forces which fostered the bilingual education movement can fruitfully be examined within the following twenty-year period: 1954 to 1974. The first date marks the beginning of a new era in judicial constitutional interpretation regarding the fundamental rights of racial minorities "to the equal protection of the laws under the Fourteenth Amendment" (Alexander, et al., 1969, 641). The second represents another landmark decision regarding the rights of linguistically different minorities to an equal education on the basis of Section 601 of the Civil Rights Act of 1964 (United States Commission on Civil Rights, 1975). Both decisions have had a significant effect on the course of the bilingual education movement in the United States. The following will be but a brief account of those events and ideas which assisted the movement.

The Black Civil Rights movement, a more positive outlook on the benefits of a culturally pluralistic approach to teaching in the public schools, and the Great Society war-on-poverty programs were some of the factors which contributed to the acceptance of bilingual education by the Congress in 1968 (Dinnerstein and Reimers, 1975). Another reason given for its acceptance in cities like New York and Chicago was that the prestige and authority of these school systems had greatly diminished. Educators in these school systems were on the defensive, assaulted by parents, community agencies and liberal scholars, for their alleged failure to educate the hundreds of Black, Chicano and Puerto Rican students (Krug, 1976).

The passage of the Elementary and Secondary Education Act in 1965 greatly contributed to the successful enactment of the Bilingual Education Act (Title VII) in 1968). The Civil Rights Act of 1964 also helped by eliminating the delicate issue of segregation. The fear of federal control over state education was assuaged by giving the state departments of education more control over the grants. The issue of blanket federal aid to the state was resolved by establishing a poverty category which would benefit the urban as well as the rural poor. The strategy pleased both northern and southern politicians who clearly wanted the votes of the newly enfranchised Blacks and Spanish-speaking minorities (Bailey, 1970).

Bilingual education in this country is not a recent phenomenon. The earliest accounts of classroom instruction being conducted in a language other than English goes back as early as 1840. The German immigrants which settled in Cincinnati, Indianapolis, and St. Louis not only established parochial schools where the German language and cultural values were taught, but they influenced the curriculum of many public schools as well (Andersson, 1969; Fishman, 1966; Kloss, 1977).

In 1963, the first publicly funded educational program in bilingual education was begun for the children of Cuban immigrants in Dade County, Florida. Initially, the children were enrolled in all English programs until Cuban parents began to favor and encourage the implementation of a bilingual curriculum. By the time serious efforts to legislate a national bilingual education law was undertaken in 1967, the Dade County bilingual program had been hailed a success and considered a likely model which other beginning programs could very well emulate (Andersson and Boyer, 1970; Mackey and Beebe, 1977).

In 1964, two other bilingual programs were begun in Texas for Chicano children. Three years later twelve more such programs were begun in various other parts of the country.

Approximately ninety percent of the proposals submitted for the 1968-69 school year involved the use of Spanish and English instruction, although the law was not limited to Spanish alone (Andersson and Boyer, 1970).

The Bilingual Education Act was signed into law by President Johnson on January 2, 1968. The Act provided for the financial assistance of those public schools engaged in the development of "imaginative elementary and secondary school programs" that would meet the "special educational needs" of children of "limited English-speaking ability." The law specifically provided that such programs would be available to those children who came from families whose annual income did not exceed $3,000 (United State Commission on Civil Rights, 1975).

In 1971 the Massachusetts legislature passed the first mandatory bilingual education law. Since then nine other states passed similar laws: California, Colorado, Illinois, New Jersey, Rhode Island, Texas, Alaska, Wisconsin and Michigan (A Study of State Programs in Bilingual Education, 1977).

Major research efforts in the area of bilingual schooling have concentrated on language, on community related studies, and on the effects of different teaching strategies on the learning achievement of linguistically and culturally different children. As noted earlier, very little attention has been given to the state, judicial and administrative policy-making process related to the enactment of bilingual education laws, court decrees and statutes. With the exception of Gordy's (1975) research on the enactment of the first mandatory bilingual education law in Massachusetts, little has been done to research how and why similar legislation was passed in other states. The present study has been an attempt to fill the current gap.

The review of literature in this chapter traced the role of the federal government in education. The contribution of social science research to the area of public policy-making was described. This literature served to shape and clarify the focus of the present study. The literature on ethnic group politics demonstrated its importance as an explanatory factor in analyzing the enactment of bilingual education laws at the state level.

CHAPTER III

HISTORICAL ANTECEDENTS TO BILINGUAL LEGISLATION

In this study four major environmental changes were identified as having had a signifcant impact on the enactment of bilingual education legislation by the Texas State Legislature between
1968 and 1972. These factors were the enactment of the federal
Bilingual Education Act in 1968, the publication of the May 25th
Memorandum by the Office for Civil Rights, the Sharpstown Scandal,
and the election results in 1972. In this chapter we will seek
to demonstrate how these environmental changes provided Mexican-
Americans in Texas with new supports and reasons for pressing
state education officials and legislators with renewed demands
for an equal educational opportunity.

Serious demands for educational reform and interest in the
educational problems of Mexican-American students in Texas Public
Schools probably would not have readily been accepted or adopted
by state legislative and education officials had it not been for
federal initiatives and financial assistance.

ESEA of 1965 and Bilingual Education

Prior to the enactment of the Bilingual Education Act in
1968, research and special projects in bilingual education had
received considerable funding under all five titles of the
Elementary and Secondary Education Act of 1965. Title I programs
for non-English-speaking students in reading, English language
arts and English-as-a-second language (ESL) instruction were
funded for well over $65 million. Seven special projects spon-
sored under Title III, costing over three quarters of a million
dollars, were funded between December, 1964 and April, 1967. The
money was spent on the creation of educational service and learning centers in various heavily populated Mexican-American communities. Major emphasis was placed on language methodology and
on the function of culture in the instructional process.
Research interests in bilingual education ranged from testing
linguistic models for ESL instruction to studying the effects
of extra-linguistic environmental influences on the learning
development of Mexican-American children. In other research
projects work was done on developing appropriate curriculum
materials in language and science in both Spanish and English.
Between 1968 and 1970 Texas had received well over $173 million
in ESEA funds (Bilingual Education Hearings, 1967; 46th Biennial
Report, 1970).

Increased federal funding to state educational departments via Title V enabled the Texas Education Agency to develop the expertise of its personnel in bilingual-bicultural education methodology through the creation of the Office of International and Bilingual Education in the winter of 1966. Under the leadership of Dr. W. R. Goodson, chief executive officer of the Latin-American Committee of the Southern Association and also the state director of accreditation, the office was formed to promote the teaching of foreign languages, to gain expertise in the area of bilingual instructional methods, and to gather information on bilingual educational programs outside the United States (A Guide for Implementing International Education Programs, 1970).

Texas educators gained even more experience in bilingual schooling through the many experimental bilingual education programs which had been started before the enactment of the federal bilingual law. Some local programs received financial assistance from ESEA funds, in other cases local districts initiated their own programs with local funds, and applied for federal funding after Title VII was passed. The first locally funded bilingual education program was begun in the Laredo United Independent School District in 1964, under the direction of Superintendent Harold C. Brantley. Five years later there were twelve more bilingual programs. When the federal bilingual education bill was enacted in 1968, Texas had the greatest number of bilingual programs in the United States (Andersson and Boyer, 1970; Hargrave and Hinojosa, 1975; Zamora, 1977).

Several other events prior to 1968 helped to create the kind of support which brought the common problems of Chicanos to national prominence. The conferences which were held in Tucson, Albuquerque, El Paso, and San Antonio laid the common groundwork for action and enumerated the basic issues being raised by Mexican-American educational and political leaders throughout the Southwest. The formal and informal discussions which were held in these forums also helped to shape the thinking of future Mexican-American politicos like Joe J. Bernal and Carlos F. Truan on the role and possible worth of bilingual instruction in the educational training of the Mexican-American student.

The Albuquerque Conference: 1966

On March 26, 1966 Chicano conferees, who had been invited to attend a conference on Mexican-American problems sponsored by the Equal Employment Opportunity Commission in Albuquerque, angrily stormed out of the official meeting, protesting "against the disinterest, condescending way in which the

hearing was being conducted" (McWilliams, 1968, Introduction).
Mexican-American conferees also felt insulted that only lower
level federal administrators had been sent to meet with them.
The American G. I. Forum, League of United Latin-American
Citizens and several other Chicano organizations were present at
the conference. The walk-out of some sixty delegates from the
official proceedings was considered to be one of the earliest
public demonstrations by Chicano leaders. In the minds of many
Chicanos this public interest symbolized the genesis of a new
era for the Mexican-American in the Southwest.

Meeting in an adjoining classroom at the University of
New Mexico, the conferees formed an Ad Hoc coalition and formulated a list of demands to present to EEOC officials. The
list of demands called for the appointment of a Mexican-American
to EEOC at the commissioner level, the hiring of more Chicanos
in Washington, D.C. and the inclusion of Mexican-American concerns on the Agenda of the White House Conference on Civil Rights
which was held later on that year. In addition, the committee
demanded a personal audience with President Johnson.

The meeting with the President in May of that year proved
to be very successful. President Johnson agreed to convene
a conference where Mexican-American leaders would be invited to
publicly present testimony on the social, economic and political
problems which afflicted and retarded the progress of the
Mexican-American citizen. He also appointed Vicente T. Ximenes
as EEOC's first Mexican-American commissioner, and created the
first Inter-Agency Committee for Mexican-American affairs
(Reveles, 1974).

The Tucson Conference: 1966

Late in October of the same year, the National Education
Association sponsored a conference on "The Spanish-speaking
Child in the Schools of the Southwest" in Tucson, Arizona. The
purpose of the conference was twofold: First, it sought to increase local and state support for bilingual instruction in
public schools for the Mexican-American student. Second, it
also urged an increase in ESEA appropriations as well as the
enactment of specific legislation on bilingual education.

The conference itself had been the result of an NEA survey
on the school related problems of non English-speaking students
in the Southwest which had been conducted the previous year.
The findings of the survey were devastatingly difficult to
accept, but confirmed what was already suspected. The Chicano
student fell short on practically every measure of scholastic

achievement. The findings of the study pointed to such things as poverty, feelings of alienation from the dominant Anglo culture, and the school's inability or unwillingness to deal with the linguistically and culturally different child as some of the possible causal factors.

As a result of these and other findings on the educational problems of Mexican-American children in the United States, the survey committee offered nine recommendations as possible ways of dealing with the issue. Five of these recommendations are particularly important, because they appear in one form or another in the Federal Bilingual Education Act in 1968, and they appear on state legislative documents in Texas in 1969 and 1973. The committee recommended that:

1. Instruction in pre-school and throughout the early grades should be conducted in Spanish and English.

2. English should be taught as a second language.

3. A well articulated program of instruction in the mother tongue should be continued from pre-school through the high school years.

4. All possible measures should be taken to help Mexican-American children gain a pride in their ancestral culture and language.

5. State laws which specify English as the language of instruction and thus, by implication at least, outlaw the speaking of Spanish except in Spanish classes, should be repealed (Bilingual Education Hearings, 1967, 155-199).

Three months after the conference Senator Ralph Yarborough, liberal Democrat from Texas, introduced the first federal bilingual education bill to the Congress. He had been one of the invited guest speakers at the conference. Dr. Monroe Sweetland of NEA had asked him to speak on how to pass legislation. However, when he arrived at the conference he soon found out that the purpose of the meeting was to educate him on the need for bilingual education. What he learned at the conference impressed and convinced him that bilingual education would be a good way of helping to meet one of the more serious problems which afflicted a large sector of the Mexican-American community (Yarborough, R., Personal communication, March 27, 1979).

The El Paso Conference: 1967

On Octover 26, 1967, the second conference on the problems of Mexican-Americans was held in El Paso, Texas. This time Chicano leaders presented their case before a panel of five cabinet level secretaries. Testimony was offered in the areas of health, employment and education. Many of the papers which were read in the area of education "insisted on elevating and maintaining the Hispanic culture on a par with the Anglo-American culture, and on the need for bilingual education" (Ortego, 1967, 625). Both demands, according to one observer, seemed to be "objectionable to the American pattern of cultural fusion" (Ortego, 1967, 625). Moreover, the suggestions seemed to go contrary to the commonly accepted notions of social scientists that it was these two factors which actually stood in the way of the social and economic betterment of the Mexican-American in the United States (Ortego, 1967).

To many Chicanos the conference was nothing more than a scheme by the Democratic party leadership to attract the support of the Mexican-American vote for the 1968 presidential elections. Many of the more vocal and critical Chicano leaders were either not invited or refused to participate. Rodolfo "Corky" Gonzales, founder of the Mexican-American Political Association (MAPA) in Colorado did not attend. Reies Lopez Tijerina, Alianza de Pueblos Libres of New Mexico, and Cesar Chavez, of the National Farm Workers, also did not participate. These critics argued that the problems of Mexican-Americans were well documented. They called for the implementation of programs and an end to useless public relations conferences.

Many of these critics argued that the primary benefactor of the federal government largess was the well-educated, Anglo-looking middle-class Mexican-American who had successfully internalized the values and standards of the dominant Anglo culture, but who still found himself being denied full and equal participation in the social, economic and political structure (Ortego, 1967).

Many of the participants may have shared similar views, but they chose to strike out for changes within the more moderate, well recognized Chicano associations. Carlos F. Truan, who would later champion the passage of the first bilingual education bill in Texas, was one of these participants. In his testimony he argued that the government had totally ignored the economic condition of the Mexican-American despite the fact that this group constituted "the major minority group in the Southwest and the one at the bottom of the scale on virtually every criterion

measuring health, wealth, education, and welfare." Truan saw
little difference between the problems which plagued the Chicano
in employment and those which hindered his educational development. In his testimoney Truan, who at the time was deputy state
director of LULAC, graphically described the general sentiment
of Chicanos at the conference:

> In the past, the Indian, the Negro,
> the Filipino, the Puerto Rican, and
> all the other peoples in a situation
> similar to that of the Mexican-
> American have been the object of
> moral responsibility. Not so the
> Mexican-American. He has been, and
> he continues to be, the most
> neglected, the least sponsored, the
> most orphaned major minority group
> in the United States (Truan, 1967,
> 199).

Much of the testimony given in El Paso on the social ills
of the Mexican-American in the Southwest was a repetition of
what had been said in other public meetings earlier that same
year. The San Antonio Conference, held in April, and the Bilingual Education Hearings, held in May, June and July, also
hammered on the same theme: the Mexican-American had been ignored
and neglected by the federal government. Mexican-American
leaders wanted a federal program which specifically addressed
itself to their unique educational needs. For many, Senator
Yarborough's bilingual bill would help meet that need.

The San Antonio Conference: 1967

On April 13 through the 15th, 700 conferees met in San
Antonio to discuss how best to improve the educational opportunity of the Mexican-American student in Texas. Invited guests
included Governor John B. Connally, Senator Ralph Yarborough,
Congressman Henry P. Gonzalez, and Texas Education Agency
Commissioner Dr. J. W. Edgar, accompanied by Dr. Severo Gomez,
assistant commissioner of the Office of Bilingual and International Education. The conference was called the "Texas Conference for the Mexican-American: Improving Educational Opportunities." It was organized to increase support for the federal
bilingual bill which had been introduced in January, to convince
more persons on the merits of bilingual-bicultural education as
a means of improving the educational achievement of the Chicano
student, and to call attention to the mandatory foreign language
bill which had been introduced in the Texas Legislature the
previous month.

At the end of the conference participants unanimously adopted 25 resolutions having to do with the education of the Mexican-American. In general the resolutions called for involvement of state and federal officials in the education problems which were affecting the Mexican-American. The resolutions emphasized local problems which still needed to be solved and they encouraged more federal participation in the social and political welfare of the Chicano. Conference participants also suggested that the greatest change was needed in the public school curriculum. They considered that their language, cultural heritage, and historical contributions needed to be included on an equal basis within the Anglo dominated curriculum. Mexican-American intellectuals argued that the tenets of cultural pluralism did not represent a major threat to national unity as some feared. The belief in national unity and cultural diversity were not felt to be incompatible goals in American society.

One of the very first resolutions to be adopted by conference participants was Governor Connally's suggestion that Texas should work toward the creation of a bilingual state. In his address, Connally stated that he supported the idea of requiring the teaching of the Spanish language beginning in the primary schools in every public school in Texas. The statement was, however, politically motivated. In 1966 Connally had been elected to his third term of office as governor, and it was rumored that he had plans of running for an unprecedented fourth term. Chicano leaders mistrusted and disliked Connally, but they knew that they could not afford to lose his support in the legislature (Bernal, J., Personal communication, March 22, 1979).

A second resolution, made by Dr. J. W. Edgar, promised to equip all Mexican-American children with the ability to read, write, and speak Spanish and English, and to contribute to their chances for employment by preparing them with marketable skills. Another resolution suggested that diagnostic tests which purported to test the intelligence or levels of academic achievement of Chicano school children be conducted in Spanish and English in order to get an accurate picture of the student's true capacity. Three years later the same suggestion would appear in the May 25th Memorandum, and in 1973 it would be enacted into law by the Texas Legislature.

Participants also demanded the adoption of revised textbooks on the history of Texas which more accurately reflected the role and contributions of Mexican-Americans in the history of Texas. They urged the governor to proclaim English and Spanish as the official languages of Texas for the year 1968, in recognition of the opening of Hemisfair in San Antonió.

Conferees also recommended support for the enactment of Senate Bill 428, the American Bilingual Education bill, which had been introduced by Texas Senator Yarborough in January. Finally, the governor and the legislature were urged by conference participants to enact House Bill 719, a mandatory foreign language bill which had been introduced to the Texas Legislature that year, a month before the conference in San Antonio (Bilingual Education Hearings, 1967).

The bill was introduced on March 2, during the 60th Legislature. By May 23 the bill was amended in response to the sharp opposition of many Texans of German and French-speaking ancestry. Instead of Spanish, the bill was then amended to require "the teaching of foreign language(s) in the public elementary and junior high schools in grades 5, 6, 7 and 8..." The law would have been permissive until the spring of 1975, and required thereafter. The bill was passed by the House on May 27, two days before the end of the session, and sent to the Senate for its consideration. In the Senate the bill was quietly set aside and never considered (House Journal, 1967, 2720, "Bilingual Education," 1967).

Few bilingual educators in Texas remember or have any knowledge of House Bill 719. Had the act been passed in its original version, it would have been unique. It would have meant that Spanish and English would have been placed on an equal footing in the public school curriculum. The bill, which was authored by ultraconservative Ralph Wagne of Lubbock, would have required instruction in the Spanish language for all Texas school children beginning in the fifth grade and continuing through to grade eight. English-speaking children would learn Spanish and would have the opportunity of speaking it without having to leave Texas, while Mexican-American children would be taught the formal structure of the language and encouraged to cultivate its maintenance.

This was the first time legislation had ever been proposed to require the teaching of Spanish early in the primary grades in Texas. However, the idea of teaching Spanish in elementary school was not new. As early as 1943 the state department of education had promoted a six-year experimental course in Spanish for elementary students in grades three through eight. It was felt that the United States had not contributed much to the political development of its neighboring Latin-American republics primarily because of American ignorance regarding their customs, traditions and languages. It was generally assumed that Americans could probably understand and be of more help to these poor and politically disorganized peoples south of the Rio Grande if they had a working knowledge of their language.

The primary objective of the course was to teach students how to speak and understand Spanish, with little emphasis given to grammar. The program was experimental because there was very little research in the area of language instruction to young children. No study had been done to determine the content of Spanish vocabulary which was appropriate for each grade level. No study had been done to determine what grammatical principles could be introduced and when. While there had been considerable progress on teaching methods and procedures, there was very little known about the development of reading readiness skills in a foreign language. The use of cultural materials to teach about the peoples of Spanish-speaking countries was also a highly disputed issue (Tentative Course of Study..., 1943).

The early impetus for bilingual education in the 1960's came principally from Texas. The long history of bilingualism and interest in foreign language instruction, and the increased federal interest in the area, accelerated the bilingual movement. Equality of educational opportunity very early became equated with bilingual education. The bilingual hearings were especially important because they represented the culmination of this interest in that they boosted the morale of bilingual advocates, and increased the possibility of subsequent state recognition and support for bilingual education after the enactment of the federal law.

Hearings on Bilingual Education: 1967

The first of six public hearings on bilingual education was held on May 18, in Washington, D.C. Members of the Special Subcommittee on Bilingual Education heard two days of testimony from thirteen expert witnesses on the subject of education and the Spanish-speaking child. Hearings were also held in Corpus Christi, Edinburg, San Antonio, and Los Angeles. The last hearing was held in New York City on July 21.

The bilingual bill had been introduced to the Senate on January 17 as a direct result of what Senator Yarborough had learned at the Tucson Conference. The available evidence seems to suggest that Senator Yarborough's actions were motivated by little else than his desire to broaden the educational opportunities of Mexican-American children. The bill was originally intended to serve only Spanish-speaking children. Senator Yarborough was especially interested in passing a bill which would help the Mexican-American student in Texas and the rest of the Southwest attain a better educational opportunity. He firmly believed that education was the key to upward social mobility. According to Yarborough,

> If we seek to raise the economic
> level of any group, we must first
> educate them. Education opens the
> door to prosperity and progress.
> Our Spanish-speaking people in
> Texas have looked at that closed
> door too long. It is time to open
> it now. That is what I am trying
> to do with my bilingual education
> bill (Bilingual Education Hearings,
> 1967, 653).

The hearings provided the leading spokesmen of well-known
Mexican-American organizations such as LULAC and American G.I.
Forum with yet another opportunity to publicly state their
reasons for supporting the enactment of a federal bilingual education law. The hearings also served to increase the knowledge
base and to strengthen the convictions of Carlos F. Truan and
Joe J. Bernal on the merits of bilingual education for the benefit of the Mexican-American child in Texas. In 1968 it would be
these two men who would introduce and push for the passage of
the first bilingual education law in Texas legislative history.
Truan presented testimony in Corpus Christi, and Bernal made a
presentation in San Antonio.

For Truan the enactment of the bilingual education law meant
that the Mexican American child would learn to appreciate his
language and culture. The law would help reduce the high school
drop-out rate among Mexican-American youth, and "help many Mexican-Americans become good taxpayers instead of tax-eaters" (Bilingual Education Hearings, 1967, 246). Furthermore, the implementation of this law would contribute to elevating the prestige
of the Spanish language and the status of the Mexican-American.
Truan spoke from personal experience when he uttered these words
at the hearing.

> I can still remember my personal
> experience as a student in school
> for the first time when I was placed
> in the so-called beginners grade and
> not in the first grade because of the
> language barrier. Also, I can still
> feel the many spankings given to me
> because I would talk in Spanish in-
> stead of English. There was no con-
> sideration given to my family environ-
> ment whatsoever. A child, an adult,
> an ethnic group needs to be respected
> for what it is, not what the ruling

> powers dictate that it should be
> according to the unwritten and many
> times written rules of conduct.
> Every citizen has dignity and worth,
> and the Mexican-American child is
> no exception (Bilingual Education
> Hearings, 1967, 225-228).

In the course of his testimony, Truan also made it a point to
stress that at the 38th state convention of LULAC the membership
had unanimously endorsed the Bilingual American Education Act.

The views of more influential, professional individuals
were also presented. Dr. Theodore Andersson, one of the pio-
neers of the bilingual education movement in Texas, wholeheartedly supported the bill and expressed the view that bilingual
instruction would do no psychological damage. He also stressed
the hope that monolingual English-speakers would also benefit
from the provisions of this law. Dr. Hershel T. Manuel, a
retired educational psychologist who had written a major educational survey of Mexican-American educational problems in the
1940's, was not as confident. He felt that state authorities
had not erred in emphasizing the teaching of English in the
schools. The English language was the native language of the
great majority of the people who lived in the Southwest and in
the Nation. It was also the primary language of the news media,
industry, commerce, government and education. According to Dr.
Manuel, English was the preferred language of this country because of:

> Conditions inherited from the past,
> not some arbitrary ruling, and not
> some attempt to Anglicize children,
> (made) it necessary for every child
> to become proficient in the use of
> (the) language if (he was) to par-
> ticipate fully in the affairs of the
> larger community (Bilingual Education
> Hearings, 1967, 216).

Dr. Manuel was firm in stressing the primacy of the English
language, but he also conceded that the state had an equal responsibility for developing the child's native language at least
in the early years because of its value to the individual and to
the community of which he was a part (Bilingual Education Hearings, 1967).

Dr. Hector P. Garcia, the founder of American G.I. Forum,
did not quite agree with Dr. Manuel's opinions, but for very

different reasons. In his opinion:

> People must be made to realize that
> an American can be a good citizen even
> through he speaks another language, be-
> longs to another culture, or has a dif-
> ferent religion than the majority. For
> over 100 years an effort has been made
> to harass and suppress the 'spoken
> Spanish.' The American democracy will
> be possible when the majority becomes
> bilingual in the Southwest. If the
> predominant class refuses to learn
> Spanish as we have learned English and
> if they hate us because we speak Spanish,
> then how will it be possible that they
> expect to understand the many Spanish-
> speaking countries in this hemisphere?
> (Bilingual Education Hearings, 1967,
> 225-228).

The testimony of Corpus Christi superintendent Dan
Williams was supportive, but he wanted the aid to be general
and felt that the Texas Education Agency should have a greater
role in developing and implementing the program. Yarborough,
however, did not agree, stating that Texas had done the poorest
job of educating linguistically and culturally different
children in the Union. In his opinion, if the job were left
up to the State agency the result would have been "tokenism
for generations." The record demonstrated that while Texas
ranked sixth in natural resources, it ranked 34th in per capita
income and 32nd in general education. In higher education,
Texas ranked 37th, and in teacher salaries it was worse with
a rank of 43. "If Texas had done a better job," he stated,
"I wouldn't have to introduce this bill (Bilingual Education
Hearings, 1967, 228).

Throughout the hearings Yarborough made a deliberate point
of emphasizing that bilingualism was not a handicap, and that
Mexican-Americans were no less intelligent than anyone else
because many spoke two languages. He complimented the Mexican-
American speakers at every opportunity for having attained their
professional and political positions in society, despite the
negative language experiences which many of them had encountered
in school and in daily life.

Senator Joe J. Bernal's testimony in San Antonio was
particularly insightful, because it illustrated the political
realities as understood by many Chicanos in Texas. Bernal, who
had been elected to the Texas Senate in 1966, had attended the

education conferences which were held in Tucson and San Antonio. He knew of the recommendations which had been made against the English-only language laws which existed in some states. His remarks to Senator Yarborough provide us with at least a partial explanation. "You know," he told Yarborough, "I attended both conferences and I didn't come out with a bill like that. I am very proud that you did. You probably would have a better chance at that than I would" (Bilingual Education Hearings, 1967, 326).

Five months after the hearings, Title VII of ESEA was passed by the 90th Congress on December 15, 1967. It was the first federal categorical grant ever legislated that addressed itself to the unique educational needs of the Spanish-speaking minority in the United States. The law's enactment came as a direct result of Mexican-American lobbying, the support of the National Education Association, and the expert, committed, and energetic leadership of Texas Senator Ralph Yarborough (Sanchez, 1973; Schneider, 1976).

Title VII of ESEA

The bilingual Education Act was signed into law by President Johnson on January 2, 1968. The Act provided for the financial assistance of those public schools engaged in the development of "imaginative elementary and secondary programs" that would meet the "special educational needs" of children of "limited English speaking ability." The law specifically provided that such programs would be available to those children who came from families whose annual income did not exceed $3,000. The kinds of activities suggested under this program included instruction which imparted to students a knowledge of the history and culture associated with their language, and the use of the native language of the child as the initial medium of instruction if the child could not handle English. The law also suggested the creation of closer ties between parents and school authorities, and encouraged the establishment of early childhood education programs. In addition, the law specifically called for the creation of programs that would help reduce the high drop-out rate of Mexican-American students. Adult education programs for the parents of children participating in bilingual education programs were also encouraged.

Another important aspect of the federal law was financial commitment. The Congress authorized a total of $265 million for the law's implementation for a four-year period beginning in 1968 and ending in 1972. Actual monies appropriated, however, amounted to only $80 million during this period (A Better Chance to Learn, 1975; Reveles, 1974).

The enactment of the Bilingual Education Act in 1968 was seen as a major achievement by many Mexican-American educators. The federal law not only approved the use of native home languages as legitimate vehicles of instruction in public schools, but it also encouraged changes in the curriculum which portrayed the historical and cultural contributions of Mexican-Americans in the Southwest. The adoption of these innovations, however, made little impact on the problem of Mexican-American school segregation. The persistence of segregated educational facilities in Texas at the time was acute.

In 1970, when the Education Division of the Office for Civil Rights issued its national origins memorandum, the segregation of Mexican-American students in many Texas public schools was still a very serious obstacle (Mexican-American Education Study, Report IV, 1971).

The enactment of the Elementary and Secondary Education Act in 1965 represented the greatest interest which the federal government had ever displayed in the area of education. Special attention was given to educationally related problems which seemed to affect the educational chances of thousands of poor and culturally different school children. The federally sponsored conferences which were held in El Paso, Albuquerque, San Antonio, and other cities throughout the Southwest between 1966 and 1968 accelerated local interest in the education of the limited or non-English-speaking Mexican-American child. The enactment of the Bilingual Education Act in 1968 focused the federal interest on those factors which seemed to limit the educational opportunities of a disproportionate number of the nation's Spanish-speaking student.

In the following section we will briefly examine some of the early history of Mexican-American resistance to segregation, summarize the "English only" language laws in Texas, and trace the development of equal educational opportunity for national origin students under the Civil Rights Act of 1964.

Civil Rights and Bilingual Education

The intentional school segregation of Mexican-Americans in Texas has been a well-documented historical phenomenon. Since 1876 and earlier local school authorities in all parts of the state established separate "Mexican" schools. The practice predominantly affected the primary grades, but it very often was extended to high school as well. Many Mexican-Americans fully resented the separate school facilities to which their children were assigned by local school officials. What was evidently more heinous to Mexican-American leaders was the dilapidated school buildings which their children were forced to attend, the paucity of textbooks and other classroom materials, and the fact that the

40

most incompetent and least experienced teachers were most often assigned to their schools (Weinberg, 1977; Weeks, 1929; Mexican-American Education Study, Report IV, 1971).

Tri-ethnic segregationist practices were very often perpetuated by locally contrived and state supported strategies. After the Civil War, Blacks were provided with separate schools by law. No such statutory provision existed for Mexican-Americans. Nevertheless, what resulted in many communities was the support of the public schools for three groups: Anglos (southwest term to describe Whites), Blacks and Chicanos. The system was very often perpetuated by permissive transfer plans, busing, and the gerrymandering of school districts. The use of "freedom-of-choice plans" and the construction of new school buildings in predominantly Chicano neighborhoods only served to exasperate any serious efforts to desegregate the schools (Rangel and Alcala, 1972). Mexican-American responses to those blatant segregationist practices very often were met head on in the various local school districts. In other instances Chicanos were able to bring their grievances to the attention of the courts.

The legal history of Mexican-American opposition to school segregation has extended over a forty-year period. From 1930 to about 1954 Mexican-Americans sought judicial relief from overt segregationist practices by relying on three basic arguments: 1) the Mexican-American was a White person, 2) the state had no statute which mandated the segregation of Mexican-American children, and 3) the 1947 opinion of the Texas state attorney general forbade the separation of Mexican-American children on the basis of language deficiencies if they were determined solely on the basis of teacher judgment. These arguments were used in two cases, but the results in each were less than satisfactory. In the case of Del Rio Independent School District v. Salvatierra (1930), plaintiffs sought to prevent school officials in the city of Del Rio from segregating Mexican-American children from Anglo children in the early grades. The Texas Court of Civil Appeals agreed with the plaintiffs, but the appellate court reversed the lower court's decision on the grounds that the school board's intent to discriminate against Chicano children had not been demonstrated. The court upheld the school board's policy of separating Chicano and Anglo children on the basis of alleged language difficulties based solely on teacher judgment.

In the 1948 case of Delgado v. Bastrop Independent School District, the "other white" and the "absence of state" law arguments proved successful. The court ordered the local school district not to segregate children of Mexican-American descent, and suggested the construction of new school buildings or other

41

measures needed to be taken in order to rectify the problem before the fall of 1949. In addition, the court specified that the segregation of first grade children would be permitted in a school if the decision was based on properly administered standardized tests. The suggestion, however, was used by school districts to perpetuate segregation.

The little progress which had been made in the courts was thwarted by the Texas Legislature. In order to prevent the state superintendent, L.A. Woods, from enforcing the court's ruling on Del Rio school officials by cancelling their state accreditation, the legislature abolished the office of superintendent, an elected office, and created the post of Commissioner of Education, an appointed post. When Del Rio school officials appealed the disaccreditation ruling which had been handed down by the former superintendent, the newly appointed commissioner, J.W. Edgar, reversed the decision (Rangel and Alcala, 1972).

The period between 1954 and 1967 yielded only two significant court victories for Chicanos. In Hernandez v. Driscoll Consolidated Independent School District (1957), the court ruled that the segregation of Chicano children in the first grade was illegal in the absence of standardized tests which demonstrated the need for separating children into different classrooms. In the case of Chapa v. Odem Independent School District (1967), Chicano plaintiffs presented convincing evidence to show that Chicano segregation was a result of traditional school board policy. The use of diagnostic tests provided school officials with a convenient cover for separating the children. Plaintiffs were able to demonstrate that teachers and administrators were not competent to deal with the educational needs of linguistically different children. They also provided evidence which showed that of the three first grade teachers in the Mexican school only one had a college degree and a valid state teaching credential. It was also found that the same materials and textbooks were used in the Anglo and the Chicano schools. In its ruling the court refused to totally accept a classificatory system which separated Anglo and Chicano students based on standardized tests (Rangel and Alcala, 1972).

The case of Mexican-American school segregation practices in Texas is a well documented fact. Mexican-American leaders never questioned the primacy and legality of the English language in the school curriculum. What they consistently opposed was the capricious segregation of their children in the absence of state statute. Chicano students very often were forced to attend crowded, substandard buildings, were assigned the worst teachers, and were subjected to a common rigid state imposed curriculum which failed to take into consideration their linguistic and cultural differences.

42

While Chicanos struggled against the imposition of locally segregated Mexican schools, the Texas Legislature enacted education laws which required English to be the only language of instruction in all public schools. The reasons for the language restrictions which were passed between 1905 and 1927 varied, but the effects of these policies on the education of many Mexican-American school children were often detrimental.

Restrictive Language Laws in Texas

The first attempt at establishing a state-wide, uniform system of public free schooling in Texas came in 1905 with the enactment of Senate Bill 218. Prior to this time, education in Texas was limited to a plethora of private, parochial and locally subsidized public schools with no uniform curriculum or officially recognized language of instruction. The language of instruction in many schools very often depended on the community. The slow development of public schooling in Texas was due in part to the widespread apprehension of increased governmental power and the lessening of individual liberties. How one educated one's children was generally considered to be an individual prerogative and responsibility. The Civil War, the Radical Reconstruction period and the reaction which followed were events which also served to retard the implementation of a centralized, state controlled system of public free schooling in Texas (McCleskey, 1966; Benton, 1966; General Laws of the State of Texas, Regular Session, 29th Legislature, 1905; Texas Public Schools, 1954).

The reorganization act of 1905 was very extensive. Among its many provisions the act called for a uniform school curriculum and determined the classroom language of instruction. Under the heading "Duties of the Teachers," the act required all certified teachers to teach exclusively in English. Section 102 of the Act stated:

> It shall be the duty of every teacher
> in the public free schools of this
> State to use the English language
> exclusively, and to conduct all reci-
> tation and school exercises exclusive-
> ly in the English language; provided,
> that this provision shall not prevent
> the teaching of any other language
> as a branch of study, but when any
> other language is so taught, the use
> of said language shall be limited to
> the recitations and exercises devoted

43

to the teaching of said lan-
guage as such branch of study
(General Laws of the State of
Texas, Regular Session, 29th
Legislature, 1905, 290).

In 1918 the Texas Legislature reiterated its position in
the primacy of the English language as the medium of instruction
in all public schools with the enactment of House Bill 128.
Section One of the Act specified:

> Every teacher, principal, and
> superintendent employed in the
> public schools of this state shall
> use the English language exclusive-
> ly in the conduct of the work of
> the schools, and all recitations
> and exercises of the school shall
> be conducted in the English lan-
> guage, and the trustees shall not
> prescribe any texts for elementary
> grades not printed in the English
> language; provided that this provi-
> sion shall not prevent the teaching
> of Latin, Greek, French, German,
> Spanish, Bohemian (Czech), or
> other language as a branch of study
> in the high school grades as out-
> lined in the state course of study
> (General and Special Laws of the
> State of Texas, 35th Legislature,
> 1918, 170).

Section Two prescribed penalities for school officials who
failed to comply with the provisions of the law. Violators of
the law would be considered guilty of a misdemeanor and, upon
conviction, were subject to a fine of not less than $25 and not
more than $100, the cancellation of their teaching certificate,
removal from office, or any combination of the above penalties.
Enforcement of the law was delegated to local school board
members, city or county superintendents, or to ex officio superintendents. They were supposed to inspect the schools on a
regular basis and were required to promptly file charges against
violators (General and Special Laws of the State of Texas, 35th
Legislature, 1918).

Nine years later the Texas Legislature slightly modified the 1918 language code. The amended law allowed school districts in counties which bordered on the Mexican and United States frontier to teach the Spanish language in elementary grades. The law stated:

> It shall be lawful to provide text-books for and to teach the Spanish language in elementary grades in the public free schools in counties bordering on the boundary line between the United States and the Republic of Mexico and having a city or cities of five thousand or more inhabitants according to the United States census for the year 1920 (General and Special Laws of the State of Texas, 40th Legislature, 1927, 267. Italics supplied.)

The law permitted the teaching of Spanish in the elementary grades, but it did not approve the use of Spanish as a medium of instruction. The law was amended because it was felt that "a knowledge of the Spanish language (was) of inestimable value to the citizens and inhabitants of such counties and cities" (40th Legislature, 1927, 268). In addition, it was considered a "fact that in order to obtain a speaking knowledge and mastery of any foreign language, it (was) imperative that instruction in such language be begun at the earliest possible period" (40th Legislature, 1927, 268). The law was approved on March 28, 1927, and went into effect 90 days after the legislature adjourned (General and Special Laws of the State of Texas, 40th Legislature, 1927, 267-268).

The 1905 law which required English to be the only language of instruction in Texas public schools seems to have been prompted primarily by the need for establishing a uniform, efficient and less confusing state controlled system of public instruction. The historical findings of Kloss and others suggests that bilingual schooling in Texas was commonly practiced in many Spanish, German and Czech-speaking communities prior to and after the enactment of this law. The penalties which were added in 1918 came in reaction to the anti-German sentiment which dominated nativist American opinion during World War I. The modification of the law in 1927 seems to have been based on the utilitarian needs of those persons who lived on the border between Mexico and the United States, rather than on a state endorsement of the equal use of Spanish and English by all Texans. Despite this authorization, many Anglo and Mexican-American school officials in these communities emphasized the primacy of English

in the school curriculum for all elementary school children.
Many Mexican-Americans in these border counties and elsewhere in
Texas grew up thinking that the law even prohibited the speaking
of Spanish on the school premises regardless of the activity
(see Kloss, 1977; Dinnerstein and Reimers, 1975; Weinberg, 1977;
Carter, 1970).

Desegregation and Bilingual Education

Mexican-Americans in Texas have historically opposed the
segregation of their children. Like other immigrants they were
not opposed to learning the officially recognized language or
disinclined to adopt the accepted customs and political practices
of the United States. In 1929, Mexican-American members of the
League of United Latin-American Citizens very early articulated
their loyalty to the United States as well as their resistance to
oppression. On the matter of school segregation and language the
early charter of the association stated:

> We shall oppose any tendency to separate
> our children in the schools of this country.
>
> The acquisition of the English language,
> which is the official language of our
> country, being necessary for the enjoy-
> ment of our rights and privileges, we
> declare it to be the official language
> of this organization, and we pledge our-
> selves to learn and speak and teach same
> to our children (Weeks, 1929, 265-266.
> Italics supplied).

Pledges of loyalty and attempts to become like the majority
culture were very often futile. Several factors worked against
the social, economic and political ascendency of the Mexican-
American in Texas. The negative opinion by the Anglo of the
Chicano seems to have been a pervasive sentiment. In the late
1940's journalist and historian Carey McWilliams described the
general attitude in these words:

> Above all it is important to remember
> that Mexicans are a 'conquered' people
> in the southwest, a people whose culture
> has been under incessant attack for many
> years and whose character and achieve-
> ments as a people, have been consistent-
> ly disparaged (McWilliams, 1968, 132).

46

Poverty, migratory patterns, segregation by occupation and residence, illiteracy and ineffective state and federal governmental policies, all contributed to the Mexican-American's political and social impotence (Sanchez, 1972; United States Commission on Civil Rights, 1968).

In the early 1960's the record of educational achievement for Chicanos was meager. By the early 1970's the picture of failure had not improved (Mexican-American Education Study, Report II, October 1971). Texas had made no positive advances toward improving the educational opportunities of Mexican-American school children. The Texas Education Agency did not collect and maintain statistics on Mexican-American enrollment in public schools. It therefore had no way of determining or accurately documenting the reason for the high drop-out rate and the low achievement experienced by thousands of Mexican-American students ("An Appalling Waste," 1963).

The report of the Governor's Committee on Public School Education in 1969 provided Mexican-American leaders with factual data with which to press the state education agency and the legislature for educational reform. The recommendations of the report did not include bilingual education, but its findings indicated that, compared to other students in the school system, Mexican-American students were experiencing an 80 percent drop-out rate (The Challenge and the Chance, Volume II, 1969, 80).

In 1967 Mexican-American leaders were still primarily concerned with the effects of school segregation practices, and many were not entirely convinced that bilingual-bicultural education would furnish Chicanos with equal educational opportunity. "The issues," according to Sanchez, "(were) not truly linguistic, but rather lie in the areas of social policy, of school organization and administration, of educational philosophy, and of pedagogical competence" (Sanchez, 1972, 49). To Sanchez, a leading Mexican-American educator, it was clear that "the retention of the Spanish language by Americans of Spanish-American descent in the southwest (had) been the function of default, rather than of any concerted popular or institutionalized effort" ("History, Culture, and Education," 1972, 49).

Paralleling the move to provide Chicanos with an equal educational opportunity by removing all vestiges of segregation in public schools was another drive to change the school curriculum to fit the cultural and linguistic needs and characteristics of the Chicano child. Linguists, foreign language teachers and educators since the early 1960's had been advocating

the use of the child's native, home or more dominant language
as a method of teaching and gradually introducing the English
language. To many educators there was a need for applying
bilingual instructional methods. To others more emphasis needed
to be placed on bridging the cultural differences which seemed
to exist between the student and the nature of the curriculum
(Ogletree and Garcia, 1975; Andersson and Boyer, 1970).

According to Dr. George I. Sanchez, Professor of history
and philosophy of education at the University of Texas for 28
years, the Texas public school system had not done a good job of
adopting its school curriculum to meet the needs of those students who entered the first grade speaking Spanish. The curriculum, he suggested, needed to be changed to meet the particular
pedagogical needs of children. It also needed to reflect the
cultural and historical realities in Texas. In the social studies curriculum he suggested that sections on the history of the
Southwest, New Spain, Indian and European culture be included.
He would place greater attention on language arts, concentrating
on oral English and on developing the child's vocabulary, and
not expect children to read any books in the first grade. Part
of the curriculum would be taught in the home language so that
the children could attain language development in a language that
was easiest for them (Hearings, San Antonio, 1968).

The segregation of Mexican-American and Anglo children was
a problem which had not been adequately addressed by Texan
educational authorities. Segregated schools fostered artificial
beliefs of inferiority and superiority in the minds of Chicano
and Anglo children. The separation often resulted in the down
grading of the language and culture of the Chicano, creating a
stigma of inferiority. In cities with distinct ethnic neighborhoods more needed to be done to integrate as many students as
possible. While conceding the need for eliminating segregated
school facilities, Sanchez emphasized that there was nothing
inherently wrong with Mexican-American children attending the
same school.

> It is the condition under which
> they are educated that can do the
> damage. It is a fact that the
> curriculum is not suited, that the
> teachers don't understand the children,
> can't communicate with the parents
> and so on, all that, of course, is
> what is harmful, not the fact that
> Spanish-speaking children are
> going to school only with Spanish-
> speaking children (Hearings, San
> Antonio, 1968, 97).

By the mid 1960's many Mexican-American leaders, parents and other educators began to reject the notion of educational and political equality attained through cultural homogenization and identical educational treatment (Rosenbaum, 1973). The mood was particularly reflected in the changed legal strategy of the Mexican-American Legal Defense and Educational Fund. While the goal of integration was not abandoned, the adoption of an educational curriculum which took the child's language and cultural distinctions into consideration was not considered inimical or incompatible with the wider meaning of equal educational opportunity (Orfield, 1978; Kirp, 1977).

In 1970 the Office for Civil Rights broadened its coverage of Title VI, Section 601 to include linguistically different children. Language difference thus became a suspect category deserving the attention of the federal government and the courts (Teitelbaum and Hiller, 1977). However, it was not "language difference" per se which merited closer governmental scrutiny, but the "common practices" of public school officials which in many cases had had the "effect" of denying linguistically different, or less proficient national origin minority children the right to an equal educational opportunity. The development of what became known as the May 25th Memorandum is traced in the next section.

May 25th Memorandum: 1970

Prior to 1970, the Office for Civil Rights (OCR) had been primarily concerned with attacking Black-White school segregation. Neither the federal courts nor the President had seriously considered the widespread practice of segregation affecting Mexican-Americans and other non-Black minority students. In 1968 the Department of Health, Education and Welfare (HEW), only required racial statistics on Blacks and Whites (Gerry, 1974). Much of the evidence documenting the continued segregation of Mexican-Americans in Texas public schools came in the form of testimony which was offered at a series of civil rights hearings in San Antonio at the end of the year (U.S. Commission on Civil Rights, San Antonio, December 9-14, 1968).

In 1960 HEW's law enforcement efforts against districts found to be in violation of the 1964 Civil Rights Act were slow and ineffective. It was not until the following year that HEW administrative officials began to pay close attention to the complaints of Mexican-Americans. One reason for the change in policy was the rising militancy of Chicanos seeking relief from local restrictive practices. The school boycotts which occurred in Abilene and Crystal City, Texas were particularly important.

In both cities students and parents who joined them in the boy-cott demanded bilingual-bicultural education, the hiring of more Chicano teachers and insisted that the ban against the speaking of Spanish on campus be repealed. Another explanation offered for this switch by OCR was the continued success which HEW had experienced in the South, thus enabling the agency to release staff to work on the problems which were still plaguing Mexican-Americans in Texas. A third reason for the change in policy is attributed to the incessant number of complaints made by Mexican-American leaders that OCR had failed to identify and investigate serious charges of discrimination and segregation against Mexi-can-Americans (Rangel and Alcala, 1972; Gambone, 1973).

It was also suggested that the increased number of adminis-trators who were brought to Washington, D.C. from California by President Nixon may have accounted for the heightened aware-ness of Chicano and Indian educational problems. Another reason offered for increased OCR involvement was that it was a deliber-ate attempt to win over national origin votes in the 1972 presi-dential elections (Gambone, 1973).

Another author suggests that that OCR May 25th Memorandum was directly influenced by a federal court case in California, Diana v. State Board of Education, which challenged "the dispro-portionate placement of Mexican-American and other linguistically and culturally distinct children in EMR classes" (Casso, 1976, 18-19). The plaintiffs in this case challenged the commonly accepted selection process and the quality of instruction in EMR classes. This and other test cases had demonstrated that the standardized tests used to weed out children for special instruction were measures of the child's knowledge of written and spoken English, rather than of his mental capacity.

Early evidence for these charges came as a result of a study conducted by the Mexican-American Education Research on 47 Mexican-American school children who had been assigned to EMR classes on the basis of English standardized intelligence tests. Using a Spanish version of the Wechsler Intelligence Scale, Escala de inteligencia Wechsler para ninos, the investi-gators found that of the 47 children tested, 27 had attained IQ scores of 80 or more, and 37 had attained IQ scores of 75 or more (Hearings, Equal Educational Opportunity, 91st Congress, 2nd Session, Part 4, 1970).

On May 25, 1970 the Office for Civil Rights issued a memo-randum to school districts with more than five percent national origin minority children who were found to be deficient in the English language. The memorandum outlined four basic areas by which future Title VI compliance reviews would be judged. The first stipulated that school districts had to take affirmative steps to rectify the language deficiency of those children who could not understand or speak English. Second, school districts could not assign students to classes for the mentally retarded or exclude them from taking college preparatory courses on the basis of tests measuring only English language skills. Third, ability grouping for the purpose of dealing with special language needs were permissible as long as they were temporary arrangements. Fourth, school districts were responsible for adequately informing the parents of national origin minority children of school activities in a language other than English if it were necessary (A Better Chance to Learn, 1975).

The Memorandum guidelines did not mention bilingual-bicultural education as one of the possible remedies which would be offered to school districts which were found out of compliance. This would be the job of the technical assistance teams which would be called upon to insure that school districts provided the services in accordance with new OCR interpretations of what kind of educational services constituted an equal educational opportunity for national minority children (Gambone, 1973).

The new guidelines influenced both the Texas Education Agency and the proponents of bilingual education in the state legislature. When TEA submitted its recommendations to the legislature in the fall of 1970, it adopted some of the language of the Memorandum. It urged the adoption of a bilingual program for those students whose inability to speak and understand English excluded them from full participation in the school's program of instruction (Recommendations for Legislative Consideration on Public Education in Texas, November, 1970).

During the 62nd (1971) and the 63rd (1973) Legislatures, Representative Truan introduced House Bill 495 and 146 respectively. Both bills were almost verbatim copies of the May 25th Memorandum. On both occasions the bills were referred to the House Committee on Public Education, but were never reported out. However, not all of the Memorandum's criteria were discarded. The provision which called for informing parents of linguistically different children of school activities in their own language was kept and incorporated into the body of Senate Bill 121 in 1973. This bill became the mandatory bilingual law which was enacted by the historic Reform Session of the Texas Legislature. Much of the interest in governmental reform which occurred during this session was directly attributable to the stock fraud disclosures which were made during the previous legislative session.

The Sharpstown Scandal

On January 18, 1971, the day before the inauguration of the
Texas state leadership, the Securities and Exchange Commission
filed a law suit which implicated high Texas political officials
in a stock fraud scheme. The case affected the proceedings of
the 62nd Legislature, and influenced the enactment of progressive
social and political legislation during the 63rd Legislature.
One of the more liberal educational measures passed during this
session would be the Bilingual Education and Training Act.

What became known as the Sharpstown Scandal grew out of a
scheme by Houston financier and real estate developer, Frank W.
Sharp, to artificially increase his bank's deposits through a
series of illegal stock manipulations through interconnected
insurance and bank companies. The suit would not have surprised
nor angered most Texas citizens had it not been for the disclo-
sure that elected officials had contributed to the success of
the scheme and had benefited from the fraudalent business transactions devised by Frank W. Sharp (Kinch and Proctor, 1972).

Preliminary results of the investigation revealed that the
Governor, Preston Smith, the Lieutenant Governor, Ben Barnes,
the Speaker, Gus F. Mutscher, along with two of Mutscher's aides
were all directly or indirectly implicated. Bill Heatly, the
powerful chairman of the House Appropriations Committee, was
also linked to the scheme. With the exception of Ben Barnes, all
of these individuals had benefited handsomely as a result of the
investments which they all had made during the summer of 1969.

The political phase of the scandal took place during the
Second Called Session of the 61st Legislature, which met between
August 27 and September 9, to consider the matter of passing a
tax increase (Kinch and Proctor, 1972).

When Governor Smith called the Second Session of the 61st
Legislature, he, along with six other politicians, had purchased
stock in the National Bankers Life Insurance Company with loans
obtained from the Sharpstown State Bank in Houston. Both companies were owned by Sharp. Sharp was interested in getting the
legislature to pass the state's own bank deposit insurance during
this session of the legislature. The passage of such a law would
have permitted him to evade the scrutiny of Federal Deposit
Insurance Corporation officials who were at the time investiga-
ting his bank's questionable loaning practices (Kinch and Proctor, 1972).

On September 5, Representative Shannon, Mutscher's right-hand man, introduced House Bills 72 and 73, the bank deposit insurance bills. Three days later Governor Smith submitted the subject of additional bank insurance to the legislature for its consideration. The matter would not have been considered by the legislature at this time if the governor had not explicitly mentioned it in his purpose for convening the legislature. On the same day, House Bills 72 and 73 were passed by the House. The next day they were quickly passed by the Senate. On September 27 Governor Smith vetoed both bills, but not before he and the others who had bought large amounts of stock in the National Bankers Life Insurance Company had sold their stocks for substantial gains (Kinch and Proctor, 1972).

The scandal which shook the foundations of Texas government in 1971 resulted in two very significant outcomes. First, it contributed to the formation of a mixed coalition of 30 House members, "the Dirty Thirty," who viewed the Speaker's leadership as tyrannical and sought to bring about "procedural reforms and ethical standards that would weaken the Mutscher team's, or any team's, control over the legislative process" (Kinch and Proctor, 1972, 87). Their opposition throughout the session kept the issue of political corruption in government and the need for reform very much alive in the minds of the voting public. Second, the revelations also dramatically shaped the outcome of the 1972 elections. In turn, the elections contributed to the re-arrangement of the internal power structure of the House. These events inadvertently aided the proponents of bilingual education legislation during the 63rd Legislature.

The 1972 Election Year

The Sharpstown Scandal, the activities of the Dirty Thirty in the House, and newspaper accounts of political irregularities in Austin contributed to the election of a reform minded legislative body in 1972. The desire for governmental reform was most evident in the House, where the new Speaker separated the first nine bills to introduce the changes in state government which he felt were needed. The second change was the election of a new legislative leadership which was committed to supporting the enactment of a bilingual education law. Another factor which aided bilingual advocates in 1973 was the surprising showing of the mostly Chicano supported La Raza Unida Party. The election of more urban, liberal minded House members was also particularly important.

The elections of 1972 resulted in one of the largest turn-overs in Texas legislative history. In the House 77 new members were elected. All of the 15 senators elected, however, had served in the House during the 62nd Legislative session. The number of Mexican-American legislators in Austin increased to thirteen. Two were elected to the Senate and eleven served in the House (Deaton, 1973; Castro, 1973).

The election results in 1972 represented the confluence of two trends in Texas political history: the politicization of the Chicano and the weakening of traditional state-wide restrictions on the political participation of the poor, Blacks and Chicanos. In 1949 V. O. Key had noted that "the presence of large numbers of persons of Spanish and Mexican descent along the Mexican border introduce(d) special problems of political organization and produce(d) special characteristics of electoral behavior" (Key, 1949, 271). Some of the more visible factors which prevented effective Chicano political participation in the past had been their over-representation in low status and low paying occupations, low educational achievement, cultural and linguistic differences, and the indifference and hostility of the Anglo majority. The result of these and other factors led to the development of the patron system in the rural, agricultural counties in the south of the state. The boss or manager of an agricultural enterprise exercised total control over the voting of his employees. Unlike the urban group politics which was practiced in many of the other northern cities, the rural Anglo-controlled machine did very little to improve the social and political position of the people whose votes they manipulated (Curtis, 1978).

Despite what seemed like overwhelming odds against the active political mobilization of Chicanos, by the mid 1960's the climate had considerably changed. Seizing on different aspects of the problem affecting the social, economic and political condition of the Chicano in the Southwest, spokesmen of various factions and associations of the Chicano Movement leveled their criticisms at an Anglo dominated system which had done very little to help the Mexican-American. Senator Joe J. Bernal pointedly described the Mexican-American sentiment in these words:

> The idealistic situation of local and
> state partnership has at times been
> adverse to the welfare of the Mexican-
> American minority in the Southwest.
> We have not had to overcome slavery;
> but oppression, yes! Ethnic discrimi-
> nation, yes! De facto segregation,
> yes! Mix these with cultural and

> ethnic pride and somewhere you
> will find the answer to why some
> people had not been aware that
> there were problems in the South-
> west. That deep rooted pride has
> caused us for many years to turn
> inwardly to find reasons or causes,
> instead of outwardly to be understood,
> or to understand ("The Role of the
> State," 1970, 365).

Dissatisfied with the slow approach of the more traditional Mexican-American organizations and the traditional lack of response of the regular state political parties, younger Chicanos decided to utilize the tactics of confrontation which Blacks were successfully using to obtain economic and political concessions from the Texan establishment.

In 1970, under the leadership of Jose Angel Gutierrez, the first Chicano political party was founded in Crystal City, Texas. In the beginning, the efforts of the La Raza Unida party were confined to wresting political power from the Anglo minority in Crystal City which, until that year, had controlled the city council and school board. Gutierrez's original plan called for building a strong regional support for the party before attempting to enter any statewide contests. In 1971, however, Gutierrez, under pressure from others in the party who looked on the victory in Crystal City as heralding the beginning of genuine political participation in Texas for the Chicano, was forced by the membership to participate in the statewide elections in 1972. According to Castro:

> Around the state there were Raza
> Unida activists who were eager to
> become politically involved. To
> many of them, Crystal City repre-
> sented a challenge. And if they
> lived in El Paso, Dallas, Fort Worth
> or Waco, South Texas was too far out
> of the way to attract their enthu-
> siasm. A statewide candidate, on
> the other hand, would give everyone
> in the state a chance to partici-
> pate (Castro, 1973).

Four candidates for the gubernatorial race appeared on the ballot in November, 1972. Of the four the most seriously considered were conservative Dolph Briscoe, Democrat and conservative Henry C. Grover, Republican. The only difference between the candidates was their party affiliation. The pre-election campaign in 1972 was essentially issueless, but the Democrat from Uvalde, Briscoe, was favored to win the contest.

Most observers had not expected a very close contest. The election results proved otherwise. Dolph Briscoe won his opponent by a margin of 99,507 votes, capturing approximately 49 percent of the vote. La Raza Unida candidate Ramsey Muniz obtained six percent, while Socialist party candidate Deborah Leonard received .7 percent of the vote. The election marked the first time since Reconstruction that a governor had ever been elected without a majority of the popular vote (Deaton, 1973; House Journal, Volume I, 1973, 1969).

Statewide, 61 percent of the Chicano voters had supported Dolph Briscoe, and 33 percent had cast their votes for La Raza Unida party candidate Ramsey Muniz. If Muniz had received 27 percent more of the Chicano vote, Briscoe would not have won the election (Levy and Kramer, 1973). Election analysts were very surprised at the results of the election. They generally conceded that La Raza Unida party had made a political impact which could not be ignored by the dominant conservative Democratic party.

The political gains which Mexican-Americans attained in 1972 came as a result of federal intervention and not through progressive, innovative state initiatives. Historically Texas policy-makers had fought practically every attempt to broaden the participation and decision-making process of the poor, and its ethnic minorities in state government. The characteristic resistance to change which Texas legislators have exhibit since 1876 has been attributed to the state's distinctive political cultural development. In his study on American federalism, Elazar (1972) hypothesized that there seemed to be a relation between the political development of a state and the migration of culturally different groups who settled in these states. He subsequently identified three cultural labels which seemed to encompass the migratory patterns he had observed: moralistic, individualistic and traditionalistic. Texas' development was characterized as a synthesis of traditionalism and individualism.

A "traditionalistic" political culture was described as one which was based on an elitist conception of government and paternalism. In Texas this meant that the right to the decision-making process was considered the domain of a small, hard-working, and deserving group of persons. The role of government was to preserve the status quo and the average citizen was not expected to take part in politics, but to passively accept the decisions of the ruling class. The "individualistic" political culture conceived of government as a tool to facilitate private gain, limited the role of government and expected very little popular participation in the political process (Nimmo and Oden, 1971). Although limited, the model has provided us with a basis for understanding the development of the state's one-party system, its parochial approach to economic and social problems, and its historic resistance to increasing the participation of the poor, Blacks and Chicanos in the decision-making process. Lockard's description of the one party dominated political system fits the pattern which developed in Texas since the radical Reconstruction Period.

> In hard fact, state governments are
> often quite unresponsive to the needs
> and desires of the people without wealth
> and organized power. In general the one
> party states represent the least responsive
> and most corrupt political systems. The
> factual confusion of noncompetitive pol-
> itics is made to order for well placed
> and powerful interests who strick bar-
> gains with irresponsible politicians
> and in inconspicuous ways to manage to
> achieve their objectives, often with
> total disregard for the interests or
> desires of wider elements of the society.
> (Lockard, 1966, 198).

The Sharpstown incident had an immediate, major impact on the usually complacent and self-perpetuating system of government in Austin. Of the 56 candidates who were elected in 1972, 51 had received the endorsement of the Dirty Thirty. Although no perfect cause and effect relation can be drawn between the election results and the Sharpstown incident, the activities of the Dirty Thirty, and the connection of defeated incumbents with the Speaker cannot be underplayed (Deaton, 1973).

There were other factors which aided the proponents of bilingual education in 1973. The broadening of the electorate in Texas also played an important role. The use of the "white primary," the poll tax, residency requirements, the gerrymander, registration restrictions, and other more subtle, informal restraints had limited the decision-making process in Texas to a select few. The earliest restrictions, the poll tax and the "white primary," were directed against Blacks shortly after the Reconstruction Period, and against rural, poor whites during

The Populist movement of the 1890's (Benton, 1966). These restrictions, although originally not enacted against Mexican-Americans, adversely limited their participation as well.

Before the general elections in 1972 a number of voting restrictions were successfully challenged in court. In the case of Beare v. Smith (1971) plaintiffs charged that the law which required annual registration between October 1 and January 31 placed unnecessary obstacles to the voter. Based on the findings of the case the court ruled against the code, stating that the requirement did not promote a compelling state interest (Maxwell, 1972). A second contributory factor was the decision of Bob Bulluck, Secretary of State, to change the residency voting requirement to 30 days. The invalidated Texas statute had required one year residency in the state and six months in the county to qualify to vote. The secretary's ruling was based on a Supreme Court decision, Dunn v. Blumstein (1972) in Tennessee, which suggested that any residency requirement beyond 30 days could be declared unconstitutional ("Voting Residency Role Cut to 30 Days in Texas," New York Times, 1 April 1972, p. 8). Chicanos and others were also successful in challenging Texas laws which discouraged many persons from seeking political office because of excessive filing fees. In Carter v. Dies (1970) the court ruled the Texas Election Code requiring a candidate for statewide or country office to file a fee unconstitutional. Before the decision Texas law required a filing fee of $1,000, for state senator and $600 for state representative, depending on the size of the legislative district. In Johnston v. Luna (1972) plaintiffs challenged the legislature's revised statute requiring a candidate to be charged no more than four percent of the salary of the office sought. The statute included a pauper's provision for those who could not pay the filing fee. However, its requirements were especially prohibitive. The court once again held that the state had not made a compelling case to justify the need to pay for elections through the use of filing fees when in other states legislators had found different and acceptable ways of paying for these expenses (Maxwell, 1972).

Another major change which affected the outcome of the 1972 elections was a federal court ruling which declared the use of the multimember legislative districts in Dallas and Bexar counties unconstitutional on the grounds that they denied minority groups freedom of association and equal protection of the laws (Maxwell, 1972).

The redistricting law, enacted during the 62nd Legislature, had been the work of Speaker Gus F. Mutscher and Representative Delwin Jones of Lubbock. The law "violated every court standard, state attorney general's opinion, and common sense principle that related to reapportionment. County line, voting precincts, natural boundaries, and socio-economic distributions were completely ignored" (Katz, 1972, 254). Nonetheless, the bill was passed into law by a conservative, Mutscher-controlled House more interested in self-preservation than in political equity.

Chicanos, Blacks and Anglo liberals challenged the legality of multi-member districts arguing that their use discriminated against minority groups by restricting the choice of candidates to conservative, business-backed members of the Democratic party. In addition, multimember districts diluted the voting strengths of minorities. The court ruling would have resulted in a legislative challenge, but Governor Smith decided not to defy the court decision sensing that the legislature would be unable to draw up a plan that would have been acceptable to the court in time for the February 6 deadline and the upcoming primary elections in May of 1972 ("U.S. Court Revises Texas Districts," New York Times, 23 January, 1972, p. 30). The results of the court ruling became evident in the fall.

Out of the 150 member House, 53 representatives were from the three most heavily populated counties in Texas: Dallas-Fort Worth, Harris, Houston, Bexar, and San Antonio. Thirty-nine of these delegates had been elected for the first time. In San Antonio only four of the eleven legislators present in the 62nd Legislature returned in 1973. Matt Garcia's defeat of House Appropriations Committee chairman Bill Finck was especially significant. It cleared the way for the appointment of a liberal as chairman of the powerful Appropriations Committee who could support the bilingual education bill. It also inadvertently brought another Mexican-American legislator to Austin who would play a key role in the enactment of Truan's bilingual education bill.

In Dallas county only four out of 18 members of the 62nd Legislature were re-elected. In Harris county, which had been redistricted before the court's decision in August, 1971, the effects were particularly noticeable. Eighteen of the 24 representatives had been elected for the first time. Of this group 14 were liberal Democrats, three were moderates and seven were Republicans. The Harris county delegation was dominated by liberals (Deaton, 1973; Pettus and Bland, 1976).

The changes which occurred in the Senate were less affected by the political fiasco and the court challenges. Most of the changes came as a result of ordinary reasons. Three senators voluntarily retired and eight had decided to run for other government positions. Of the 20 incumbents left, nine ran unopposed. In eleven contests where incumbents were running for another term, four were defeated. However, of all the Senate races, only three of the senators were ever questioned concerning their role in the Sharpstown affair.

Several reasons are offered to explain why Senate members were less affected by the political scandal. The feud between the Speaker and the Dirty Thirty was centered in the House. Public attention, was, as a result, focused on the governor, the Speaker and the Dirty Thirty. The difference in size between House and Senatorial electoral districts was also suggested to be an important factor.

The election of 1972 produced no extraordinary changes in the political climate of the Senate. The four senators who were defeated were replaced by conservative Democrats. The Senate during the 63rd Legislature was tightly controlled by conservatives, "and was the 'death chamber' for lobby-opposed bills" (Deaton, 1973, 154-156).

During the 1972 election year a series of unexplained events worked to the advantage of the advocates of bilingual education legislation in Texas. The Sharpstown revelations played an important role in helping to alter the make-up of the House. More than half of the chamber's representatives were replaced by reform-minded, urban and liberal oriented House members. Attracted by Price Daniels, Jr.'s commitment to refor in state government, these newly elected officials overwhelming ly elected him to the Speaker's position. This, in turn, clear the way for the appointment of liberal and sympathetic House me bers to key legislative committees to which the bilingual educa tion bill would have to be referred for consideration.

Two other factors seem to have had a positive effect on th passage of the bilingual education bill in Texas. The Chicano voter turnout on behalf of La Raza Unida party seems to have had a sobering effect on the leadership of the Democratic party It became evident to many legislators that the Mexican-American vote could no longer be taken for granted. Federal interventic in the areas of voting rights, participation in public office and equal legislative representation worked to the advantage of bilingual proponents in 1973.

Four factors in the political environment of Texas were identified as having influenced the enactment of bilingual education legislation in 1969 and 1973. Three of the events, the May 25th Memorandum, the Sharpstown Scandal, the 1972 Elections, indirectly contributed to a favorable, more receptive political environment to the demands by Mexican-Americans for educational reform during the 63rd Legislature (1973). The enactment of the federal Bilingual Education Act in 1968 had a more direct effect on the passage of similar legislation the following year in Austin.

The impetus for and the subsequent passage of the federal Bilingual Education Act was strongly influenced by professional educators and Spanish-speaking minorities from the Southwest and Northeast. The nine conferences which were held between 1966 and 1967 served to define the needs of Chicanos and to devise a common advocacy strategy. In the mid 1960's equal educational opportunity became synonymous with bilingual education.

The issuance of the May 25th Memorandum was made in response to Mexican-American demands for aid in their fight against segregationist practices in public schools. The new criteria developed by the Office for Civil Rights served to encourage bilingual instruction methodology and influenced state educational policy-makers.

The political scandals created an unfavorable climate which altered the routine legislative transfer of power in Austin. The disclosures of political corruption in the legislature affected the election results in 1972. A series of unexpected court challenges against the electoral system and legislative apportionment also greatly contributed to the election of a completely new legislative leadership which would be more sympathetic to the demands for bilingual education legislation. Lastly, the interventionist effect of third party La Raza Unida on the traditional Democratic vote served notice on party elites in Texas that Chicano demands for a greater share of the state's resources needed to be placated.

CHAPTER IV

MEXICAN-AMERICANS, BILINGUAL EDUCATION AND
LEGISLATION: 1969 and 1971

The enactment of the bilingual education bill by
the Texas legislature in 1969 was significant. It marked the
first time that a major piece of legislation had ever been initiated and successfully passed through both Houses of the legislature by a Mexican-American legislator.

The passage of such progressive legislation was as much a
product of the legislative process as it was an indication of the
political, social and economic changes which had occurred in
Texas within a period of scarcely twenty years. The political
and social changes which considerably altered the Texas political
environment during this period, as shown in the preceding chap-
ters, account in part for the enactment of what can be considered
landmark legislation in the area of state educational curriculum
policy-making.

The environmental factors, however, only partially explain
the enactment of bilingual education legislation in Texas.
According to Meranto:

> External changes do not automatically bring
> about innovation in the system and in its policy
> outputs for the simple reason that the institu-
> tional structure of the system is rigged against
> producing change (Meranto, 1967, 110).

Explanations for new policy outcomes must also be sought within
the framework of established customs and institutions. The
objective of this chapter will be to describe the events and
actions of the various actors, demand articulators, which contributed to the successful passage of bilingual education legislation in 1969. We shall then examine the attempt which was made
to expand the provisions of the bilingual law in 1971 and why
it failed. In the last part of the chapter we will describe
the part which Mexican-American organizations played in influencing the introduction and passage of bilingual education legislation. Finally, we will describe the role of the Texas Education Agency in the enactment of bilingual education legislation.
The strategy devised by advocates of bilingual education was
cautious and incremental. The first step was to make bilingual
instruction in the state of Texas legal. The second would
attempt to expand the original provisions of the law and obtain
state funding.

In a 1953 study of the Mexican-American in Texas, Clinchy noted that there was little evidence of interest by the legislature on the educational problems of this group. Most of the work which had been done on behalf of Mexican-Americans had been shouldered by state educational agencies on a piecemeal basis. With the sole exception of one bill, which established the Good Neighbor Commission in 1945, actual legislation which addressed itself to the needs of Mexican-American citizens did not exist. Texas legislators, it was noted, were extremely cautious when it came to enacting legislation which would directly benefit minority students. The sentiment of the legislature at the time seemed to be marked by "a resistance to direct governmental action. . . , but (with) a willingness to experiment with gradual change. . ." (Clinchy, 1974, 124, 180, 202).

One such experiment came in the form of two bills which were introduced in the legislature in 1943 and 1945. The first bill (H.C.R. 105) was introduced in the form of a resolution. The first part of the bill stated that "All persons of the Caucasian Race" within the state of Texas were entitled to equal access and use of all accommodations in public places. The second part of the resolution admonished its readers that those persons who failed to abide by this principle would be "violating the good neighbor policy" of the state. The bill was a harmless concurrent resolution with no law enforcement provision. It omitted the Blacks and safely avoided addressing the issue of discrimination against Mexican-Americans by labeling them "Caucasians."

In 1945, Senate Bill Number 1 was authored by Senator J. Franklin Spears of San Antonio during the 49th legislative session. The bill was different from the previous resolution in two respects. It specifically mentioned Mexican-Americans, commonly referred to as Latin-Americans, as being the victims of discrimination in Texas. The bill's prohibition of discriminatory practices applied to all public accommodations and imposed a penalty of imprisonment, a $500 fine, or both (Clinchy, 1974). The bill never left the committee to which it had been assigned.

With the exception of a 1959 pre-school law, known as the Little School of the 400, Mexican-American educational problems were not addressed or seriously considered in the legislature until the convening of the 61st Legislative Session in 1969.

The 61st Legislature - 1969

The federal Bilingual Education Act was a year old when the 61st Legislature convened in Austin on January 14 to consider the business of the state. Preston Smith, who had served as lieutenant governor during the previous six years, had been elected governor. Ben Barnes was elected lieutenant governor after having served as Speaker of the House for two terms.

The powerful Speaker's position went to a newly elected House member from East Texas, Gus F. Mutscher. All three were conservative Democrats and not necessarily interested in the economic and social problems of the Mexican-American as they were in protecting the corporate interests of the state. Nothing in their previous legislative records would necessarily associate them with the needs and demands which Texas Chicanos would bring to their attention. Yet, without their support or consent, the bilingual education bill which was proposed and passed during the 61st Legislature would have had little success.

In 1969, ten Mexican-American legislators were in the 150 member House. In the Senate, Joe J. Bernal, known respectfully as "mi senador" by his Chicano colleagues, had successfully won his bid for a second term of office from San Antonio. He and the newly elected Representative from Corpus Christi, Carlos F. Truan, would initiate and push for the passage of the first bilingual education law in Texas.

Senate Bill 46

Fifteen days after the beginning of the 61st Legislative Session, Senator Bernal introduced Senate Bill 46. The bill's purpose was to repeal the state's prohibition against the use of another language as a medium of instruction, and to permit local school districts to implement bilingual instruction if it was deemed advantageous for the student (Senate Journal, Volume I, 1969, 94).

Throughout the entire legislative session Truan and Bernal repeatedly emphasized three things to their colleagues: one, the law's enactment would allow the state of Texas to receive up to $3 million in new Title VII federal funds; two, the law would in no way jeopardize the local autonomy of the school districts; and three, the use of another language as a medium of instruction would not supplant the officially recognized language--English.

By December of 1967 Bernal had been fully convinced that the bilingual-bicultural approach to teaching Mexican-American students provided one of the best means for their educational success. As a former teacher, he intuitively believed that this method of instruction would be far better than what the educational system was offering (Bernal, 1970).

Seven months after he had presented testimony before Senator Yarborough's committee on bilingual education in San Antonio, he wrote a letter to the Office of Education mentioning the positive gains in student performance which had been demonstrated in the Harlandale School District of San Antonio.

"These startling successes," he wrote, "would provide for me a firm base of support for future state legislation in the area of . . . bilingual-bicultural education" (Letter to Armando Rodriguez, 12 December 1967).

The following year Bernal wrote a letter to Dr. J. W. Edgar, commissioner of the Texas Education Agency (TEA), informing him of the availability of new federal funds and of the state's language restriction.

> The Congress and President of the United States recently approved an $80 million federal program for bilingual education. Presently, Texas law restricts public schools to conducting classes in English, therefore, I would appreciate your office drawing up a bill to amend this law thus permitting this state to participate in the above-mentioned federal program (Letter to Dr. J. W. Edgar, 1 January 1968).

Dr. Edgar's response was assuring and supportive. He informed Senator Bernal that a State Task Force had been created to administer the program. In addition, he promised to prepare a bill that would amend the restrictive law (Letter to Bernal, 2 June 1968).

The momentum for the advocates of bilingual education in Texas mounted. On April 6, the State Board of Education had approved the agency's plan to develop a state plan for bilingual education and to establish an advisory committee on bilingual education. By August 24, fifteen appointees to the advisory committee had been confirmed (Official Agenda, State Board of Education, April 6, 1968, August 24, 1968). Both Senator Bernal and the newly elected House member, Carlos F. Truan, were members of this committee.

Work on the preparation of a bilingual bill that could be enacted went on at TEA and at the Texas Legislative Council. On November 22 the first draft of what would be Senate Bill 46 was sent to Senator Bernal by a Council staff member. The bill was modeled after a much earlier permissive statute on bilingual education which had been enacted in California in 1965 (Geffert, et al., 1975). The draft consisted of three sections: the first emphasized the school's authority to determine when and if bilingual instruction could be utilized; the second called for the repeal of Article 288 of the Penal Code of Texas, and the last section included the emergency clause, giving the bill priority (Letter to Bernal, November 22, 1968).

On the same month TEA published its first recommendation to the state legislature on the subject of bilingual education in Texas. The document reflected the emerging interests in ethnic pride and the ideals of cultural pluralism, stressing the importance of becoming bilingual in Spanish and English for all public school children in Texas. The Spanish-speaking population was described as a valuable resource which could contribute to the state's development. The introduction also emphasized the promising research findings which had been made on the nature of language, language acquisition and on the psychological and cultural development of children. These new insights into language learning and early childhood development provided educators with more hope for educating both the English and Spanish monolingual child. Texas, it was hoped, would make all of its public school children bilingual in Spanish and English.

The Agency then made three specific recommendations to the legislature:

1. English shall be the basic language of instruction in all schools.

2. The governing board of any school district and any private school may determine when and under what circumstances instruction may be given bilingually.

3. The policy of the State is to ensure the mastery of English by all pupils in the schools, provided that bilingual instruction may be offered in those situations when such instruction is educationally advantageous to the pupils. If bilingual instruction is authorized it should not interfere with the systematic, sequential, and regular instruction of all pupils in the English language (Recommendations for Legislative Consideration on Public Education in Texas, November, 1969, 39).

House Bill 103

When Representative Truan arrived in Austin on January 14, it was the second time he had ever visited the Capitol. Two years earlier he had come to Austin as a representative of LULAC to testify in favor of the enactment of a minimum wage bill on behalf of migrant farm workers. His interest in politics had been shaped to a great extent as a result of his involvement with LULAC sponsored anti-poverty programs, the national conferences which had been convened by the federal government, and

67

his involvement with the Civil Rights Commission. It was during this time that he became even more conscious of the political, social and economic powerlessness of the Chicano in Texas. His enthusiasm, concern and natural leadership qualities did not go unnoticed by the leadership of LULAC and American G.I. Forum. Before the hearing on bilingual education was held in Corpus Christi in the Spring of 1967, he had been asked to run for state representative by Dr. Hector P. Garcia and Tony Bonilla. According to Senator Yarborough, it was arranged to give the promising LULAC leader a chance to present testimony at the bilingual education hearings scheduled for Corpus Christi, in order to give him local visibility in anticipation of the November elections in 1968. When he won his bid for election on November 5, he was the second Chicano to have ever been elected from this predominantly populated Mexican-American city (Truan, C. F., Personal communication, February 20, 1979).

Salesmanship and Legislative Advocacy

In the winter of 1969 Representative Truan went to Austin with what seems to be one central thought in mind. He knew it was important to pass a bilingual education bill. The language restrictions were an eye-sore for the state, especially when the primary impetus for the federal bilingual education law had originated in Texas. Truan's past experiences, his willingness to take leadership positions and his idealism prepared him for his new role as legislator.

Born and reared in Kingsville, a cattle and agricultural community about 20 miles southwest of Corpus Christi, Truan had personally experienced the results of the "no Spanish" rule in the all "Mexican" primary school he was forced to attend. By the time he was a senior in high school, the rule had become an accepted way of life. As a student leader he recalled how he promoted an "English only" campaign among the student body to encourage other students who had apparently not accepted the norm.

After graduating from Texas A and I University in three years with a B.S. degree in business administration, Truan went to Corpus Christi to find a job. After several weeks of searching, it became clear to him that regardless of how qualified, he was not going to be employed by any local company. His application for employment with the Humble Oil Company (now called Exxon) was turned down, because he was informed the jobs were held for the sons and daughters of company employees. Eight years later he would learn the real reason he was not hired. Bewildered by his inability to find employment, despite his qualifications, he went to the Texas Employment Commission. They suggested that he try selling insurance.

Truan's decision to become an insurance salesman was fortuitous. It gave him the freedom and the economic independence that he would need later on to become an active leader in LULAC, to become involved in the organization of the early anti-poverty programs, and to fully participate in the Chicano Movement of the mid 1960's. As a member of the State Advisory Committee to the U.S. Commission on Civil Rights, Truan was able to gain first hand knowledge on the social and economic discrimination suffered by Mexican-Americans in Texas. It became very clear to him that no matter how qualified, there were certain sectors of the economic and social system which were closed to the Mexican-American.

In 1967 he and several other active Mexican-Americans organized La Primera Conferencia de la Raza Unida in the City of San Antonio. The conference served to unite various groups and individuals who had become conscious of the way Mexican-Americans had been denied social, economic and political opportunities in Texas. It was a signal to local, state and federal officials that Mexican-Americans would no longer be denied full participation in the economic, social and political life of Texas. Conference speeches were very often followed by action. Truan's exposure of Humble Oil's hiring practices was one example. Conference participants were informed that the Humble Oil Company in Corpus Christi had purposely discriminated against Mexican-Americans. Out of 428 employees, only eight were Mexican-Americans. Conference participants voted to boycott the company and, to demonstrate their dissatisfaction and unwillingness to accept these practices, over 100 Humble Oil credit cards were mailed to the company's headquarters in Houston with letters of protest.

When Truan returned to Corpus Christi, he was contacted by Senator Yarborough and asked if he could organize the hearings on bilingual education scheduled to be held in May of that same year. It was at these hearings that Truan's past experiences in school converged with the kind of testimony which was offered. Like Yarborough, he too became convinced of the merits and justification for bilingual education instruction.

In 1969, 1971 and 1973 it was Truan who provided the advocacy role in the Texas State Legislature. With the asistance of Manual Garza, LULAC lobbyist, Representative Truan was introduced to the Speaker and the Lieutenant Governor, two of the most powerful officers in the Texas Legislature. Without their help, no major or local bill of any substance could be enacted. By the time the 61st Legislative session was into its second week, Truan had been appointed to all of the committees which he had requested. The education committee, made up of 21 members, was important because it was to this committee that his first bill on bilingual education would be sent for consideration.

On February 5, House Bill 103, entitled, "An Act requiring that English shall be the basic language of instruction in all grade schools. . ." was introduced into the House, read for the first time and referred to the Committee on Public Education. By March 5 the bill was reported favorably out of committee with a "do pass" recommendation. This bill passed through the committee hearings unopposed. No person or interest group had raised any significant objection to the bill's proposal. When it became certain that the bilingual bill had a chance of clearing the scrutiny of the education committee, legislative representative for the Texas State Teachers Association, L. P. Sturgeon, attempted to take credit for the bill's introduction and authorship.

TSTA Maneuvers to Champion Bilingual Education

The Texas State Teachers Association (TSTA) is the largest and most powerful teacher organization in Texas. TSTA's legislative lobbying interests have almost exclusively been in the area of teacher salaries and retiree benefits. Its interest in the allocation of federal funds in Texas seems to have been limited except if it were related to a state enacted legislative bill (Berke and Kirst, 1972). Prior to 1969 the association seems to have demonstrated little or no interest in the educational problems of Mexican-American school children. Its leadership had provided no testimony in support of bilingual education during the Senate subcommittee hearings on bilingual education which were held in San Antonio and Corpus Christi in 1967. The association may have offered a favorable resolution or two on bilingual education instruction, but it never included it in any of its legislative proposals to the Texas legislature between 1969 and 1973. Hence, the referral of another bilingual education bill endorsed by TSTA surprised the 21 member Public Education Committee.

House Bill 103 had been in the Education Committee for eight days when Representative Menton J. Murray of Harlingen introduced House Bill 334, entitled "An Act requiring that English shall be the basic language of instruction in all grade schools . . ." into the House (House Journal, Volume I, 1969, 237). The bill, which was a verbatim copy of Truan's bill, was referred to the Committee on Public Education. When representative Murray appeared before the Committee on its first public hearing on the bilingual education bill, it became clear to the members, after questioning him on the particulars of the bill, that he knew absolutely nothing about bilingual education, nor could he clearly state what the bill was supposed to do. It was soon discovered that Representative Murray, who represented a heavily populated Chicano district in the valley, had been

asked by L.P. Sturgeon, executive secretary of TSTA, to introduce
the bill. When Sturgeon was questioned about the bill he claimed
that the bill had been originally drafted by TSTA. Truan
objected to the claim, declaring that his bill had been drafted
by TEA with the help of the Advisory Committee on Bilingual
Education during the summer of 1968.

It appears that TSTA, after learning that the bilingual
bill stood a good chance of passing, had requested Representative
Murray to introduce the bill for two reasons. Murray, whose
twenty years in office was being contested back home, thought
that his chances for re-election the following year would be much
better if he could demonstrate that he had authored a bill that
would benefit Mexican-Americans. TSTA, which was the major
lobbyist organization representating the interests of teachers
in the state of Texas, was anxious to receive the credit for
having authored or suggested such innovation. The maneuver,
however, did not work.

LULAC and the State Legislature

Both the President of the Senate, Lieutenant Governor Ben
Barnes, and the Speaker of the House, Gus F. Mutscher, had
been approached by LULAC representative Manual Garza very early
in the session concerning Mexican-American interests in the
enactment of permissive bilingual education. In return for
their support of this bill, LULAC would promise to back them in
their bid for higher elected office. The bill was harmless and
did not affect any major business interest. In addition, it
did not call for any new appropriations.

LULAC's direct involvement in state politics represented
a major departure from its position of nonalignment in political
activities. The enactment of the federal bilingual education
law in 1967 encouraged the LULAC leadership in Texas to take a
more participatory role in local and state politics. It became
obvious to the new Chicano leadership that the state educational
agency was limited in what it could do to implement the kinds
of educational changes which they felt were needed. Hence,
Truan's candidacy and eventual election in 1968 was no mere
coincidence, but a planned effort on the part of LULAC and
American G. I. Forum leaders to increase Mexican-American representation in Austin.

LULAC's new political activism was not unanimously shared
by all. Some still feared that direct confrontations with the
Anglo would do more harm than good. The younger leaders in the
organization could not agree with the policy of accommodation.
LULAC's support of a migrant strike in the Valley for higher
wages in 1966 represented a major turning point for the

organization.

On July 17 the LULAC leadership voted in favor of supporting the proposed march to Austin as well as migrant workers' demands for a minimum wage law. Most agreed to give moral support for the march, but were divided on whether LULAC should participate. Both Mario Obledo, LULAC State Director, and Carlos F. Truan, Deputy State Director, favored LULAC's active participation in the march and also the demands for a minimum wage law starting at $1.25 per hour. Those who supported the migrant workers argued that the migrant workers' demands for a better standard of life for themselves and their children in no way conflicted with the goals of the organization.

The era of accommodation had come to an end. The new Chicano leadership would no longer accept a sit and wait attitude ("LULAC's Approve Valley Strike Aid," 1966; Truan, C. F., Personal communication, February 20, 1979).

The 61st Legislature and the Political Leadership

The 61st regular session of the Texas Legislature was a tranquil legislative session. With the exception of three bills--bilingual education, minimum wage, pre-school program-- no major innovative social or political legislation was enacted by this legislature. The governor's almost record setting 55 vetoes did not significantly alter the legislative process. Perhaps the most troublesome aspect of the session was Governor Smith's veto of the $2.8 billion annual appropriations bill at the end of the session. The veto forced the legislature to prepare a two year budget with a $349 million tax increase. The original appropriations bill would not have required a tax bill (Kinch and Proctor, 1972).

Of the 2,341 bills which were introduced by House and Senate members, 944 were finally enacted. Legislative proposals during the session included such costly items as a proposed $9 billion water development plan, overdue salary increases for teachers, the construction of three new medical schools, and the creation of the first four year university to be constructed since 1923. Drug and law enforcement proposals received special attention. The legislature renewed and tightened restrictions on the use of hallucinogenic and other kinds of drugs. The governor was also given more authority to quell possible public demonstrations (Accomplishments, 1969).

It was very important for the advocates of bilingual education legislation to win the support or the consent of the Speaker of the House and the President of the Senate for the enactment of their bill. It was also equally vital to obtain

VRJC LIBRARY

the support of the committee chairman to which the bilingual bill
would be referred. Without this preliminary work the bilingual
education bill would have had very little chance of passing. The
key to the successful enactment of H.B. 103 and S.B. 46 then lay
with the political leadership of the 61st Legislature.

The presiding officer in the Senate with whom Truan, Garza
and Bernal had to deal was the new lieutenant governor. In 1968
Ben Barnes had become the first lieutenant governor to ever carry
all 254 counties in Texas and to get over two million votes in
an election. Barnes was a conservative Democrat whose success
in state politics was due more to establishment team efforts
than to his own intelligence, interest in good government or
personal crusade for egalitarian causes (Katz, 1972).

When the author of S.B. 46 and other Mexican-American legislators informed him of the intent of the bill he nodded his
approval. The bill was harmless in that it neither sought
funds nor required local school districts to implement bilingual
instruction. Another reason for Barnes' tacit approval was his
recognition of a growing Chicano constituency and of its potential in future elections.

The lieutenant governor in the Texas Senate exercises more
influence over the legislative process than the governor. While
in other state legislatures the office is merely an executive
position, in Texas it has developed into the most influential
legislative position. As the presiding officer in the Senate he
is responsible for the appointment of all standing committee and
subcommittee chairmen and vice chairmen. The lieutenant governor
has a direct hand in writing the Senate rules of procedure and
in their interpretation during the session. The President of the
Senate also refers all bills to the various standing committees
and, as presiding officer, has the power to recognize members
wishing to take up bills for floor action out of their regular
order on the calendar (Pettus and Bland, 1976).

The Speaker of the House, Gus Franklin Mutscher, was
another legislative officer with whom Truan and Manual Garza
had to strike an amicable agreement. Mutscher succeeded Ben
Barnes as Speaker of the House in 1969 after serving nine years
in the legislature. He too was a staunch conservative Democrat
who ruled the mostly conservative House with military precision.
Mutscher, like Barnes, was a loyal follower of the established
power arrangements in the Texas legislature. His connection and
strong support of Ben Barnes in the House earned for him the
chairmanship of the House Redistricting Committee in 1967. In
1969 it was known that Mutscher was looking forward to succeeding
Ben Barnes or going to Washington, D.C. The plan which Barnes
and he had devised to run the legislative business of the state

73

was quite traditional. "Neither house would question minor
legislation initiated by the other" (Katz, 1972, 95). Differences on major bills would be settled among the leaders of
both houses with the various business interests consulted every
step of the negotiation process (Kinch and Proctor, 1972).

The bilingual bill which TEA had recommended and Mexican-
Americans wanted was considered "minor legislation" and thus its
passage was not interfered with by the political leadership. In
the House Public Education Committee, where controversial or
unwanted bills are very often buried, Chairman George Hinson
offered no resistance to the bilingual bill either. The next
possible obstacle which Truan faced was the quixotic behavior
of newly elected Governor Preston Smith.

Smith's election as governor in 1968 was the fulfillment
of a boyhood dream. Of the three legislative leaders, he had
had the longest experience in state government. Preston Smith
was also a Democrat with an ultraconservative political philosophy. In his inaugural address to the Legislature, Smith
emphasized the need for law and order, stricter enforcement of
narcotic laws and the strengthening of the technical and vocational program of the state. Preston Smith provided very little
leadership throughout his two terms in office. Although his
office was the weakest link in the legislative process, he did
have the last word when it came to the enactment of a bill.
Apparently, none of the bilingual education advocates in the
legislature at the time ever openly solicited his help throughout the entire process. It seems as though few feared that he
would oppose the bills which the legislature sent him. His near
record 55 vetoes clearly demonstrated otherwise. However, he
did not oppose the enactment of H.B. 103 (Kinch and Proctor,
1972; "The New Establishment," 1968).

House Bill 103 Becomes Law

By the second week in March, H.B. 103 and S.B. 46 had passed
in the House and Senate with no opposition. When H.B. 103 came
up for floor action on March 10, Truan moved that the constitutional rule which required a bill to be read on three separate
days be suspended. The motion prevailed by a vote of 132 Yeas,
11 Nays. House Bill 103 was subsequently laid before the House
members on its third and final passage. The bill passed comfor-
tably by a vote of 141 Yeas, with eight absent (House Journal,
Volume I, 1969). Immediately after the vote was taken Truan
invoked House Rule IV, Section 9. The rule called for a recon-
sideration of the bill and a motion to table further debate on
the bill in question (House Journal, Volume I, 1969). The par-
limentary maneuver effectively closed any opportunity by any
member of the House to challenge the bill on any point there-

after.

On March 12 House Bill 103 was sent to the Senate for their consideration. The bill was kept 49 days in the Senate Education Committee, finally being reported out on May 1 (Senate Journal, Volume II, 1969). Bernal, who was a member of the Education Committee, recalled that at the time there were a number of bills which he was working on. As the only Chicano senator his support and advice on bills introduced by his fellow Mexican-American colleagues in the House was always sought. In general a great deal of the legislative activity of senators and representatives is concerned with the passage of bills which would directly benefit their respective constituencies and thus increase their chances for re-election. Carlos F. Truan would work with the House members from Corpus Christi, and Bernal would work with the members for San Antonio (Bernal, J., Personal communication, March 22, 1979). The bill may have been delayed in committee for other reasons.

Some evidence seems to suggest that Bernal may have been postponing action on H.B. 103 in the Senate until his bill was safely reported out of the Education Committee in the House and returned to the Senate. Senate Bill 46 had been introduced on January 29 and was referred to the State Affairs Committee. On February 19, twelve mostly liberal senators signed on as co-authors of S.B. 46. Five of them, Bates, Bridges, Jordan, Kennard and Schwartz were members of the 21 member State Affairs Committee. By March 13 the bill had been read a third time and passed by a majority vote. Five days later C.S.S.B. 46 was read for the first time and referred to the House Education Committee on which Truan sat. On April 23, 37 days after the bill had been referred to the committee, it was reported favorably out of committee (House Journal, Volume I, 1969). The long delays may have centered on the issue of "pride of authorship," or of being known as the author of new landmark legislation. There were other reasons as well. Bernal could very well be given the major credit for sponsoring and introducing the first bilingual education law in Texas. As it turned out, Carlos F. Truan became the name associated with the first bilingual education law.

Bills on the same subject are generally introduced in both Houses of the legislature. According to the informal, traditional rules of the legislature, once a bill gets through one House the sponsor of the same bill in the other House of the legislature substitutes that bill for his own.

Since Truan's bill had been reported out of the House first, Bernal was expected to have substituted his bill for the House version, but he did not do this right away. The 49 day delay of H.B. 103 in the Senate Education Committee may have been a deliberate tactic. On the other hand, the delay could have been for other reasons. Bernal was tied up with a number of different education bills which he wanted to pass. As the only Chicano legislator in the Senate he was very frequently saddled with a host of other bills which his Chicano colleagues on the House side wanted him to push for them. During this particular session he and Wayne Connally, former governor Connally's brother and the senatorial representative of 17 counties in the southwest part of the state, were waging a battle over a bill which would authorize the establishment of a new four year University of Texas campus. Bernal wanted the university to be constructed in his senatorial district in San Antonio. This bill in addition to his other commitments may have possibly overshadowed his interest in the bilingual education bill.

Truan, being a new representative and not committed to any particular projects in his own district, poured most of his energy into passing the bilingual bill. Moreover, several members on the committee were not on friendly terms with Senator Bernal. He had served in the House and had apparently made a few enemies. Since Truan's bill had been reported out of the House first they strongly felt that Bernal should not be considered the author of the bill (Bernal, J., Personal communication, February 22, 1979; Truan, C. F., Personal communication, July 3, 1979; "Cities Vie for New Schools," 1969).

Both Traun and Bernal claim that the delay had nothing to do with "pride of authorship." Both men were more concerned with passing the bilingual bill than it its historic significance. Bernal, since he had introduced his bill first, still wanted Truan to pass his bill through the House even though Truan's bill had passed out of the House first. Bernal's interest in passing Texas' first permissive bilingual education legislation was understandable, considering the time and effort he had spent on it prior to the 61st Legislature. However, the members of the House Education Committee informed Truan that they were not going to pass Bernal's bill because his bill had passed out of the House first.

Truan subsequently talked to Bernal about the impasse in the House Education Committee. Bernal, after learning about the dispute which was stalling his bill in committee, decided that it would be best to pass Truan's bill before it got too late in the session.

By the end of April the legislative pace becomes hectic. Texas constitutional law limits the legislative session to 140 days. Both House and Senate calendars are jammed with bills which must be taken up. Not all bills, however, are of equal importance, and the Rules Committees of each house ultimately makes all final decisions on the order of bills for floor action.

By this late date in the session it became increasingly clear to Truan that the bilingual bill might not be enacted before the end of the session on June 2. Bernal's bill was laid before the House on April 30 on its second reading. Had it been acted on and passed by the House, the bill still had to be returned to the Senate for any final action and the President's signature. The procedure would have meant a possible delay of from one to two weeks after the bill had been sent to the Senate. In the Senate its consideration would depend on the kind of priority Lieutenant Governor Ben Barnes would give it and on how long it took the Senate Rules Committee to decide on which day the bill would be considered. In the Senate at the time no vote could be taken on the passage of any bill during the last 24 hours of the session (Senate Journal, Volume I, 1969). Since the last few days of the session are spent primarily on tying up the appropriations bill, it leaves the Senate and House members little time to consider other bills which have received no appropriations.

It seems quite likely that sometime before April 13, Bernal and Truan worked out a solution to the predicament. When C.S.S.B. 46 was introduced to the House on its second reading, Truan made a motion to postpone further consideration on the bill until May 14. When House Bill 103 came up for second reading before the Senate on May 7, Bernal offered his amendments to the bill. The substitution was accepted, read a third time as amended, and passed unanimously (Senate Journal, Volume I, 1969). On the same day, the House, which had been informed of the passage of H.B. 103 as amended, immediately concurred with the amendments by a vote of 142 Yeas (Senate Journal, Volume I, 1969). Seven days later, when C.S.S.B. 46 came up for consideration again in the House, Truan moved that the bill be laid on the table subject to recall. There was no objection offered and C.S.S.B. 46 was consigned to legislative oblivion (House Journal, Volume II, 1969).

In its final form, House Bill 103 had affirmed the primacy of English as the basic language of instruction in all public and private schools. It provided local school districts with the option to provide bilingual instruction if the method were considered pedagogically advantageous for those pupils who found it difficult to understand, speak, write or read English. The law also permitted bilingual instruction to be offered only to the sixth grade. Instruction in Spanish beyond the sixth grade, however, would require the permission of the Texas Education Agency. Approval for such an extension would be granted to the school authorities subject to reapproval after three years.

Section one of Article 2893 was amended with the omission of the words: "and shall make the English language the basis of instruction in all subjects." Articles 288 and 298, which prescribed punishments for the infraction of this article, were both repealed.

The final part of the law was a paraphrase of what had been stated in TEA's recommendation to the legislature. It affirmed the axiom that a child in his formative years learns best in a language he understands. It also emphasized the importance of learning Spanish in a hemisphere where it was spoken by as many people as spoke English. Knowledge of a second language in an increasingly technical and scientific world was considered vitally important and the Texas Legislature was urged to take immediate action.

The 62nd Legislature - 1971

When the 62nd Legislature convened on January 12, 1971, the bilingual education advocates were already prepared to submit another bill that would broaden the coverage of House Bill 103 and also provide the program with state funding. The Texas Education Agency, with the advice and assistance of the Advisory Committee on Bilingual Education, and the approval of the State Board of Education, submitted its formal recommendation to the legislature for expanding the bilingual program.

The 1970 elections had not changed the political leadership of the Texas legislature. Governor Preston Smith and Lieutenant Governor Ben Barnes were both re-elected for a second two-year term of office. The Speaker, Gus F. Mutscher, had retained his seat and the leadership of the House. Two of the major issues facing the legislature during this session were taxes and reapportionment. The third issue which overwhelmed and dominated the entire session was the Sharpstown Scandal, a stock fraud case which implicated most of the political leadership in the Texas Legislature. The decisions which key individual legislators made during the 62nd Legislature regarding the scandal and its effect on state government affected the outcome of the bilingual education bill.

TEA Submits Another Recommendation

The Educational Agency requested state funds to provide for the training of bilingual teachers and paraprofessionals, the development of bilingual instructional materials, and monetary incentives for local school districts to develop bilingual education programs.

The state funded bilingual program was needed for several reasons. According to TEA, approximately 21 percent of the student population in Texas spoke Spanish as their first language. Moreover, almost 50 percent of these students came to school with little competence in English. As a result the student was inadvertently excluded from effectively participating in the school program. In addition, most schools were not adequately staffed to meet the needs of these linguistically different students. The result of all these factors was a highly unacceptable dropout rate of almost 80 percent.

In order to meet the educational needs of the Mexican-American student in Texas, the Agency made two recommendations to the Legislature:

    1.   The Foundation Program Act should be amended to include funds for bilingual education, and the State Board of Education should be authorized to develop policies for bilingual education.

    2.   House Bill 103, Sixty-first Legislature, should be amended to include the following:

> Where inability to speak and understand the English language excludes linguistically different children from effective participation in the education program offered by a school district, the district must take affirmative steps to implement a bilingual education program in which children continue their intellectual development through the use of their mother tongue and simultaneously develop facility in English, thus becoming proficient in two languages (Recommendations for Legislative Consideration on Public Education in Texas, November, 1970, 13-14).

The whole tone of this recommendation represented a drastic change from the one which had been made in 1968. This recommendation was not made on behalf of all the school children of Texas, and it did not reiterate the importance of enabling both monolingual English and Spanish-speaking students to become bilingual. This time school districts would be required to modify their instructional programs in order to meet the academic, social and psychological needs of linguistically different school children.

The language and the intent of the TEA recommendation was strongly influenced by the May 25th Memorandum which had been published by the Office for Civil Rights that same year. In lieu of the phrase "national origin-minority group children" the TEA recommendation substituted "linguistically different children." The phrase " . . . to rectify the language deficiency . . ." was changed " . . . to implement a bilingual education program . . ." It should be noted that some of the members of the Advisory Committee on Bilingual Education were also consultants to the Office for Civil Rights and had participated in the conference proceedings which had been held in Denver and San Diego shortly after the May 25th Memorandum had been issued.

Mexican-Americans and the Legislative Leadership

The Speaker and the Lieutenant Governor and other legislative members were well aware of the interests of LULAC and American G. I. Forum. They were, for the most part, sympathetic and were willing to allow the enactment of legislation which would benefit Mexican-Americans, if it meant having the support of the Mexican-American voter (Garza, M., Personal communication, March 9, 1979).

The increased militancy of Chicanos during the early 1970's had its indirect effects on the legislative leadership. They were faced with the choice of dealing directly with militant, leftist leaning organizations such as the Mexican-American Youth Organization (MAYO), and La Raza Unida party, or with the more moderate, conservative organizations such as LULAC and the American G. I. Forum. Legislators chose to negotiate with the older organizations.

During his bid for re-election Lieutenant Governor Ben Barnes had courted and received the full support of LULAC and American G. I. Forum. At the time it was felt that he would have been the kind of governor which would have supported the concerns and interests of the Mexican-American community in Texas. LULAC leaders were also very much aware of Speaker Gus F. Mutscher's ambitions to preside in the Senate and eventually become governor too. There was no mystery nor conflict in what these Mexican-American organizations were doing. If the political leadership supported or consented to legislation which benefited Mexican-Americans, these organizations would make it their business to inform the Mexican-American constituency. According to Garza, "There was no conflict to what we were getting ourselves committed" (Garza, M., Personal communication, March 9, 1979).

The understandings which had been made at the beginning of the 62nd Legislature, however, soon disintegrated when public disclosures on the Sharpstown Scandal disrupted the usual legislative process in Austin. Early on in the fight against the established control of the Speaker, Carlos F. Truan joined the ranks of the Dirty Thirty.

On March 15, Truan decided to vote in favor of Representative Frances Tarlton Farenthold's House Concurrent Resolution 87. Mrs. Farenthold, a liberal Democrat from Corpus Christi, and a staunch opponent of the Mutscher regime, called for an in-depth joint legislative investigation of the Sharpstown Scandal. The resolution called for the formation of a joint House-Senate committee whose members would be appointed by the legislature rather than by the Speaker. The Speaker's refusal to recognize Mrs. Farenthold's motion for immediate consideration of the resolution was appealed to the floor of the House by first term Representative Lane Denton of Waco. After much debate, the Mutscher controlled House voted 118 to 30 against further consideration of the resolution. This event triggered the formation of the Dirty Thirty and contributed to the death of House Bills 495 and 1024, the bilingual education bills which were introduced by Representative Truan during the 62nd Legislative Session (Deaton, 1973; Katz, 1972).

House Bills 495 and 1024

On February 11, Representative Carlos F. Truan introduced House Bill 495. This was the first of two bills on bilingual education which he introduced during the 62nd Legislative Session. The bill made the following recommendations:

1. The governing board of a school may provide for bilingual instruction.

2. When linguistically different children are excluded from educational participation, school districts may implement a bilingual program which will develop a mastery of English.

3. Linguistically different school children shall not be placed in classes for the mentally retarded, nor denied college preparatory courses.

4. Parents of linguistically different children may be notified of school languages other than English.

The bill was a diluted version of the four major areas which appeared in the May 25th Memorandum. Representative Truan's legislative assistant, Jose E. Camacho, had extracted the four provisions from the report and recommendations which had been unanimously adopted by the Advisory Committee on Bilingual Education on August 10, 1970. The provisions which dealt with bilingual instruction and parental notification were permissive. One of the Advisory Committee's strongest recommendations, however, did not appear in the bill's final draft. It called for the mandatory implementation of a bilingual education program in any school district where the enrollment of linguistically different children exceeded five percent (Official Agenda, State Board of Education, September 12, 1970).

The bill was kept in the Committee on Public Education for over two and one half months before it was released with a favorable recommendation on May 5 (House Journal, Volume II, 1971). Truan's decision to defy the authoritative leadership of the Speaker strongly affected the fate of the bill. On order from the Speaker, the bill was held pending in the House Rules Committee until the close of the session.

Earlier in the session, Truan, realizing that House Bill 495 did not stand a chance of surviving in the Mutscher controlled House Education Committee, decided to introduce his second bill on bilingual education on March 11.

House Bill 1024 introduced with eleven co-authors, nine Mexican-Americans and two Anglos, was sent to the Committee on Public Education for consideration. On April 6 the committee held public hearings on the bill.

The Committee heard testimony from state educational experts and were treated to a brief demonstration of bilingual skills by ten pre-school and first grade Mexican-American school children from Edinburg. Texas State Teachers Association executive secretary, L. P. Sturgeon, appeared before the committee and indicated his sympathy for the expanded program. Mr. Oather Raynes, representing the Texas Classroom Teachers Association, read the organization's approval of the bilingual program. The Texas Education Agency was represented by Dr. Severo Gomez, assistant state commissioner for International and Bilingual Education, and Deputy Education Commissioner Marlin L. Brockette. Other witnesses who appeared in favor of H.B. 1024 included Dr. Theodore Andersson, professor of foreign languages at the University of Texas and a member of the State Advisory Committee on Bilingual Education; Alphonso R. Ramirez and Harold P. Dooley, from the Region One Education Service Center in Edinburg, and Javier F. Chacon, LULAC State Education Committee chairman (Gomez, S., Personal communication, February 14, 1979; "Children

Show Results of Bilingual Ed," 1971).

Part of the testimony given by Chacon succinctly summarized the changed attitude which LULAC had undergone toward the use of Spanish and English in the education of the Mexican-American.

> We are taking the right steps in this bill, because now instead of making Juan Garcia, a child who speaks only Spanish and who probably has been made to feel inferior in a school environment that utilizes only English, we will make Juan Garcia learn English with the use of the Spanish language that he knows, rich with all its idiomatic expressions, colloquialisms and regionalisms. We are taking the first steps to an education program that should have been implemented years ago ("Migrant Students Display Skills in Two Languages," 7 April 1971, San Antonio Express, p. 10).

On April 21, seventeen days after the public hearings, House Bill 1024 was reported favorably out of the Education Committee. Committee Chairman Charles Jungmichel of La Grange may have been impressed by the bilingual performance of the ten children, and may have sympathized with the evidence which had been presented by experts on the need for bilingual education, but these demonstrations alone did not move the members of the committee and its chairman to vote in favor of the bilingual bill.

Throughout the session the Speaker did everything possible to ignore the protests and concerns of the Dirty Thirty. By controlling the processing of their bills in committee and by stalling them on the various House calendars, he had hoped to make them yield to his wishes. The tactic, however, did not debilitate the resolve of the thirty House members to bring an end to the unbridled power of the Speaker. Jungmichel, a Mutscher appointee, was a loyal supporter of the Speaker and the legislative ethos which had placed both of them in positions of power in the legislature. Mutscher knew that Truan was working hard to pass the bilingual bill. He requested Jungmichel to delay the bilingual bill by assigning it to a hostile, Mutscher-supported subcommittee. The bilingual bill probably could have been killed at this stage, had it not been for the agreement which Truan and Mutscher made a month before the end of the legislative session.

In return for Truan's vote on a Mutscher-supported constitutional amendment, the Speaker promised to move the bilingual bill out of committee and on to the House calendar for considera-

tion. Mutscher needed a two-thirds vote on an amendment that
would have allowed liquor-by-the-drink in Texas in order to
insure that the measure would take effect immediately after it
had been voted on by the public in a specially scheduled election
in May. Without the 100 votes, the measure, if approved by the
Texas public, would not take effect until 90 days after its
approval.

The Speaker was being pressed by liquor and business lobbyists to push for immediate passage of the bill. Mutscher needed
five more votes to get the necessary two-thirds majority. After
talking with Truan and with other House members who had voted
initially against the measure, Mutscher brought the subject
before the House for a second time. The second vote on the
measure registered 102 in favor. Several members of the Dirty
Thirty were not pleased with the way Truan had voted. Truan,
however, was not the only one who had switched his vote. Neil
Caldwell and two other Dirty Thirty members also changed their
minds for other reasons. Truan felt that the vote against the
measure was but a symbolic gesture against the Speaker's leadership since the amendment, if approved, would have eventually
become law. It made more sense to bargain with the Speaker when
there was an opportunity to do so, and get the bilingual bill
out of committee (Katz, 1972; Truan, C. F., Personal communication, July 3, 1979).

The bilingual bill was reported out of committee, but it
still had to wait its turn for floor debate on one of the eight
calendars in the House. Here too Truan's bill was deliberately
held up by the Speaker and House Rules Committee Chairman, Jim
Nugent. House Bill 1024 languished on the calendar for 31 days
before it was finally reported on to the House floor for debate.

On May 26 the bill was read a second time and was approved
by a 125-17 vote. After a minor committee amendment was added
and approved, the bill came up again for its third reading and
final passage. The bill picked up an additional four votes,
passing with 129 Yeas and 17 Nays. After it passed the Speaker
announced that the bill was funded provided the Comptroller of
Public Accounts certified there was money for this expenditure
(House Journal, Volume IV, 1971; Constitution, Article III,
Section 49a).

The recommendations included in House Bill 1024 differed
from the proposals of House Bill 495 in that they specifically
addressed the three areas which the Educational Agency had
mentioned in its recommendations to the legislature. This time
the language of the bill neither was influenced by the text of
the May 25 Memorandum nor did it implicitly accuse school
administrators and teachers of placing a disproportionate number

of Mexican-American school children in classes for the mentally retarded. Another item not repeated in H.B. 1024 was a paragraph which indirectly accused educators in Texas of tracking a high percentage of Mexican-American students into dead end curricula.

With these parts omitted, the bill's three main points included the establishment of teacher training institutes, salary schedules for bilingual education teachers, and the acquisition of bilingual textbooks. The last section included a description of the position and the kind of preparation which was required to obtain a bilingual teacher certificate. It also included the number of monthly payments which would be authorized under the Texas state public education compensation plan for bilingual education teachers. The bill called for a funding level of $5.8 million through the State's Minimum Foundation Program.

Although Mutscher had managed to keep control of the House throughout most of the session, he had not diluted or destroyed the coalition of the Dirty Thirty who had mounted an all-out attack against the Speaker and the system. At one point in the session Mutscher approached the LULAC lobbyist and asked him to "dump" Carlos F. Truan in return for his support of the bilingual bill.

LULAC, early on, had committed itself to helping Mutscher in his quest for a higher political office, but his suggestion to abandon Representative Truan was not considered an acceptable arrangement. "Come hell or high water," declared Manual Garza, "we were going to stick to Carlos Truan" (Personal communication, March 9, 1979). It was strongly felt that a move against Carlos would also be a blow against all the Mexican-American legislators. "The Mexican-Americans were going to stick together" (Ibid.).

House Bill 1024 was subsequently introduced in the Senate on May 27, four days before the end of the session, and was referred to the Committee on State Affairs. Senator Moore, chairman of the committee, held up action on the bill for two days. On May 30, a Sunday, Bernal, sensing that the bill might never be reported out of committee, made a motion to withdraw the bill from the Committee on State Affairs and had it referred to the Committee on State Departments and Institutions, which was chaired by liberal Senator Chet Brooks. Bernal was also a member of this committee. By unanimous consent Bernal was able to quickly move the bill out of one committee and into another more hospitable committee. The maneuver caught Ben Barnes by surprise and momentarily undermined his control over the passage of the bill in the Senate. Before making the motion for unanimous consent, a senate rule (Number 51) which required

a majority vote of the members elected to the senate, he made
sure that he had the votes of all the senators who were present
in the chamber. By unanimous consent Bernal prevented the bill
from being printed (Rule Number 36). Had he not invoked
this rule the bill would have had to be printed, and perhaps
would not have been ready and available for each senator until
the last day of the session (Senate Journal, Volume I, 1971;
Bernal, J., Personal communication, February 10, 1979).

Senator Bernal was informed by Ben Barnes that he could
not guarantee that the bill would be funded for the fiscal year
beginning in September, 1971. Bernal then offered to compromise
by amending the effective funding date of the bill to September
1, 1973. This was acceptable to the Senate President, and the
bill was subsequently passed with its committee amendment by a
vote of 27 Yeas agains 4 Nays. All four senators who had voted
against the bill (Aikin, Creighton, Moore and Snelson) were
members of the Committee on State Affairs (Senate Journal, Volume
I, 1971). The bill was sent back to the House on the same day,
one day before the close of the session.

The last two days of any legislative session in the House
are long and arduous--they are tests of endurance. It is at this
time that legislators try to make up for lost time, and also
comply with the 140 day legislative limitation, by attempting to
pass practically every bill which the Speaker places before them
for consideration. A traditional legislative maneuver to expe-
dite pending bills has been the liberal and sometimes abusive
use of the Local and Consent Calendars. On these calendars the
leadership frequently places what it considers to be minor bills
of local, general and statewide applicability on which little or
no floor opposition is expected or desired (Pettus and Bland,
1976).

On May 30 the House Rules Committee assigned a total of 102
Senate bills on the Consent Calendar. This had been the same
device which was used to pass the Sharp inspired bank insurance
bills during the Second Called Session of the 61st Legislature
in 1969. The Dirty Thirty, however, planned to slow down the
process so that House members could have more time to study,
debate and possibly amend any of the bills which were brought up
for floor action.

The afternoon session began with opponents raising a number
of objections against the use of the consent calendars. All of
the points of order were overruled by the Speaker. To silence
any further objections De Witt Hale, of Corpus Christi, made a
motion to suspend the House Rules in order to consider the
consent calendar. The motion was approved by 110-31 vote.
Anticipating this motion, opponents invoked a seldom used rule

which called for the removal of any bill on the Consent Calendar
with the presentation of a written objection by five House
members (House Rules, 1971, IX, Section 9-4, 57). The Dirty
Thirty had prepared 102 written slips. The rule could have been
defeated by a two-thirds vote on each bill, but the Speaker
decided not to use it.

The tension in the House chamber slowly mounted as each
bill which was brought up for floor action was taken off the
calendar. The Speaker's lieutenants tried to discredit the
opposition by accusing them, via press releases, of vindictive
selfishness and irresponsibility. Members of the press received
the press releases with little enthusiasm. First term House
member Mike Moncrief, of Ft. Worth, was allowed to address the
House. He delivered an emotional, but naive speech on his concept
of good government, and how the tactics of the Dirty Thirty were
an affront to the people of Texas. Representative Tom Moore,
from Waco, responded on behalf of the Dirty Thirty. The speech
totally shattered the Speaker's opposition. During the remaining
hours of the session, each bill was considered on its individual
merits (Katz, 1972).

The House session had been convened at 2:00 p.m. on Sunday,
and did not recess until 1:00 a.m. the next morning. Sometime
during these last hours in the session House Bill 1024 was returned to the House by Senator Bernal with the amendment
changing the effective date of the bill. Without the amendment
the bill would have been of little value, since everyone of its
provisions called for state funding. Truan intuitively suspected
that Mutscher, infuriated by the delaying tactics of the Dirty
Thirty, might not recognize him. But he had little choice.
In order for the bill to pass as amended it was necessary to
submit the bill for a vote of concurrence. Truan tried desperately to be recognized by the Speaker so that he could ask
House members to concur on the senate amendment. It would have
been a simple procedure and would not have taken much time, but
the Speaker refused to recognize him, effectively preventing
the bill from being enacted (Truan, C. F., Personal communication, February 20, 1979).

Representative Clayton and House Bill 105

During the previous legislative session few if any of the
legislators who had voted against the permissive bilingual bill
were concerned or even knew much about bilingual education to
plan a personal attack against the bill or to introduce different
legislation. The situation changed in 1971.

On January 26, 1971, Representative Bill Clayton, a conservative Democrat from the northwest corner of the state, expressed

his opposition to the further expansion of bilingual education in Texas by introducing his own version of the bilingual bill. House Bill 105 was referred to the Committee on Public Education. Representative Truan was a member of this committee. The bill never received any tangible support from the 22 member committee, and it was not reported out of committee.

Had the bill been enacted it would have dealt a serious blow to the advocates of bilingual education in Texas. The provisions of the bill were strict and they also carried harsh penalties for violators.

The bill was divided into three sections. The first part declared that English was the basic language of instruction in all of the state schools, and that its mastery by all children was one of the school's primary objectives. The second section restricted bilingual instruction to the third grade. It allowed for bilingual instruction above the third grade only with the expressed approval of TEA, subject to reapproval at the end of the three-year period. It also provided for remedial English reading classes beyond the third grade for those students with language deficiencies which tended to impede their scholastic progress. The last part stipulated that violators, teachers and school administrators, would be guilty of a misdemeanor and, if convicted, would be subject to a fine of $25 to $100, cancellation of their teaching certificates, removal from their jobs, or any one combination of the prescribed penalties (House Journal, Volume I, 1971).

Several factors contributed to the successful enactment of House Bill 103 during the 61st Legislature in 1969. The legislative leadership did not oppose a bill whose provisions were permissive, required no state funding, and increased the amount of federal aid available for Texas. Both Speaker Mutscher and Lieutenant Governor Ben Barnes were contemplating to run for higher elected positions in government. Consequently, it was to their own advantage to secure what they perceived to be a potentially important Mexican-American constituency.

When the bill was introduced very few legislators knew what bilingual instruction meant. Fewer still could care less. Another factor which helped was the bill's ambiguity. It stressed the primacy of the English language in Texas and the term "bilingual instruction" was not explained. In addition, the bill did not include the teaching of history or culture to be a vital or necessary component of this kind of instruction. In contrast, the federal bilingual education bill considered the teaching of the history and culture associated with the native language of the children to be an integral part of any bilingual instructional program. It was this model which most federally funded bilingual programs in Texas attempted to implement.

Few, if any, bills which are introduced during a legislative session are ever enacted purely on their intrinsic merit. Truan's advocacy was an important factor in the enactment of Texas' first permissive bilingual education law. Without his strong lobbying efforts the bill might not have been considered during the 61st Legislature.

During the 62nd Legislature (1971) the proponents of bilingual education legislation introduced bills that would have expanded the bilingual program and provided state funding. Representative Truan introduced two bills on the subject of bilingual instruction. House Bill 495 was directly influenced by the May 25th Memorandum which had been issued by the Office for Civil Rights the previous year. The bill was killed in the House.

The second bill, House Bill 1024, was introduced later on in the session when it became clear that the first bill stood little chance of passing. This bill reflected the legislative recommendations of the Texas Education Agency. Had it not been for the activities of the Dirty Thirty and Truan's connection with this group, the bill would have been enacted, although it would not have gone into effect until the fall of 1973.

CHAPTER V

THE 63rd LEGISLATURE - 1973

When the 63rd Legislature convened on January 9, 1973 the
top leadership of Texas government had totally changed. Conservative Dolph Briscoe, a millionaire rancher and banker from
Uvalde, won the race for governor. William P. Hobby, president
and executive editor of The Houston Post, and an independent
conservative, was elected lieutenant governor. The speaker's
position went to Price Daniel, Jr., a liberal, member of the
Dirty Thirty, and a son of a former Texas governor.

The November elections also altered the composition of both
houses of the legislature. Over half of the House members were
freshmen representatives. In the Senate fifteen new senators
had been elected. The Sharpstown incident and the activities of
the Dirty Thirty throughout the entire 62nd Legislature Session
contributed to the election of a reform minded legislative body.
It would be a legislature that would respond to the demands of
Mexican-Americans more than any other in Texas legislative
history (Clinchy, 1974).

The 63rd Legislature is remembered in Texas legislative
history as the "reform legislature." Practically all of the new
legislators in the House had campaigned on one issue: reform in
state government. Governor Dolph Briscoe and Lieutenant Governor
William P. Hobby had both campaigned against political malfea-
sance. Price Daniel, Jr. was elected Speaker of the House on
the strength of his reform platform. "All concerned had a vivid
memory of the Sharpstown fiasco, and all wanted to be able to
conclude the session with good, clean records of achievement"
(Accomplishments of the 63rd Legislature, 1973, 1). Part of
this record would include the enactment of the Bilingual Education and Training Act as well as the Adult Education Law.

Legislators during this session were faced with several
issues: consumer protection, judicial reorganization, environmental legislation, constitutional revision, school finance. Determining a more equitable system of financing the state's public
schools represented one of the most challenging issues (House
Journal, Volume I, 1973).

The subject of inequitable school finance in Texas had been
brought to the attention of state officials in the case of
Rodriguez v. San Antonio Edgewood I.S.D. (1968). Mexican-American parents had filed a class action suit against the State
Board of Education and three other defendants, charging that
Texas' method of funding public schools discriminated against
poor and minority students who lived in school districts with a

91

low property tax base. In 1973 the state's highest court ruled the Texas system of school financing public education to be unconstitutional under the Fourteenth Amendment (<u>Mexican-American Education in Texas</u>, 1972; Alexander, et al., 1975).

In the winter of 1973 the case was argued before the Supreme Court, but a decision was not expected before the end of the legislative session. It was clear to many elected officials, however, that something had to be done to equalize or minimize the differences which existed between rich and poor school districts. The governor and legislators opted for supporting bilingual education legislation, while they waited for the Supreme Court's decision.

When Representative Carlos F. Truan, who had been elected to his third term in office, returned to Austin, he was not only interested in correcting past legislative abuses, but was thinking of introducing another bill on bilingual education. In the House Truan would be the author of the bill, but in the Senate it would be Senator Chet Brooks, a liberal Democrat from Pasadena, who would get the support of all the senators for his mandatory bilingual education bill.

Senator Joe J. Bernal, <u>mi senador</u>, had lost his bid for a third term in the Senate. His defeat, however, did not deter him from actively lobbying among many of his former legislative colleagues on behalf of the bilingual education bill. The advocates of bilingual education would also have the support of thirteen Mexican-American legislators, ten in the House and three in the Senate, who would vote in favor of the bill whether they believed the claims made on its behalf or not. Another factor which would contribute to the bill's passage would be the unexpected support of the Texas Association for Continuing Adult Education and the Texas Association of School Boards. Another very important factor in favor of the bill's enactment during this legislative session would be the new governor's public support and last minute intervention to insure its passage and funding. During this legislative session the leadership of the Senate or the House would not be opposed to the bill. The League of United Latin-American Citizens and the American G.I. Forum had actively supported Dolph Briscoe in the 1972 gubernatorial race. Now they sought his help in the enactment of bilingual education legislation in 1973.

Building Support for Bilingual Education

The defeat of House Bill 1024 at the end of the 62nd Legislature did not deter the advocates of bilingual education. For the rest of 1971 and into 1972 Truan, Bernal and others continued their efforts to increase support for the bilingual and the adult education bills which Representative Truan was thinking of introducing in 1973.

By mid April of 1972 Truan, Bernal and Joe Christie, a senator from El Paso, were urging Governor Preston Smith to include the subject of bilingual education in his call for a special legislative session scheduled to be held in June. The main purpose for the session was to write the General Appropriations Bill for fiscal year 1973. But, other subjects could be taken up if clearly stated by the governor. In his address to the Third Called Session of the Legislature, however, Governor Smith did not mention bilingual education ("Bilingual Education Push Gains," 1972; Senate Journal, 1972).

By this time, Gus F. Mutscher, the former Speaker of the House, had been convicted of conspiracy to accept a bribe, and Rayford Price, a former friend and legislative colleague of Mutscher, had captured the speaker's position in time for the special session (Deaton, 1973; "Mr. Speaker Daniel," 1973).

With Mutscher out of the way bilingual proponents felt confident that they could pass the bilingual bill during the special session if the governor specifically included the subject as part of his reason for convening the session. During a National Conference on Bilingual Education which was held on April 14 and 15 in Austin, Truan, Bernal and Christie publicly stated their support for bilingual education, as well as what they intended to do in order to insure the enactment of the bilingual bill during the 63rd Legislature. Senator Joe Christie, who was running for lieutenant governor that year, promised to advocate "full and complete funding of the Bilingual Education Bill." He was a member of the Senate Finance Subcommittee that would be helping to write the appropriations bill that summer (Truan, 1972; "Bilingual Education Push Gains," 1972).

Governor Preston Smith, running for a third term of office, demonstrated a willingness to cooperate with his Mexican-American colleagues if it meant getting the support of the Mexican-American vote in the Democratic primary on May 6. Although he was defeated in the primary, he still included a $6.4 million recommendation in his Executive Budget for the establishment of a new bilingual education program (Deaton, 1973; House Journal, Volume I, 1973).

Governor Smith's request for additional funds in bilingual education in no way bound the legislature or the new governor to honor such a commitment, but the fact that money for bilingual education had been included, enabled bilingual proponents to urge newly elected Dolph Briscoe to include money for bilingual education in his Executive Budget for fiscal years 1974 and 1975.

On June 15, 1972 Carlos F. Truan and TEA officials appeared before the joint legislative committee hearing on state finance. In a written statement Truan identified himself as the author of the bilingual and adult education bills, and urged the committee to include TEA's request of $1.9 million for bilingual education, and $2.5 million for adult education in that year's legislative budget.

Representative Truan made it a point to stress that at its March meeting the State Board of Education had voted unanimously to request the governor to include bilingual education legislation in the Third Called Session of the 62nd Legislature. Citing statistics which had been compiled by the Report of the Governor's Committee on Public Education (1968), Truan argued that the drop-out rates for public school children had been great among Mexican-American children. The drop-out rate among Anglos had been calculated to be about 33 percent, whereas among Mexican-American youth it was estimated to be close to 80 percent.

The problem was quite serious and merited the state's immediate attention. It was an established fact, according to Truan, that the high drop-out rate among Mexican-American school children was caused by their limited knowledge of the English language. Another reason for supporting a greater state role in the bilingual instructional program was the apparent success which federally funded programs were having. Studies on the effects of these programs on scholastic achievement and acquisition of language skills in Spanish and English had demonstrated encouraging results.

Since 1964 the demand for more bilingual education programs had increased considerably. As the statewide bilingual program expanded, the need for bilingual teachers would become greater. Truan argued that there were about 8,500 Mexican-American teachers in Texas in 1971, but that it was not enought to take care of the projected needs. Finally, he urged the committee to take into account the special needs of approximately 12 percent of the public school population who came to school with limited skills in the English language, and pleaded for the training of bilingual and monolingual teachers to take care of the future demand for that kind of instructional program.

Truan's testimony also included a special plea for adult education. The main reason for Truan's interest and advocacy seem to be his recognition that a large sector of Mexican-American adults in Texas were oftentimes illiterate in both languages, or, could not speak, write or understand English. Their needs were just as serious as those faced by Mexican-American children. It made little sense to educate the children and neglect the needs of their parents. Both problems could more effectively be addressed together (Testimony presented by Representative Carlos F. Truan before House Appropriations Committee and Senate Finance Committee, January 15, 1972, "Truan Endorses Plea for More Bilingual Education Funds," 1972).

The Alliance: Bilingual and Adult Education

Controversial bills are seldom legislated without the support of some active lobbying group. In 1972 the advocates of bilingual education legislation in Texas were not well organized. The Texas Association for Bilingual Education was barely gaining the support of its few members. The only consistent support which Carlos F. Truan could count on was from individuals such as Dr. Jose A. Cardenas, Dr. Theodore Andersson, and Dr. Hector P. Garcia. Although these individuals were well known and respected by many Texan legislators, what they could do to push for the bill's passage was limited as their support seemed "special pleading." Truan realized that he needed more outside support in order to pass the bilingual bill during the 63rd Legislature.

In the early half of 1972, Truan was approached by Harvey E. Owen, president of the Texas Association for Continuing Adult Education, and asked to sponsor a bill that would establish a state funded program of adult education in Texas. On the Senate side, Mr. Owen had asked Senator Chet Brooks to carry the bill. Since Senator Brooks was already sponsoring a related bill in the area of vocational education, it was felt that he would be more receptive to the idea of authoring an adult education bill in the Senate.

The association president also made it his business to inform Senator Aikin, a respected and highly influential legislative expert on education legislation, about his interest in the enactment of an adult education bill. Senator Aikin, however, demonstrated little interest in the bill. Mr. Owen, suspecting that Senator Aikin might thwart their efforts to pass an adult education bill if he chose to do so, contacted the district director of the association from the senator's district. He urgently suggested that he contact two or three of the senator's most generous campaign supporters and ask them if they would be willing to travel to Austin to have a conference with Senator Aiken on the merits of the bill. After the meeting, Senator Aikin, although not fully convinced, decided he would not oppose its introduction and passage (Owen, H., Personal communication, April 1, 1979).

By the time the joint legislative committee on finance met in June, 1972 to consider the next year's budget, Representative Truan had devised a legislative strategy he hoped would insure the enactment of both bills. In a meeting with TEA Commissioner J. W. Edgar, Truan proposed to introduce the bilingual bills (H.B. 145 and H.B. 146) and the adult education bill (H.B. 147) as a package. He suggested that in order to get the votes they would have to support both bills. Bob Allen, director of the Adult Education Division at TEA, and his assistant, Manual Garza, were also present at this meeting. It had been their suggestion that led Mr. Owen to ask for Truan's sponsorship of the education bill (Camacho, J. E., Personal communication, February 15, 1979; Truan, C. F., Personal communication, February 20, 1979).

The strategy served to bring the complete support of the Texas Association for Continuing Adult Education on behalf of both bills. When Mr. Owen was informed by Bob Allen that the sponsor of the adult education bill would not push for its enactment unless the bilingual bill was also supported, the president agreed to actively lobby for the passage of both bills. The lobbying efforts of the association on behalf of both bills completely surprised legislators. What could be wrong with a bilingual bill that was also supported by Anglos from all parts of Texas? (Camacho, J. E., Personal communication, February 15, 1979).

The association deluged legislators with a blitz-krieg letter writing campaign. Letters supporting both bills came from all parts of Texas. Adults in federally sponsored programs were provided with stationery and stamped self-addressed envelopes and encouraged to write to their legislators. No effort was made to correct the letters for spelling errors, punctuation, or sentence structure. The need for adult education programs, it was hoped, would be self-evident (Watson, B., Personal communication, May 24, 1979).

Prior to 1973 the adult association had not been active. Its leadership had done nothing to influence the legislative process. During two previous legislative sessions attempts to pass an adult education bill had not been successful. The change in leadership which occurred in the fall of 1971 represented a crucial turning point for the association.

After the disastrous results of the 1971 legislative session, it became evident to Harvey E. Owen, Billy Watson, and other more active members throughout the state that the association needed to develop a more active legislative advocacy role in order to pass a state funded adult education program. With the cooperation of Bob G. Allen, who had been hired by TEA three months before the 1971 legislative session, the newly elected

officers began to raise state-wide support for the passage of
an adult education bill in 1973 ("New Leaders of TACE Named at
Fall Conference," 1972; Owen, H.E., Personal communication,
April 1, 1979).

Owen and Watson were not timid individuals. They understood that making direct contacts with key legislative officials
was important. Owen, who was from Lubbock, was personally acquainted with Governor Preston Smith. He also knew and personally met with newly elected Governor Dolph Briscoe on several
occasions during the 63rd Legislature.

Adult association officials made a deliberate effort to
contact the legislative leadership. Late in 1972 Price Daniel,
Jr. was invited to speak at a TEA sponsored state conference of
adult education directors in Dallas. In his speech Representative Daniel publicly endorsed the passage of a state funded
adult education bill ("Boost for Adult Education," 1973).
Daniel's invitation seems to have been a part of a well calculated strategy of TACE officials, because by this time it was
well known by legislative observers that he would be the next
speaker of the House during the 63rd Legislature.

When Truan introduced his bills to the legislature in the
winter of 1973 over half of the House membership signed on as
co-authors. The lobbying efforts of the association played a
major part in defining public support for bilingual and adult
education in Texas (Camacho, J. E., Personal communication,
February 15, 1979).

TEA Recommends Bilingual and Adult Education

In 1972 the State Board of Education once again requested
the governor and the legislature to enact a bilingual education
law that would benefit Mexican-American school children. The
recommendations were essentially similar to the ones which had
been made in 1970.

The legislators were informed that most of the bilingual
education programs in Texas were federally funded. Consequently,
only a small percentage of the children needing bilingual education were actually being served. Another problem mentioned was
the need to train more teachers in the methods and philosophy
of bilingual instruction. It was noted that while less than
five percent of the teachers were capable of teaching in two
languages, twenty-two percent of the school population was
Spanish-speaking.

These were the conditions which were considered unacceptable by the Texas Education Agency. It was suggested that

97

school districts with children who could not function effectively in all English curriculum should be helped with a bilingual instructional program. It was also suggested that the few bilingual teachers in existing programs should be given 11 and 12 month contracts so they could develop the badly needed curriculum materials. They also wanted the legislators to allow the agency to develop another method for obtaining the necessary bilingual textbooks, apart from the general textbook provisions for English written textbooks (Recommendation for Legislative Consideration on Public Education in Texas, November, 1972).

The agency also recommended the creation of a state funded adult education program. The report stated that there were many adults in Texas who were unable to obtain a high school education because there were no state funds. The money which was provided by the federal government was too limited to adequately finance the kind of program which was needed. Moreover, the federal Adult Education Act was restrictive in that it provided for educational programs only up to the eighth grade level and limited its services to those persons who had had some schooling in Texas. Statistics compiled by TEA showed that three million adults over the age of 25 had not completed high school. Of this group over one million had not completed eight years of formal schooling, and one of six thousand had not completed one year of school. In order to meet this need the agency estimated that it would need about $5.1 million annually (Recommendations . . , November, 1972).

House Bills 145, 146 and 147

One of the many changes which significantly contributed to the enactment of the bilingual bill during the 63rd Legislature was the appointment of Carlos F. Truan as chairman of the 21 member Human Resources Committee on January 12. Truan worked diligently to get Price Daniel, Jr. elected as Speaker. In exchange Price Daniel, Jr. appointed him chairman and promised to support the passage of his bills. On the other side of the Capitol rotunda Chet Brooks had also been appointed chairman of the 11 member Human Resources Committee in the Senate. The collaboration of both chairmen was a major force in the enactment of both bills. Truan would introduce his bills in the House, and Brooks would introduce two companion bills in the Senate (Camacho, J. E., Personal communication, February 15, 1979).

On January 22, 1973, Reprsentative Truan introduced House Bills 145, 146 and 147 (Appendix F, G, H) as a package to the House. He then put out an announcement on the desk of each of the 150 members inviting them to be co-sponsors of the bills. Seventy-seven House members responded by placing their signatures on all three bills. By obtaining the signatures of more than half of the House members on his bills, he had committed them to either supporting the bills to the end of the enactment process or to support any other substitute bill. Truan's committee chairmanship as well as the strong lobbying efforts of the Texas Association for Adult and Continuing Education were both very important factors.

Truan's bilingual bill carried no mandatory provision, but the bill which Senator Chet Brooks would introduce later on in the session would carry mandatory requirements. Truan's bill still emphasized the local school districts' option to implement a bilingual education program or not, mainly because Truan did not want to arouse undue suspicion about a bill whose primary beneficiary would be the Mexican-American. He was cautious and was not going to jeopardize the passage of the bilingual education bill in this session ("Trying Again on Bilingual Ed.," 1973).

Senator Chet Brook's sponsorship of the bilingual bill was very important, because it lessened the chances of it being labeled a Mexican bill. In Truan's opinion, former Senator Joe J. Bernal, as respected as he was in the Senate, could have never passed a mandatory bill in the Senate (Truan, C. F., Personal communication, February 20, 1979).

All three bills were subsequently referred to the House Committee on Education for consideration. The commitee's chairman, Dan Kubiak, a liberal Democrat from Rockdale, wholeheartedly supported the bilingual and adult education bills which Truan had introduced. Representative Kubiak, like the Speaker and Truan, had been a member of the Dirty Thirty during the 62nd Legislature.

House Bill 145 was the same as the bilingual bill (H.B. 1024) which Truan had introduced during the last regular session. The bill called for the development and implementation of teacher training institutes for the preparation of professional and paraprofessional public school personnel in the philosophy and methods of bilingual instruction. The institutes would be directed by TEA officials, and participants were to be reimbursed for expenses incurred in the course of the training program. In addition, the bill requested funds for the development of bilingual instructional materials and salaries for bilingual teachers.

House Bill 146 was also similar to the first bill (H.B. 495) which Truan had introduced during the 62nd Legislature. The wording of this bill was strongly influenced by the text of the May 25th Office for Civil Rights Memorandum. The bill mandated the use of a bilingual education program in school districts which had enrolled students who could not function well in the regular school curriculum because of an "inability to speak and understand the English language." It prohibited school district authorities from assigning linguistically different children to classes for the mentally retarded or to low achievement tracks on the basis of tests which purportedly measured English language skills and mental ability. It forbade the tracking of students into dead end programs. It also warned against denying linguistically different students college preparatory course work. Lastly, it demanded that school districts send school announcements in the language of the parents. The bill suffered the same fate as its predecessor. It was referred to a subcommittee and never reported out of the education committee.

House Bill 147, the Adult Education bill, was favorably received in the House Education Committee. On February 2 the bill was reported engrossed and by the 12th it was reported out of committee with a favorable report. The bill's main provisions called for the establishment of a state funded adult education program, required the use of bilingual education instruction for non-English speaking students, authorized the creation of a state advisory board, and sought appropriations. When the bill was released from committee two major changes had been made. In both instances the bill's mandatory provisions were changed to permissive ones. Bilingual education would not be required, but it could be used "for students who do not function satisfactorily in English whenever it is appropriate for their optimum development." The second change permitted rather than authorized the State Board of Education to establish an adult education advisory committee.

Representatives Truan and Garcia, San Antonio, negotiated the bilingual bill during the floor debate and amending process which occurs so frequently in the Texas legislative process on February 19, 1973. In addition to the amendments which were offered, there were two parliamentary maneuvers which were employed to prevent the passage of the bill. Representative W. J. Blythe, a Republican from Houston, raised a point of order against further consideration of the bill on the grounds that it violated Rule XIX, Section 30 of the House Rules. The rule prohibited the Speaker from laying any bill having to do with appropriations before the House during the first 120 days of a regular session, before the Comptroller General's approval of the general appropriations bill (H.B. 139). Speaker Price Daniel, Jr. considered the objection, and then overruled the point of order (House Journal, Volume I, 1973).

The second attempt to sidetrack the bill was a motion by
Lindon Williams, a Democrat representing District 96 in Houston,
to postpone consideration of H.B. 147 until March 19. Truan
responded quickly by moving to table the motion to postpone.
The motion to table Representative William's motion prevailed by
a vote of 83 to 55. The major objection to the bill was its
cost. In five years the Legislative Budget Board had estimated
that it would cost Texas taxpayers about $28 million. Represen-
tative Forrest Green, from Corsicana, thought that it was inap-
propriate to consider the funding of any new state programs before the Appropriations Bill had been considered and introduced
to both Houses for floor debate. Moreover, he felt that,
although not against voting funds for the adult education bill,
it was a mistake to be committing money to projects before the
priorities and revenues had been determined by the legislature
(House Journal, Volume I, 1973). Despite the objections raised
on the grounds of fiscal restraint, the bill was passed on
February 20 and sent to the Senate for its consideration. About
two months later, May 5, the bill was returned to the House for
the Speaker's signature. Two days later the bill was formally
sent to the governor's office for his signature. The law took
effect on August 27, 1973.

Senator Chet Brooks and Senate Bill 121

Six days after Representative Truan had introduced his
three bills, Senator Brooks introduced Senate Bill 121 (Appendix
I), a bill related to bilingual education programs in the Texas
public schools (Senate Journal, Volume I, 1973). Brooks' bilingual bill was the most detailed and comprehensive of all the
bills which were submitted on this subject during the 63rd Legislature. Moreover, Brooks' bilingual bill was mandatory.

Senator Brooks worked closely with the leaders of the Texas
Association for Adult and Continuing Education and with Bob
Allen, director of the Adult Education Division at TEA, and his
assistant, Manuel Garza. According to Senator Brooks, both men
played a major role in the decision to introduce a mandatory
rather than a permissive bilingual bill in the Senate. Brooks
and bilingual proponents who were actively pushing for the passage of the bilingual bill felt that if it were not mandatory
TEA officials would not have authority to force tenacious and
unwilling school district authorities into complying with the
law's provisions. It was also felt that the law's mandatory
requirement would make it compatible with recent federal mandates
concerning the educational rights of national origin minority
students (Brooks, C., Personal communication, June 5, 1979).

The mandatory bilingual education bill which was enacted in 1973 represented a radical departure from the accepted schooling practices in Texas. The bill's introduction, which was an adaptation of Massachusett's Declaration of Policy statement on transitional bilingual education in 1972, set forth the basic rationale for the change in state educational policy.

> The legislature finds that there are large numbers
> of children in the state who come from environ-
> ments where the primary language is other than
> English. Experience has shown that public school
> classes in which instruction is given only in
> English are often inadequate for the education of
> children whose native tongue is another language.
> The legislature believes that a compensatory pro-
> gram of bilingual education can meet the needs of
> these children and facilitate their integration
> into the regular school curriculum. Therefore,
> pursuant to the policy of the state to insure
> equal educational opportunity to every child, and
> in recognition of the educational needs of chil-
> dren of limited English speaking ability, it is
> the purpose of this subchapter to provide for the
> establishment of bilingual education programs in
> the public schools and to provide supplemental
> financial assistance to help local school dis-
> tricts meet the extra cost of the programs (Gen-
> eral and Special Laws of the State of Texas, 63rd
> Legislature, 1973, 860).

In its final form the bilingual bill required a school district which had an enrollment of 20 or more children with limited English-speaking ability, to establish a program in bilingual education for the children in each language classification. The bill provided for the grouping of students for instruction in their native language and for English-as-a-second language classes. It also provided for the full integration of these students with their monolingual English-speaking counter-parts in subjects such as art, music, and physical education.

The bill also required that such bilingual programs be offered to a student for three successive years or until he achieved a level of English language proficiency which enabled him to perform successfully in classes in which instruction was given only in English. A child could not be continued in such programs for longer than a three-year period without the approval of the school district and the child's parents. On the other hand, no school district could transfer a child out of a bilingual program prior to his third full year of enrollment without the express approval of the parents in writing or an examination score which indicated that the student had acquired English language skills appropriate to his grade level.

The section of the bill which referred to finances stated in a very general manner that school districts operating TEA-approved bilingual education programs would be allotted special allowances to be determined by the Agency for supplies, materials, and textbooks. The cost of transporting bilingual education students was to be reimbursed based on the number of actual miles traveled times the district's official extra-curricular travel per mile rate. The Foundation School Program Fund Budget Committee was instructed to include such costs in their estimates of the funds needed for the Foundation School Program.

The program was to be funded for the 1974 and 1975 biennium, according to the appropriations which were allotted for the program in the Appropriations bill of the 63rd Legislature. The first year of the program was used to prepare teachers and materials. The actual instructional program would not begin until the fall of 1975.

Texas Association of School Boards

The two year phase-in of the program had been a suggestion of the Texas Association of School Boards. The association was not opposed to the bilingual education program which had been recommended by the State Board of Education, but it had strong reservations against provisions which would weaken the decision-making authority of local school boards. In mid February, TASB Executive Committee members voted to oppose any measure in House Bill 145 or Senate Bill 121 which would lessen local control. In addition, members were urged to write to Senator Longoria, Ogg and Santiesteban about their concern or, if possible, to attend the public hearing which had been scheduled for the senate version of the bilingual bill (TASB Legislative Report No. 5, February 15-22, 1973).

The association was really not comfortable with the whole notion of bilingual education. However, in the absence of association board policy which absolutely opposed bilingual instruction, Dr. Richard Hooker, who was associate director of TASB, decided to push for a transitional bilingual education program. On an informal level Dr. Hooker was Governor Briscoe's major advisor on education legislation. He urged the governor and TASB officials to support a transitional bilingual education program similar to the one which had been enacted by the Massachusetts legislature the previous year (Hooker, R., Personal communication, June 7, 1979).

On May 17 TASB members were informed on the progress of the bilingual education bill.

> The press of time has caused the author of H.B.
> 145 to substitute S.B. 121 for his bill on the
> House Floor. This action removes the necessity
> of having to seek the passage of H.B. 145 in
> the Senate. Since the House accepted this move
> and passed the bill it appears that the measure
> is destined to be a statute (Newsletter, Issue
> #17, 1973).

The news release was deliberately written to keep the bilingual education issue as low key as possible. The major difference between the two bills was not mentioned. Moreover, lack of time was not the actual reason for Truan's decision to substitute Brooks' bill for his own in the House.

Senate Approves Bilingual Bill

Brooks' bill was referred to the Senate Committee on Education on the 30th of January for its consideration. It was not reported out of committee until April 11. Sixteen days later Senator Brooks filed a notice of intent with the secretary of the senate, scheduling Committee Substitute Senate Bill 121 for floor action on April 30. On the same day Senators McKinnon, Traeger and Wolff requested and were granted consent to be shown as co-authors of S.B. 121.

By April 20, when the bill came up for its second reading before the Senate, Senator Brooks had obtained the cooperation of the entire Senate on S.B. 121. As chairman of the Human Resources Committee, Brooks wielded considerable influence in the Senate. In addition, Senator Brooks was also a respected and well known member of the Senate. Despite his denials to the contrary, it seems very unlikely that Brooks could have convinced the 30 other senators to vote in favor of the bill solely on its merits. Chet Brooks was in a position where he could make deals or trade-offs with the rest of his colleagues. If he wanted the bill badly enough he had to offer something in return for their support of the bill (Camacho, J. E., Personal communication, February 15, 1970; Hooker, R., Personal communication, June 7, 1979; Garcia M., Personal communication, June 5, 1979).

When Senator Brooks requested a unanimous consent to suspend the order of business to consider S.B. 121, Senator Blanchard, from Lubbock, objected. By a vote of 29 to 1 the Senate consented to Senator Brooks' motion not to follow the regular calendar. When the bill came up for its third and final reading it was overwhelmingly passed by a vote of 30, with the absence of

104

Senator Don Adams of Jasper noted (<u>Senate Journal</u>, Volume I, 1973).

On May 1 Senate Bill 121 was sent to the House for its consideration. By this time Representative Truan seems to have decided to wait for Brooks' bill, even though his bill had been reported out of committee on March 26, and technically could have probably been sent to the Senate before Brooks' bill was sent to the House. On the same day Representative Dan Kubiak, chairman of the Education Committee, announced a public hearing for the bill to be held on May 3. During the hearing Truan made a motion to substitute his two bills, H.B. 145 and 146, for Senate Bill 121. Truan was apprehensive because he knew that Brooks' bill was mandatory, whereas his bill was not. After some discussion the motion making the bill mandatory was passed with no objections and with no points of order being raised by any of the members of the Education Committee. Five days later the bill was reported favorably out of the education committee and placed on the Consent Calendar, on which all uncontested bills of general or statewide interest are placed. On May 12, due to the objection of five House members, the bill was removed from the Consent Calendar and placed on the Major State Calendar. This Calendar lists all measures of primary importance and which have general applicability. The change in the Calendar was a prelude to what awaited the bill when it came before the House for floor action. By removing the bill from the Consent Calendar, opponents had prevented the bill from easily being passed through the House by a simple voice vote. More objections and points of order would come later when the bill was introduced for final action on May 15 (<u>House Journal</u>, Volume II, 1973).

The Governor Supports Bilingual Education

Bilingual education advocates were hopeful that the newly elected governor would support their bill in 1973. During the campaign, Briscoe had claimed that he was better acquainted with the needs and concerns of the Mexican-American community, because he was from South Texas. Briscoe appointed Rodolfo "Rudy" Flores, his friend and the vice-president of his bank in Uvalde, as his special administrative assistant to deal with the issues which the Mexican-American leadership considered to be important. Flores made it a point to emphasize that if Dolph Briscoe were elected, he had every intention of hiring more Mexican-Americans on his staff than any other previous Texas governor (Garza, M., Personal communication, February 9, 1979). During the 1972 campaign, Briscoe also promised the support the passage of bilingual education legislation (Flores, R., Personal communication, March 21, 1979).

After Dolph Briscoe had won the elections in November, LULAC representatives and Dr. Hector P. Garcia turned to him for support of the adult and bilingual education bills which Carlos F. Truan would be introducing again during the 63rd Legislature. Throughout the year the Mexican-American leadership cautiously approached all of the candidates who were running for governor and presented their demands for their share of the economic, political and social opportunities in Texas.

In 1972 Ben Barnes, the lieutenant governor for the last two terms, was the first to announce his candidacy for governor. Mexican-American leaders generally considered that the main contest in the runoff elections would be between Dolph Briscoe and Ben Barnes. On the evening before the primary, LULAC representatives confident of a Barnes victory, met with the candidate, members of his staff and other supporters at the Forty Acres Club in Austin, to bargain for key positions in state government. The results of the May 5th primary, however, stunned most of the political analysts. Ben Barnes and Preston Smith both lost. Dolph Briscoe, on the other had, managed to capture 45% of the vote and Frances Farenthold, a liberal and leader of the Dirty Thirty during the 62nd Legislature, came in second with 28% of the vote. In the runoff on June 3, Briscoe defeated Farenthold, and subsequently went on to win the elections in November (Deaton, 1973; Garza, M., Personal communication, February 9, 1979).

It is difficult to determine when particular events may have taken place, but the evidence does suggest that spokesmen of the two leading Mexican-American organizations frequently extracted promises of support for their programs from various candidates. In a meeting among Mexican-American politicos in San Antonio Preston Smith expressed his support for the bilingual education program wh ich he knew Mexican-American leaders wanted. Smith's credibility, however, was shattered when he stated with all apparent sincerity or naivete that in his opinion there was no discrimination in the state of Texas against any ethnic group in the areas of education, administration of justic or employment (Cardenas, J. A., Personal communication, February 28, 1979). After this meeting the Mexican-American leadership abandoned any hope of supporting Preston Smith, even though he had expressed an interest in promoting bilingual education programs.

Governor Preston Smith lost his bid for a third term of office. The Sharpstown Scandal terminated any hopes he might have had. Despite his loss, Governor Smith, in his address before a joint session of the Texas legislature on January 10, 1973, mentioned that his Executive Budget did include the establishment of a new bilingual education program with a funding level of $6.4 million (House Journal, Volume I, 1973).

As he had promised, newly elected Governor Dolph Briscoe
included adult and bilingual education in his recommended budget
for the 1974-1975 biennium. For the bilingual program he recommended $1,622,000 for the first fiscal year, and $4,913,500 for
the second. The adult education program was allotted $5 million
for each fiscal year. Budgetary recommendation must also include
the method of financing each line item. Money for the proposed
bilingual program was to be funded through the general state
revenues (Executive Budget, Governor Dolph Briscoe, 63rd Legislature, 1974-1975 Biennium, IV-2 and IV-3).

The Appropriations Process and Bilingual Education

The governor's budget, unlike the budget of the legislature,
is influenced more strongly by his objectives, goals or campaign
promises. Former Governor Smith's recommendation to the legislature that it consider the creation of a bilingual education
program in no way obligated the legislature or the new governor,
but the statement did strengthen the advocacy appeal of bilingual
proponents.

In his inaugural address before the joint session of the
Texas Legislature on January 16, 1973, Governor Briscoe further
demonstrated his support for the bilingual bill. He stated that
as a part of his objective to create an environment in which
every person had the "opportunity to rise to the maximum of his
or her potential" he supported the enactment of "an adequate
bilingual educational program" (House Journal, Volume I, 1973,
114-115). The next day the governor reiterated his position
on bilingual education. In his statement before the legislature
the governor linked the need for bilingual education to the
Texas school finance case which at the time was being reviewed
by the United States Supreme Court.

> I am concerned by the problems which the state
> will encounter in public education if the
> Rodriguez Case is upheld in the Supreme Court
> of the United States. I will consider carefully
> all of the reports and recommendations coming
> from the various study groups prompted by this
> case.
>
> Until the court acts, we cannot define the mag-
> nitude of these problems. It may well be that
> the case will not be settled until after adjourn-
> ment of this Regular Session. But, regardless of
> the timing, and regardless of the outcome, I
> believe very strongly that the opportunity for

a quality education must be available to
every child, including bilingual teaching
where needed. Quality should not be determined by where a child lives or the wealth of
his community. By the same token, I also be-
lieve very strongly in local control and
equitable local participation in the costs
of public education (House Journal, Volume I,
1973, 140. Italics supplied).

Briscoe's statements in support of bilingual education
were brief and cautious. It seems quite likely that he was not
entirely convinced about the merits of the bilingual bill which
Truan and others wanted him to endorse. However, he had promised
the Mexican-American leaders that he would endorse and work for
the bill's enactment (Camacho, J. E., Personal communication,
February 15, 1979).

The governor's inclusion of line items for bilingual and
adult education as a part of his budget was important, but it
did not assure that the programs would be enacted or funded.
Unlike most states where the budgetary preparation phase of the
appropriations process is handled by the governor, in Texas this
aspect of the budget is initiated and concluded by the legislature exclusively (Pettus and Bland, 1976). The appropriations
process in Texas involves the preparation of two budgets: the
governor's executive budget and the budget which is recommended
by the Legislative Budget Board.

The Legislative Budget Board to a great extent determines
what new demands for state funding are included or left out of
the budget. By law the Board is composed of ten legislators.
The Lieutenant Governor and the Speaker of the House serve as
the Board's chairman and vice-chairman. The chairmen of the
Senate Finance Committee, State Affairs Committee, the House
Appropriations Committee, and the Committee on Taxation and
Revenue are automatically members of the Board. Two other
members from each House are appointed by the Speaker and the
Lieutenant Governor (Bowhay and Thrall, 1975).

In 1973, although the governor included two new line items
in his budget, these same items did not appear in the legislative
budget because there was no prior legislation authorizing appropriations for bilingual and adult education. The availability
of funds to pay for new programs and the political compromises
which are agreed to among the various actors during and in the
final days of the legislative session are among the two most
important factors which determine the enactment of new legislation which is supported by the governor.

The appropriations process begins seven months before the legislature convenes on every odd-numbered year. Administrators of the various agencies submit their budget requests to the Legislative Budget Office and also the Governor's Budget Office between May and September of even-numbered years. Public hearings and analysis of the proposed two year budget are independently held by both offices. The analysis of budget requests and recommendations in the Legislative Budget Office is handled by a professional staff hired by the legislature. After all requests and recommendations are considered, the director of the office with the aid of his staff present the budget to the Legislative Budget Board. The Board, in turn, examines the budget and makes final last minute changes in the appropriations budget which it recommends to the legislature no later than December, several weeks before the beginning of the regular legislative session in January (Bowhay and Thrall, 1973).

The Governor's Budget Office follows a similar procedure, with the governor playing the decisive role in the process. After the governor reviews, approves or disapproves of the recommendations and requests on the proposed budget, it is mailed to all members of the legislature, state agencies and to the Legislative Budget Board by December 15. Seven days after the legislature convenes for the regular session, the Director of the Legislative Budget Office submits a copy of the budget prepared by the Legislative Budget Board to all legislators and to the governor (Bowhay and Thrall, 1973).

Thus, legislators in Texas receive two budgetary documents, but work closely with the budget recommendations which are prepared by the Legislative Budget Board. The governor's budget represents a revenue plan for funding old and new programs, while the legislature's budget represents a unified method of spending state funds (Pettus and Bland, 1976).

After the initial budget has been submitted to the legislature at the beginning of the session the budgetary preparation is continued by the legislative leadership and the Senate and House financial committees. The negotiating process continues in both committees until very late in the session. The final task of forming an acceptable budget is done by the conference committee. This committee is tightly controlled by the Speaker and the Lieutenant Governor and, to a lesser degree, the Governor. The legislative leadership controls by appointing the membership of the committee. The governor's influence over the final product of the appropriations budget comes at the end of the session, when his power to line item veto increases his leverage over the process to some extent (Pettus and Bland, 1976). In 1973 the proponents of the adult and bilingual education bills worked diligently in influencing the funding of both bills in the House

Appropriations Committee and in the joint session of the conference committee.

The Funding Process

Very early in the session Representative Neil Caldwell, chairman of the House Appropriations Committee, assured Representatives Matt Garcia and Bob Vale that they would be given an opportunity to present their request for funding the adult and bilingual education bills to the full committee. Committee members were not overly receptive to the idea of providing funding for the bilingual and adult education bills, but Garcia and Vale continued to press for their inclusion. It was not until the last days of the committee hearings that they were able to squeeze out a total of $7 million for both bills. Without the help of the committee chairman it is very doubtful that they could have obtained any funding for two bills which at the time had no legislative authorization. When the House budget was submitted for floor debate the funding level for both bills was not changed. It was not until the House budget was considered in the conference committee that the funding of the bills ran into serious problems. The House version of the budget included line items for adult and bilingual education, but the Senate version did not. According to the new rules which were adopted during the 63rd Legislature to govern the function of the Conference Committee, the committee could not recommend a greater amount than that which had been recommended if the item appeared in only one version of the appropriations budget (Garcia, M., personal communication, June 5, 1979; Bowhay and Thrall, 1975).

Towards the end of the 63rd Legislative Session, between May 8 and 23, the adult and bilingual education bills lost the funding which Matt Garcia and Bob Vale had worked so hard to include in the House version of the budget. The main objection raised by some of the conferees in the Conference Committee was that the bills had not been passed by the legislature and thus could not legally be appropriated funds (Garza, M., Personal communication, March 7, 1979). Other opponents of the bills argued that the legislature would be funding programs which were not proven. This was especially the case regarding the bilingual education bill. The legislators were well aware that the major beneficiary of these bills would be the Mexican-American population, and many of them made that the central argument against appropriating funds for such a program. Another argument which was used was that the legislature was dangerously close to expending monies which would not be certifiable by the state comptroller. Legislators who supported the bilingual bill looked upon this last argument as being a direct attack on the Mexican-American, since most of the funds would be utilized to help Mexican-American children. It was noted that the same argument was not used against funding highway construction, or bills to eliminate fire ants and other programs (Garcia, M., Personal communication, June 5, 1979).

The Mexican-American legislative caucus and Bob Allen of the Adult Education Division of the TEA wanted to ensure the passage of both bills with the funding which had been obtained in the House version of the appropriations budget. With the help of the Dental Association, Truan was able to call a LULAC Legislative Seminar to which he invited the governor and his wife, Kelvin Guest, Chairman of the state Democratic Committee, Rudy Flores, Manuel Garza, and the members of the Mexican-American caucus.

During the meeting Truan did most of the talking. He pleaded with the governor and his staff to lobby for the reinstatement of funding for both bills. He reminded him that LULAC had supported him in his campaign for governor. They had stayed out of the primaries, and had supported him in the November elections. Moreover, he stressed that the Mexican-American caucus unanimously favored the bill. Briscoe agreed to push for the reinstatement of funds when the legislature reconvened that afternoon.

Kelvin Guest and Rudy Flores actively lobbied for the funding of both bills. By the end of the day the intense lobbying had succeeded. Funding for both bills was restored, but it was contingent upon their enactment by the 63rd Legislature. The compromise which was worked out netted both bills a total of $7 million. The adult education bill was appropriated $4.3 million, evenly divided for the 1974 and 1975 biennium. The bilingual education bill was appropriated a mere $700,000 for the first year and $2 million for the next (Garza, M., Personal communication, March 7, 1979; General and Special Laws of Texas, 63rd Legislature, 1973).

The amount of money which was finally approved by the Conference Committee for the adult and bilingual education programs was not decided according to any predetermined formula. The funding which was approved was based on what money Garcia and Vale were able to extract out of the House Appropriations Committee. Funding also depended to a great extent on what the committee was willing or felt that it was able to provide for each program.

Another factor used to determine the amount of money which could be made available was the past history of each program. It was felt that the bilingual education program was a new, untested program, in contrast to the adult education program, and that therefore it would be best to start the program with seed money to prepare teachers and produce the necessary materials that would be used in the classroom. The following fiscal year the funding level would be increased to reflect the actual classroom instructional program.

At the time no one actually knew how much money it would take to fund a minimally acceptable bilingual program. There was little data on how a bilingual program would differ from a regular monolingual program in terms of cost per child. The first attempt to empirically determine the cost of funding a bilingual education program was not undertaken until November, 1973, six months after the enactment of the Bilingual Education and Training Act (Cardenas, Bernal, Kean, 1976; Garcia, M., Personal communication, June 5, 1979).

Throughout the legislative session and even during the funding crisis TEA officials of the Office of International and Bilingual Education never actively intervened in the legislative process. Had it not been for the independent course of action which Truan, Garza, Garcia, Rudy Flores and others had taken in pushing for legislative authorization and appropriation for both bills, it is questionable whether the bills could have been funded during that legislative session. With both bills assured of funding, the next step was to make sure both bills were enacted.

House Bill 147 was passed in the House in mid February and was approved by the Senate in early May. There was little hostile opposition to this bill. The only problem encountered had been the issue of funding. Senator Brooks' bilingual bill, however, still had not passed the House.

House Debate and Passage of S.B. 121

On May 15 Senate Bill 121 was introduced on the floor of the House on its second reading and in place of Truan's House Bills 145 and 146. Immediately following the bill's introduction, Representative Bill Hollowell of Grand Saline, and Representative Hilary B. Doran of Del Rio both raised a point of order against the further consideration of the bill. They claimed that the bill had not been in the member's box 24 hours before its announcement on the floor of the House. They also claimed that S.B. 121 was not a companion bill to House Bill 145. The Speaker, Price Daniel, Jr., sustained the point of order. He then laid House Bill before the House on its second reading and final passage to engrossment. The bill was read a second time, whereupon Truan made a motion to postpone further action on the bill until Friday, May 18 at 10:00 a.m. The motion was accepted without any objections (House Journal, Volume II, 1973). Truan postponed further action on his bill in order to allow S.B. 121 to be re-introduced after its compliance with the 24 hour rule.

On Thursday, May 17, the Speaker re-introduced S.B. 121 for consideration in the House. Representative Hollowell quickly raised another point of order against further consideration of the bill on the grounds that it violated Rule VIII, Section 13 of the House Rules. After the objection was raised the Speaker placed the House at ease for 24 minutes while he prepared a written answer to Mr. Hollowell's objection. The rule which was cited required that a five day notice be given of any public hearing by a committee or sub-committee. Mr. Hollowell was contending that this had not been done. The objection raised was more a delaying tactic than it was a substantive objection, because in the same section the rule clearly exempted a senate bill which was the same as a House bill from the five day notice provision. In addition, according to the House and Joint Rules, the Speaker had the authority to place any Senate bill on the House Calendar in place of a similar House Bill (Rule XIX, Section 13; Joint Rule 15).

The Speaker, who supported the bilingual bill, overruled the objection raised by Hollowell, stating that the point of order raised, assuming the point of order was valid, should have been made during the committee hearing. Since the point of order was not raised at that time, the objection was moot. Senate Bill 121 was once again placed before the House for its consideration. This time the Speaker reminded the members that it was a Senate Bill Day, according to Rule XIX, Section 14, Joint Rule 16, and that the bill had been placed on the Major State Calendar. Opposition to the bill, however, was not over.

Representative Doran then objected to further consideration of S.B. 121 on the grounds that it contained more than one subject in its title and it therefore was in violation of the Texas Constitution and the House Rules (Article II, Section 35; Rule XIX, Section 2). Speaker Daniel promptly overruled that objection too, stating that the bill had but one subject, although the bill had been divided into two parts.

Neil Caldwell, chairman of the House Appropriations Committee, was then recognized. He offered to amend the bill by inserting a subparagraph which specified that the cost for funding the act for the fiscal years 1974 and 1975 would be maintained at the level which had been agreed to in Conference Committee several days earlier. The amendment was adopted without any objections, but the fight over the bill was not quite over.

Representative Bennie Bock, who came from the predominantly German-American community of New Braunfels, commented that the bill was a Mexican bill and that its main beneficiaries would be Mexican-Americans. He then suggested that the word "bilingual" be changed to "multilingual" wherever it appeared in the text of the bill. In response Matt Garcia challenged Bock to find one sentence in the bill where the word Mexican or Mexican-American appeared. Representative Garcia then raised a point of order against further consideration of the Bock amendment on the grounds that it represented a different subject from that being considered and therefore, was not germane to the bill (Rule XX, Section 7). The Speaker then noted that the bill dealt with "bilingual education programs" and did not specify which two languages could be taught. The Bock amendment, on the other hand, would have required the state to fund the teaching of many languages. The objection was sustained.

Two more amendments to the bill were offered by Representatives James Nugent, of Kerrville, and James Cole, of Greenville. The first amendment stated clearly and emphatically that it was a matter of state policy to insure that all pupils who attended Texas public schools master the English language. However, bilingual instruction would be permitted in those situations where such instruction was considered necessary in order to insure "reasonable efficiency in the English language so as not to be educationally disadvantaged." The second amendment required each school district to offer a program of bilingual instruction beginning in the fall of 1974 if it had an enrollment of 20 or more limited English-speaking ability students in any language classification in the same grade during the preceding school year. Bilingual instruction would be offered in the first grade in 1974, then it would be increased by one grade each year until it was offered in each grade up to the sixth. The local school board was given discretionary powers to decide on an appropriate program of instruction if there were less than twenty limited English-speaking ability students. Both amendments were passed with no objections (House Journal, Volume II, 1973).

The final attempt to amend the bill was initiated by Representative Tom Craddick, a Republican from Midland. He suggested stricking out the requirement of having to teach the history and culture "associated with the native language of the children of limited English-speaking ability" who were enrolled in bilingual programs. Truan moved to table the Craddick amendment. The move to table prevailed by a vote of 92 to 48 with nine members recorded absent. Craddick offered another amendment which would have limited the program to the third grade. Truan quickly moved to table that motion too, and won by a vote of 104 to 35 with eight recorded absent. Finally, in a last desperate attempt to block the bill, Craddick objected that the bill contained two subjects, and was therefore in violation of Rule XIX, Section 2 of the House Rules. The Speaker once again overruled that point of order and promptly granted a request for a vote on the bill. Senate Bill 121 was passed to third reading by a vote of 114 to 27 with eight recorded absent. Truan swiftly moved to reconsider the vote by which the bill had been passed to third reading, and to table any further motion to reconsider. The motion to table was passed (House Journal, Volume II, 1973).

Representative Tom Massey, of San Angelo, was so strongly opposed to the bill that he asked that his objection be placed on record.

> I voted against SB 121 because it goes much
> too far. I favor bilingual education, but it
> should be limited to the first three grades.
> Bilingual education programs in Texas should be
> limited to Spanish-speaking students and should
> not require teaching the native cultural history
> of all the minorities involved. This bill re-
> quires all of this (House Journal, Volume II,
> 1973, 4020).

The following day, Truan, assured of S.B. 121's passage, moved to have further consideration of his bilingual bill tabled subject to recall. No one objected. On May 23, Senate Bill 121 was passed by a vote of 112 to 20, with 15 members recorded absent (House Journal, Volume III, 1973). The Senate concurred with the House amendments on the same day (Senate Journal, Volume II, 1973). Two days later the bill was signed by Price Daniel, Jr. and William P. Hobby. On June 13, 1973, the Bilingual Education and Training Act was signed by Governor Dolph Briscoe.

The enactment of the Texas Bilingual Education and Training Act during the 63rd session of the legislature seems to have been the result of a number of factors. The bilingual education bill received the full support and endorsement of the legislative leadership. The legislative advocacy of the Texas Association for Continuing Adult Education, along with the active lobbying efforts of TEA Adult Educational Division personnel, helped to insure overwhelming legislative approval for bilingual education legislation in 1973.

Newly elected Governor Dolph Briscoe had promised Mexican-American leaders that he would support the enactment of bilingual education legislation. Before the 63rd legislative session began he included a line item in his budget for adult and bilingual education. In his address before a joint session of the legislature he mentioned that bilingual education legislation was one of the goals of his administration. During the session, Rudy Flores, administrative assistant to the governor, personally presented testimony on behalf of both bills in Senate and House public education committee hearings. The governor's last minute intervention in the appropriations process was crucial in assuring funding for both bills.

The election of Price Daniel, Jr. as Speaker of the House was a very important link in the enactment of Representative Truan's two bills. His appointment of Representatives Truan, Garcia and Vale to key House committees strategically contributed to the uninhibited passage of the adult and bilingual bills. During the House debate on S.B. 121, it was his parliamentary expertise which prevented the bills from being altered or killed by hostile opponents.

The active lobbying support of the Texas Association for Continuing Adult Education and the leadership which Bob G. Allen and Manuel Garza provided was also very valuable. Senator Brooks and Representative Truan relied heavily on their expertise and willingness to present formal testimony as well as information in an informal, behind the scenes manner to legislators at every step of the process. They filled a role which TEA bilingual educational personnel were unwilling to play. As a result, TEA's input into the legislative process on behalf of the adult and bilingual education bills was not significant.

CHAPTER VI

SUMMARY

This study was undertaken to identify the factors which may have contributed to the enactment of the Texas Bilingual Education and Training Act in 1973. An examination of the literature on politics and education revealed that little attention had been given to the study of ethnic group politics and its influence on state educational policy-making in the United States. In a review of the social science literature on bilingual education, Fishman noted that little historical research had been done to document the most recent developments in bilingual education policy-making by federal courts and state legislatures (1977).

Meranto's model for explaining legislative outcomes was used to organize the study. The model called for an examination of the political changes which occurred within the legislature at the time the bilingual bill was being considered. It was assumed that specific structural or informal activities which may have occurred in the legislature at the time would help to account for the enactment of the bilingual bill in Texas. The model also stressed the importance of examining those external political environmental changes which may have contributed to the legislative process and outcome.

Using Meranto's environmental categories we isolated eight variables for the study. Under Circumstantial Conditions we included four factors: 1) the enactment of the federal Bilingual Education Act in 1968, 2) the publication of the May 25th Memorandum, 3) the Sharpstown Political Scandal, and 4) the 1972 elections. Under Demand Articulators were included: 1) two Mexican-American voluntary associations, 2) two state education associations, 3) the Texas Education Agency, and 4) the governor. The study primarily focused on the events which contributed to bilingual legislation in 1973. However, since this had not been the first bilingual law enacted in Texas, attention was given to four-year period beginning in 1969 and culminating in 1973.

The first bilingual education law was enacted in 1969 by the Texas Legislature in the 61st legislative session. In this session House Representative Carlos F. Truan, Corpus Christi, and Senator Joe J. Bernal, San Antonio, introduced House Bill 103 and Senate Bill 146 respectively on the subject of language and instruction in the public schools of Texas. In its recommendation to the legislature the Texas Education Agency suggested local school districts be given authority to decide on the use of the language of instruction and urged that the language restriction and penalty be repealed.

During the 61st Legislative Session Truan and Bernal agreed that their proposal would allow the state of Texas to receive more federal funds for education. Local participation in the new ESEA Title VII federal demonstration projects was optional and required no state expenditures. The bills were not opposed by the legislative leadership or by committee members in either House of the Legislature. House committee member's personal opposition to Bernal's authorship of the bill, and the intervention of TSTA were the only two obstacles which could have seriously hampered the bill's final enactment. On May 22, 1969 the Texas Legislature formally approved the state's first permissive bilingual education law.

During the 62nd Legislature in 1971 House Representative Carlos F. Truan introduced H.B. 1024 and H.B. 495. House Bill 495 was introduced first. The text of the bill was an almost plagiarized version of the May 25th Memorandum which had been published by the Office for Civil Rights the previous year. This bill was not passed by the Legislature. The second bill, House Bill 1024, proposed the establishment of teacher training institutes, salaries for bilingual teachers, and the acquisition of textbooks. Participation by local school districts was still optional.

The first major opposition to the proponents of an expanded version of the first bilingual education law came during this session. House Representative Bill Clayton introduced a bill which would have restricted bilingual education instruction to the third grade and would have imposed strict criminal penalties on school officials who disregarded the law's restrictions. The bill was killed in committee. In the final days of the session House Bill 1024, which was not opposed by the legislative leadership on its merits, also failed to receive the endorsement of the House. Truan's connection with the Dirty Thirty had made him an enemy of the Speaker of the House. By refusing to recognize Truan's request for House concurrence on a last minute senate amendment the Speaker prevented the bill from being voted upon.

During the 63rd Legislative Session of the Texas Legislature advocates of bilingual and adult education joined forces to influence the legislative process. Truan, who had been asked to support an adult education bill by the Texas Association for Continuing Adult Education, astutely decided to introduce the bilingual and adult bills as a package. In order to get the votes to pass the adult association bill, Truan informed TEA Adult Education Division officials and the leaders of the adult association, they needed to support both bills. When he introduced his three bills to the House he received 77 co-sponsors on each bill. The personal lobbying and the intense letter writing campaign which had been mounted by Bob G. Allen, Manual Garza and by the association, however, was only one of the factors which helped push the bills through the legislature.

A new and supportive legislative leadership and the strategic House committee appointments which were made by Speaker Price Daniel, Jr. also contributed to the authorization and the funding of both bills. Daniel appointed Truan chairman of the House Resources Committee. His position and the importance of the committee in the House worked to safeguard the passage of the bilingual and adult education bills. Daniel appointed liberal and pro-bilingual advocate Dr. Dan Kubiak chairman of the Public Education Committee. The powerful appropriations committee chairmanship was given to liberal Neil Caldwell. The speaker also appointed bilingual proponents Matt Garcia and Bob Vale to this committee. In addition, Bob Vale, a Chicano from San Antonio, was appointed chairman of the House Rules Committee.

In the Senate Human Resources Committee chairman Chet Brooks co-sponsored the bilingual and adult education bills. This move was crucial because it served to detract opponents from claiming that the bill was a "Mexican" sponsored and supported bill. Although arguments of this kind were raised against the bill when it was considered by the House, Senate Bill 121, which carried mandatory requirements, was finally approved by the Texas Legislature. On June 13, 1973 the Bilingual Education and Training Act received the statutory approval of both Houses of the Legislature.

Analysis

A review of the historical data which was collected and examined in the study suggests that the enactment of the Texas Bilingual Education and Training Act in 1973 was not the result of any single dominant factor. Consequently, it was important to highlight several factors which were found to have a particular impact on the enactment process. The following factors were examined: 1) the role of the federal government, 2) the function of legislative ambiguity, 3) the primacy of the English language, 4) the support of the governor and ethnic group politics, 5) the support of the speaker, 6) the adult and bilingual education coalition, and 7) the role of the Texas Education Agency.

1. Federal Role

In 1969 federal initiatives in the area of bilingual education accelerated the slower local pace. The enactment of permis-

sive bilingual education legislation in Texas in 1969 received
its major impetus from the enactment of the federal Bilingual
Education Act in 1968. Increased federal funding provided local
school districts and the Texas Education Agency with a major in-
centive to participate in another educational program. The federal act provided state advocates with legitimate reasons to ask
for the elimination of restrictive language codes. The evidence
suggests that prior to 1969 Chicano legislators could not have
proposed the repeal of school language restrictions and have been
successful. When bills were introduced the arguments were cautious, low key and well within the acceptable Texas political
value system.

In 1971 Representative Truan's two bills on bilingual education were still optional. The first bill (H.B. 495) was a sub-
dued paraphrase of the May 25th Memorandum which had been sent to
school districts having five percent or more national origin minority student enrollment the previous year. The second bill
(H.B. 1024) increased TEA control over the training of bilingual
instructional personnel, the disbursement of funds and the preparation of teaching materials.

The influence of the federal mandate on the education of
linguistically different national origin minority school children
on the introduction of bilingual bills in 1973 was even more evident. Senator Brooks' bill (S.B. 121) was heavily influenced by
the spirit and language of the May 25th Memorandum.

2. Legislative Ambiguity

The manner in which the first bilingual law was written provides us with an important insight into the enactment process.
The bilingual bills were not clear statements on all of the objectives of bilingual education as advocates would have preferred. Instead each bill stressed the importance of English as the
primary language of instruction, called for the repeal of certain
language restrictions, and gave local districts the option to
participate in new federal education programs. According to Rein
and White, controversial legislation is frequently enacted in
this fashion. They noted that very often:

> Legislation requires ambiguity in the statement
> of its goals so that coalitions can be formed in
> support of it, and each group can believe that
> the legislation serves its own special purposes
> (Footnote in Boyd, 1978, 584).

It is evident that in Texas legislators viewed the bilingual bills in different ways. Anglo legislators perceived the bilingual bills as being a program designed to aid poor, non-English-speaking Mexican-American school children master English. Mexican-American advocates of bilingual schooling, on the other hand, viewed the passage of bilingual legislation differently. To many the use of Spanish as a medium of instruction was a symbol of prestige and increased social status for the Mexican-American in Texas. Often the pedagogical significance of bilingual schooling has been of secondary importance. From the evidence in this study it seems quite clear that arguments which emphasized the advantages of bilingualism and laid claim to legal or human linguistic rights would not have successfully convinced Texan legislators.

Mexican-American legislators and other advocates of bilingual-bicultural education diffused what could have been a highly controversial issue by down playing the cultural component of the bilingual education bill. The tactic of bilingual advocates in the legislature was to stress the transitional nature of the program by emphasizing the "primacy" of the English language.

3. Primacy of English Language

It is important to note that major emphasis was given to the primacy of the English language in each of the bills which were introduced in 1969, 1971 and in 1973. In both the permissive and mandatory versions of the bilingual bill mastery of the English language by all public school students was declared to be official state policy.

In 1973 the Texas Legislature had approved a transitional bilingual education program. It was modeled to a great extent on the bilingual law which had been enacted in Massachusetts the previous year. The objective was to use the child's native language as a medium for classroom instruction while he gradually learned English. The maintenance of linguistic and cultural distinctions was not the law's intended purpose. It is doubtful whether any bill not having a statement on the primacy of English could have been passed. During the House debate on S.B. 121 one of two last minute amendments introduced and passed concerned the rightful place of the English language. It seems clear that state legislators had not approved legal authorization for a bilingual state when they enacted bilingual laws.

To most of the legislators lack of English was the root cause for the Mexican-American's low socio-economic status in

Texas. Capitalizing on the business ethos of Texas politics, advocates of adult and bilingual education argued that there was a direct relationship between English language proficiency and economic benefits and productivity.

4. Governor's Support and Ethnic Group Politics

The role of Governor Dolph Briscoe in the enactment of S.B. 121 was crucial. The newly elected governor delivered on his campaign promises to the Mexican-American leadership by requesting over $16 million in new appropriations for the adult and bilingual bills. The strong and unexpected electoral showing by La Raza Unida party in 1972 was another reason for Briscoe's concern for Mexican-Americans. The elections had demonstrated to Democratic party leaders the potential threat which independent Chicano voting could pose to the dominance and stability of the conservative Democratic party.

Bilingual education was a La Raza Unida party platform. By enacting a bilingual law the Democratic party weakened the appeal of La Raza Unida, and at the same time helped to strengthen Chicano confidence in the dominant party. The passage of the bilingual law vindicated the arguments of liberal and conservative Chicanos who chose to work for changes within the system. It seems clear, however, that Chicano political efforts on opposite sides of the ideological spectrum were both instrumental in suggesting immediate legislative considerations on behalf of Mexican-Americans in Texas.

Furthermore, the evidence shows that at no time during the advocacy process was the governor made aware of any organized opposition to bilingual education by any influential segment of the Mexican-American community. The G. I. Forum, LULAC and other Mexican-American voluntary associations presented a united front on the issue of bilingual instruction in Texas public schools.

5. Support of the Speaker

. Senate Bill 121 had the full support of the legislative leadership in both Houses of the legislature. Speaker Price Daniel, Jr.'s support in the House for bilingual education was very important. Without his support it is doubtful the bill would have survived the massive House debate. Price Daniel, Jr.'s strategic House committee assignments were the key to the bill's success in the House. His appointment of Truan to the influential post of Chairman of the Human Resources Committee was a decisive move. In this post Truan was in a much better position to make deals with colleagues in exchange for their votes on the bilingual bill. The speaker's appointment of sympathetic House members to committees to which the bilingual bill would be referred for consideration were calculated and deliberate. Speaker Daniel had not forgotten the help which Truan had extended to him in his bid for the leadership of the House. Truan's loyalty and hard work as a member of the Dirty Thirty during the 62nd Legislature did not go unnoticed or unrewarded.

6. Adult and Bilingual Coalition

In addition to the support which he received from the governor and the Speaker of the House, Truan was keenly aware that he also needed some kind of strong, external public support for his bills.

The involvement of the Texas Association for Continuing Adult Education filled the public advocacy void which neither bilingual educators, Mexican-American parents and educators, nor the Texas Education Agency and its officials in the Division of Bilingual Education would or could do. Through their intense, personal lobbying efforts and the barrage of letters which they sent representatives, they were able to sensitize and influence over half of the House members on the subjects of bilingual and adult education. The association was not actually concerned with bilingual education per se, but in their minds there was little difference in the goals of each bill. One bill addressed the educational problems of the young Mexican-American child, while the other encompassed the needs of the adults.

The newly elected officers of the association and the two officials in the division of adult continuing education of TEA were goaded by some very practical considerations. They all knew that federal funds for adult education were limited, that the use of these funds was restrictive, and that there was always the threat of these funds being cut or decreased. Both the adult and bilingual programs were federally funded. However, the adult program had been in existence since 1966, whereas the other program had only begun in 1969.

The idea to merge both interests into one concerted legislative strategy that would insure the enactment of both bills came from Representative Truan. In Truan's mind both bills were policies that needed to be "sold" to his colleagues in the House and

Senate. One bill insured Mexican-American children in the primary grades from having to fial because of linguistic limitations or negative self-concepts. The other bill insured that the parents of these children were not denied the opportunity that they were not able to have in their youth.

7. The Texas Education Agency

From 1968 to 1972 the Texas Education Agency acted as a facilitator and responded to external demands for change which emanated from within the state or from Washington, D.C. The Agency provided a formal, structural link between the demands of the Mexican-American community and the legislature. .

Formal linkages, however, were not enough to assure the passage of new and controversial education legislation. Between 1969 and 1973 the Agency never actively lobbied for the enactment of any of its new educational proposals. The bilingual and adult education bills were no exception. The Agency made its formal requests for legislative consideration of both bills as prescribed by law, but personnel in the bilingual division of the Agency did not actively push for their passage or funding. With the exception of Bob G. Allen and Manuel Garza, TEA officials did not actively lobby for the enactment of either bill.

The Agency's failure to push for the passage of its legislative recommendations was rooted in its image as an impartial, professional and non-political organization, obedient and subservient to the expressed will of the people of Texas through its elected lawmakers.

Although the need, the interest, and much of the early expertise and support for bilingual education came from Texas, it was not ehe first state to enact a mandatory bilingual education law. The advocates of bilingual education legislation were successful in articulating their demands for educational change at the federal level before they were able to influence the passage of similar state legislation. In general, the evidence obtained in this study suggests that the enactment of bilingual education legislation in Texas in 1969 and in 1973 was influenced by Mexican-American demands for innovative changes in the state's public school curriculum. In addition, the evidence demonstrates that the strategy and tactics which Mexican-American legislators adopted to pass the bilingual bills was a reflection of the political culture, as it was an explicit illustration of the nature and extent of the federal influence on state educational policy-making.

Notwithstanding the above factors, the evidence strongly suggests that the most important factor in accounting for the successful passage of the Texas bilingual education law seems to have been the role of the powerful Speaker of the House. Without his active support the bilingual bill could have never been passed by the 63rd Texas Legislature in 1973.

It took four years to enact a mandatory bilingual education law in Texas. Incremental and non-incremental educational policy-making went on simultaneously. The push for enacting a bilingual law was low-keyed. Earlier legislative successes and possibly the successful enactment of similar laws in other states were used to broaden the demands of Mexican-Americans for the enactment of bilingual education legislation in 1973. Finally, the study suggests that Mexican-American demands for bilingual-bicultural schooling were partly the result of a long history of educational neglect. Segregated schools, serious financial disparities among school districts, and the indifference and prejudice of the majority culture compounded a problem which could have been more seriously and ably met by local and state public officials.

Chapter VII

Bilingual Education Legislation
1975-1981

The enactment of the mandatory Bilingual Education and Training Act in 1973 represented a major political victory for Mexican-American legislators, educators, and the leaders of LULAC and American G.I. Forum. The victory, although quite significant, was not complete. The law had failed to include children enrolled in kindergarten and made no provision for meeting the instructional needs of limited English proficiency students in junior or senior high school. Another issue which seriously limited the law's full reach and effectiveness was the low level of funding. It was clear to the advocates of bilingual education that future legislative efforts needed to be focused on increasing the level of funding as well as ensuring the maximum participation of those students who stood to benefit from a bilingual and English-as-a-second-language instructional program. The legislative accomplishments in 1973 encouraged them to demand more changes in the law during subsequent legislative sessions. Between 1974 and 1981 bilingual education lobbyists successfully amended many sections of the original 1973 law. The changes which were adopted by the Texas legislature during this period were substantive. The instructional program was expanded to include primary and secondary school students, and the stigma associated with language and scholastic underachievement was removed from the original text of the law.

In 1973 we found that the successful enactment of bilingual legislation in Texas had been influenced by several internal and external political factors. Changes in the bilingual law were incremental and occurred within a period of four years. Between 1975 and 1979 the speaker of the House temporarily thwarted the efforts of bilingual education advocates to amend the bilingual education law. In 1981 the influence of the federal government once again enabled Mexican-American legislators to make significant changes in bilingual education legislation.

During the period 1975 to 1981 several factors contributed to the effective legislative advocacy of bilingual education proponents. By 1981 the Texas Association for Bilingual Education (TABE) was far more organized than it had been eight years earlier. With the leadership of former state senator Joe J. Bernal, the organization published a legislative manual for the purpose of educating its members on how they could influence the legislative process in a more systematic manner. The manual's publication would not have been possible without the assistance of other Mexican-American professional educators and the support of the San Antonio based Intercultural Development Research Association (IDRA). The association, founded in the late 1960s, played a very important role in converting bilingual education philosophy, theory, and methods into legislative mandates. The evidence strongly suggests that Senator Carlos F. Truan and others relied quite heavily on the professional expertise of education leaders Jose A. Cardenas, director of IDRA, Gloria Zamora and Albert Cortez. These educational experts collectively contributed to the dynamics of the ethno-educational curriculum policymaking process in Texas. The actions of Mexican-American organizations like LULAC, American G.I. Forum, and the Mexican-American Legal Defense and Education Fund also contributed to the changes in bilingual education legislation which were adopted by the 67th Legislature in 1981. The efforts by Mexican-American legislators on behalf of bilingual education cannot be underestimated. In 1981 the Mexican-American caucus unanimously supported the curriculum innovations which Senator Truan and Representative Matt Garcia had introduced for legislative consideration.

What follows is a synopsis of some of the factors which influenced the passage of new bilingual education legislation during the 64th, 65th, 66th, and 67th Legislative Sessions.

THE 64th LEGISLATIVE SESSION

The 64th Legislature was convened on January 14, 1975. The legislature worked on several important bills. Early on it approved Senate Joint Resolution 11, a proposal calling for the first revision of the state's constitution in 100 years. The proposed constitutional amendments affected 11 of its articles. The changes submitted included the creation of single-member legislative districts, redistricting after each federal census, annual legislative sessions, the creation of the commission to set legislative salaries, the lifting of an $80 million ceiling on public assistance funding. On November 2, 1975, the voters of Texas rejected the proposed amendments that would have modernized state government. Other issues before the legislature included consideration of a new voter registration law, public school finance reform, the creation of a superport, strip-mining safeguards, criminal reforms, and how it would spend a revenue surplus of $1.5 billion (Accomplishments of the 64th Legislature, 1975; Bernal, 1978).

In November of 1974 the State Board of Education submitted its first recommendation to amend the Bilingual Education and Training Act of 1973. The Board suggested the inclusion of the kindergarten level as part of the bilingual education sequence. It also requested increased funding for the preparation of kindergarten teachers and teacher aides, the employment of additional administrative staff at TEA, and the hiring of "bilingual instructional personnel in the education service centers to promote bilingual-multicultural education" (Recommendations, November, 1974).

The election of a new Speaker in the House affected the course of bilingual education legislation. On January 14, House members overwhelmingly elected Bill Clayton as Speaker of the House. Clayton received 112 votes and his opponent, Carl Parker, received the support of 33 House members. Representative Truan and other Mexican-American legislators did not vote for Clayton. The opposition to Clayton's election was due to his conservative political views, and his unwillingness to support bilingual education legislation (House Journal, Volume 1, 1975).

The Speaker's power over the legislative process in Texas lies in his authority of appointment. There were 24 Standing Committees in the House to which were assigned 2,249 bills for consideration during the 64th Legislative Session. None of the representatives who had voted against Clayton were appointed as chairmen of any of the 24 committees. With the lone exception of Representative Powers, who sat on the Committee on Elections, none of those who opposed Clayton's election were assigned the post of vice-chairman. Other changes affected the course of bilingual education legislation. The Human Resources Committee was changed to the Committee on Health and Welfare, and Representative Truan lost his post as chairman of this very powerful committee. Whatever leverage Truan may have had during the previous legislative session was lost. The appointment of Representative Tom Massey as chairman of the Committee on Public Education was calculated to thwart the legislative efforts of bilingual education proponents (House Journal, Volume 1, 1975).

On January 22, Governor Dolph Briscoe delivered his second state of the state address to a joint session of the legislature. In his speech he urged the legislature to expand the coverage of

the bilingual education law enacted in 1973 by including kindergarten. This was the second time Governor Briscoe had publicly
endorsed the use of bilingual education instructional goals and
methods for Mexican-American school children in Texas. Public announcements, however, are just one way of measuring the extent of
a person's commitment to an issue. During the 63rd Legislature the
governor's staff exerted considerable influence on behalf of bilingual education legislation. One year later the governor's support
for bilingual education had waned (House Journal, Volume 1, Bernal,
1978).

Four bills on bilingual education were introduced during the
64th Legislature. In the House Representative Tom Massey introduced House Bill 1640, and Representative Truan filed House Bill
289. In the Senate Senators Brooks and Ogg introduced Senate Bills
102 and 96, respectively.

Both Truan's and Brooks' bills were similar. They called for
the inclusion of kindergarten in the bilingual education sequence,
and its continuation through the sixth grade. Instruction was to
be given in the child's primary language in all required subjects
of the curriculum, and in the English language when the child acquired proficiency in English. The bill called for the development
of reading, writing, listening and speaking skills in both languages with "continued skill development of the English language."
The curriculum was supposed to include the history and culture of
the United States and of the minority language group (Appendix J).

A provision of the bill which had not been recommended by TEA
called for the voluntary enrollment "of children whose primary language was English, in order that they may acquire an understanding
of the language and cultural heritage of the children of limited
English-speaking ability for whom the particular program is designed."

The bill included the allocation of funds to TEA "for research
and development in the areas of curriculum, materials, and assessment and evaluation instruments." In addition, the education
agency was given full responsibility for the training of teachers,
administrators, paraprofessionals, and parents. The education
agency was responsible for the development of bilingual education
training programs in all colleges and universities in the state.

The bill's most radical changes were written into its preamble. In this section the authors were asking Texas legislators to accept the difference theory on the nature of language and culture, and to reject the law's remedial and compensatory image, an inherited legacy of the Great Society anti-poverty programs of the 1960s.

> The legislature finds that there are large numbers of children in the state who come from environments where the primary language is other than English and who have a cultural heritage that differs from that of the speakers of English as a primary language. Experience has shown that a primary means by which a child learns is through the use of his or her language and cultural heritage and that public school classes in which instruction is given only in English are often inadequate for the education of children. The legislature believes that large numbers of children of limited English-speaking ability have educational needs that are best met through bilingual instruction to facilitate their integration into the regular school curriculum (Statement of Policy, H.B. 289, 1975).

The introduction of Representative Tom Massey's bilingual bill (H.B. 1640) exacerbated the debate over the proposed changes. His bill called for the introduction of a permissive law, and a limitation of bilingual instruction to the third grade. School districts which opted for continuing a bilingual program beyond the third grade would not receive state assistance. One of the most damaging provisions of this bill was the authority it gave to local school districts to discontinue a bilingual program at any time (Appendix K).

By the end of the session it was evident that the proposals in both H.B. 289 and S.B. 102 would not be supported by the respective education committees. In the Senate Senator Brooks' bill was shunted aside in favor of Senator Ogg's bill, S.B. 96. This bill received the full endorsement of TEA officials because it included funds for the establishment of Service Centers with bilingual education personnel and bilingual kindergarten classes. In addition, Senator Ogg's bill did not have any changes in its Statement of Policy. In the House Representative Truan's bill (H.B. 289) was kept in abeyance in the Calendars Committee. When the amended ver-

sion of S.B. 96 was sent to the House for its endorsement it met
the same fate as H.B. 289 (Bernal, 1978).

On May 12, after considerable debate and compromises, the
amended version of S.B. 96 was attached to H.B. 1126, the public
school finance bill, as section 16, subsection (b) Section 21.453
of the Texas Education Code (House Journal, Volume II, 1975). On
June 1, the House agreed with the amendments added to H.B. 1126 by
the Senate although with strong reservations by many House members.
There was an attempt by Representative L. Jones to scuttle the
Senate amendment. He favored a conference committee to settle the
differences in the two bills. But a motion by Representative Tor-
res to table the substitute motion of Representative Jones resulted
in the defeat of the motion by a vote of 120 yeas and 27 nays, and
3 not voting (House Journal, Volume III, 1975).

The final version of the bilingual education bill included
mandatory bilingual education programs in kindergarten, first
grade, and second grade by the 1975-76 school year and also in the
third grade by the 1976-77 school year. Bilingual instruction
could be offered in the fourth and fifth grades for students who
had not made sufficient progress to participate in the regular
school curriculum. Any bilingual instructional program beyond the
fifth grade would not be funded by the state (General and Special
Laws of the State of Texas, 64th Legislature, 1975).

THE 65th LEGISLATIVE SESSION

The 65th legislative session began on January 11 and ended on
May 30, 1977. In the House 439 bills were enacted into law out of
a total of 2,267 which had been introduced. In the Senate 458
bills were enacted out of a total of 1,336. One of the most important issues during this session was school finance reform. In 1975
the legislature had failed to make any major changes in the school
finance law. During this session no action was taken on school
finance either. The legislature was more successful in enacting
legislation relating to the cost of malpractice insurance, crime
control, teacher retirement benefits, highways, and rules governing
the use and display of the Texas flag (Accomplishments of the 65th
Legislature, 1977).

In 1977 Carlos Flores Truan returned to Austin as senator of
the 20th senatorial district. In the Democratic primary Truan ran

132

against three Anglo candidates and won. On November 2, 1976, Truan successfully ran against James T. Smith and won by a margin of 30,068 votes (Senate Journal, Volume I, 1977).

During the 65th legislative session only two bills on bilingual education were introduced. In the Senate Carlos F. Truan submitted for consideration S.B. 307. In the House Representative Matt Garcia introduced companion bill H.B. 1767. Senator Truan's bill was the same as the one he had introduced during the previous legislative session. The bill called for the establishment of a program of bilingual instruction from kindergarten to the fourth grade during the 1977-78 school year, and required the program's implementation by one grade each year until it was offered in each grade through the sixth grade. The House version of the bill was the same. Both bills were sent to the education committees of both houses for consideration (House Journal, Volumes I, II, III, 1977; Senate Journal, Volumes I and II, 1977).

In 1976 the Texas Education Agency made no new requests for amending the state's bilingual education law (Recommendations, November, 1976). Also, Governor Dolph Briscoe, in his third term of office, made no mention of bilingual education in his address to the joint session of the Texas legislature as he had done in 1973 and 1975 (House Journal, Volume I, 1977). Instead he endorsed a reduction of state appropriations allocated for bilingual programs from $9.3 million to $5.2 million (General Appropriations Bill for 1978-79 Fiscal Years, 1977).

Prior to 1976 the Texas State Teachers Association (TSTA) had not shown much interest in sponsoring bilingual education legislation. The evidence suggests that the largest teacher union in Texas was concerned about more mundane issues, i.e., salary increases, retirement benefits, health insurance, which directly affected the lives of its members. According to one TSTA official, support for any kind of legislation had to come from local TSTA officials. If an issue was not brought to the attention of the TSTA executive leadership at one of its conventions, it was not taken up as part of the union's business. Prior to 1976 Mexican-American educators who were members of the association had apparently failed or had been unable to place the subject of bilingual education before the union leadership and the membership at large for its consideration and endorsement.

In a meeting of the Association's House of Delegates in the

spring of 1976, this body approved of the creation of a Special Committee on Bilingual Education. Three persons were appointed to sit on this committee by the president of the association. The members were Virginia Reyna, chairperson, teacher for the Mission Independent School District; Donroy Hafner, a supervisor from Region 13 Education Austin; and Mazie Mack, counselor from Freeport. The committee members were charged to collect information on the subject of bilingual education from specialists throughout the State of Texas (Texas Outlook, November, 1976).

The committee members met on three separate occasions to gather information on the subject of bilingual education. The meeting which was held at TSTA headquarters in Austin on December 7, 1976 seems to have been particularly important. The concerns and issues which were raised during this meeting greatly influenced the content of the six recommendations which the committee subsequently presented to the Association's House of Delegates in the spring of 1977. Speakers at this meeting included the assistant commissioner for International Education at TEA, Dr. Severo Gomez; Arturo L. Gutierrez, director of the Division of Bilingual Education at TEA; Dr. José A. Cardenas, director of the San Antonio based Intercultural Development Research Association (IDRA); and others who presented testimony on the subject of bilingual education. TSTA officials were urged to broaden the participation of school children in bilingual education programs by allowing English-speaking children of different ethnic groups a chance to learn another language and culture. They were asked to sponsor legislation which would allow TEA to enforce the provisions of the Bilingual Education and Training Act of 1973. Officials of the association were also asked to help encourage the preparation of adequately trained teachers. It was suggested that approximately 80% of the teachers working in bilingual education programs at the time did not have the necessary preparation (Texas State Teachers Association, Committee on Bilingual Education, 1976).

As a result of this and two other meetings the members of the Special Committee on Bilingual Education made six recommendations to the TSTA House of Delegates in the spring of 1977. The report received the approval of the Executive Committee without discussion, and it passed the House of Delegates with no objections. Ranked according to their priority, the committee recommended that:

1. The Texas State Teachers Association encourages that the Texas Education Agency be given full

authority to mandate and oversee its compliance.

2. The Texas State Teachers Association should encourage acceptance of the philosophy and concepts of bilingual education and work toward presenting the Bilingual/Bicultural Program in a positive vein. The Association should strive for the inclusion of bilingual education as part, not a deficit model, of the general educational program in Texas.

3. The Texas State Teachers Association should support legislation in the area of bilingual/bicultural education in the next regular session of the Texas Legislature.

4. The Texas State Teachers Association should recommend that school districts be encouraged to hold preservice and inservice training in bilingual education conducted by the staff of the Texas Education Agency and/or other agencies.

5. The Texas State Teachers Association should support the statewide adoption of multicultural textbooks and materials and that textbooks be adopted on the basis of "need" rather than "grade level."

6. The Texas State Teachers Association should recommend that the Texas Education Agency be given the adequate staff necessary to function in a leadership and a regulatory role (TSTA, Special Committee on Bilingual Education, Recommendations on Bilingual Education, Spring, 1977).

The endorsement of bilingual education legislation by the largest and strongest teacher union in the state may have increased the prestige of bilingual schooling as an alternative and legitimate instrument of education, but it did very little to change the legislative priorities of Texas legislators during the 65th Legislature. When the legislature concluded its business on May 30, the bilingual education bills which had been introduced by Senator Truan and Representative Garcia remained buried in the Calendars Committee of the House. Representative Bill Clayton, elected for his second term as Speaker of the House,   successfully prevented the passage of both bills. The Speaker was not opposed to individuals wanting to become bilingual, but the thought of forcing Texans to become bilingual by law was not right. The United States was an English-speaking nation, and schools should carry out the instructional process in English (Bernal, 1978).

THE 66th LEGISLATIVE SESSION

During the 66th Legislative Session, January 9 through May 28, 1979, Senator Truan and Representative Garcia of San Antonio once again introduced two bills on bilingual education, S.B. 195 and H.B. 1328. On January 22 Senator Truan filed S.B. 195 for consideration in the Senate. The bill was sent to the Education Committee and did not surface on to the floor of the Senate until April 5 as Committee Substitute S.B. 195. The bill as originally introduced underwent several changes before it was finally released for floor action (Senate Journal, Volume I, 1979; Appendix L).

The bill's Statement of Policy (Section 21.451) created considerable difficulty for some of the Senate education committee members. The statement on language and culture read as if the only difficulty confronting Mexican-American and Anglo students in schools was a "difference" in the language they spoke and the cultural heritage which they had inherited. Gone from the statement were all indications that the program was justified because the students could not perform ordinary classroom assignments due to their linguistic, social, or economic limitations. Nowhere was there any mention of the acquisition of the English language as being the primary goal for the enactment of a bilingual education law. A comparison of the statement which was initially introduced with the one which was finally approved by the Senate's Education Committee follows. A close comparison of these statements reveals the philosophical differences between advocates and adversaries on the nature and use of language and culture in the public school curriculum. The words which are underlined represent the substantive changes which were being proposed. The first statement of policy read:

> The legislature finds that there are large
> numbers of children in the state who come from en-
> vironments where the primary language is other
> than English and who have a cultural heritage that
> differs from that of speakers of English as a pri-

mary language. Experience has shown that a primary means by which a child learns is through the
use of his or her language and cultural heritage
and that public school classes in which instruction is given only in English are often inadequate
for the education of children. The legislature
believes that large numbers of children of limited
English-speaking ability have educational needs
that are best met through bilingual instruction
and the fullest use of multiple language and cultural resources. Therefore, pursuant to the policy of the state to insure equal educational opportunity to every child, and in recognition of
the educational needs of children of limited
English-speaking ability, it is the purpose of
this subchapter to provide for the establishment
of bilingual education programs in the public
schools and to provide supplemental financial assistance to help local school districts meet the
extra costs of the programs (S.B. 195).

The statement which was amended by the Education Committee stated:

The legislature recognizes that the mastery
of basic English skills is a prerequisite for effective participation in the state's educational
program and that those who do not understand English are certain to find their classroom experiences wholly incomprehensible and in no way meaningful. Experience has shown that the most effective means by which a student learns is through
the use of his or her language and cultural heritage. The legislature believes that large numbers of students with limited English language
skills have educational needs that are best met
through bilingual instruction and the fullest use
of multiple language and cultural resources.
Therefore, pursuant to the policy of the state to
provide a thorough and efficient system of public
education, and in recognition of the educational
needs of students with limited English language
skills, it is the purpose of this subchapter to
provide for the establishment of programs for students with limited English language skills in the

public schools and to provide supplemental financial assistance to help local school districts
meet the extra costs of the programs (C.S.S.B.
195).

The bill mandated TEA to develop a plan to identify students
in elementary and secondary schools with limited English language
skills (LELS). It called for the establishment of bilingual education education programs in those districts which had an enrollment of 20 or more LELS students in any language classification in
the same grade level in kindergarten through the fifth grade. In
grades 6-12 the bilingual program was optional. Any program beyond
the fifth would be at the school district's expense. In those
school districts where there were less than 20 students who could
benefit from such instruction the district was obligated to provide what was called "a language response program." This was defined as a program which was especially designed to meet an LELS
student's particular language and other curricula needs. A regular
language arts program designed for monolingual English-speaking
students would not be accepted as a "language response program."

Students in the Bilingual Education and Language Response Program would be required to remain in the program until they had
gained a mastery of English language skills "sufficient to enable
[the student] to perform successfully in classes in which instruction was provided in English." In addition, the bill once again
called for the inclusion of no more than 40% Anglo or English-
speaking student enrollment in the program.

Since the late 1960s proponents of bilingual education in
Texas continually lobbied federal and state governmental officials
on the efficacy and basic soundness of this pedagogical approach.
Demands for educational change were simultaneously made by professional Mexican-American educators on three levels of government.
In the state legislature Senator Truan and Representative Matt
Garcia pushed for changes in the state's bilingual education law.
American G.I. Forum and LULAC used the legal services of the Mexican-American Legal Defense and Education Fund (MALDEF) to press for
curriculum innovation through the federal courts. Bilingual education advocates also worked on enlisting the support of the majority
of the 23 members of the State Board of Education and the administrators of the Texas Education Agency.

Between 1975 and 1978 the state's policies for meeting the

educational needs of national origin minority children came under close scrutiny by federal officials from the United States Office of Education (USOE) and the Office for Civil Rights (OCR). Federal officials were comparing the state's policies and practices with the Lau remedies which had been written in the summer of 1975. The Texas Education Agency's response to federal proposals was slow. By January 19, 1978, OCR had cited 17 school districts as being out of compliance on the basis of Title VI. On March 8, TEA officials presented OCR representatives in Dallas with the state's "Plan for Bilingual Education: A System for Meeting the Needs of Limited English-Speaking Students in Texas Public Schools, Grades K through 12." The Agency claimed that this proposal satisfactorily met all of the requirements under Lau and Title VI. Three months later 40 districts which had applied for funding under the Emergency School Aid Act (ESAA) were cited for noncompliance with Title VI of the Civil Rights Act. Approximately $14 million in ESAA funds were withheld from 26 school districts which had not met the federal standards. Texas Education Agency officials protested the actions of OCR to Health, Education and Welfare secretary Joseph Califano and voiced their displeasure at an oversight hearing of the subcommittee on Elementary, Secondary, and Vocational Education in Washington, D.C. on August 15.

While letters of protest were exchanged between Austin and Washington, D.C., the State Board of Education met hastily on June 10 and adopted emergency policy and administrative procedures to implement TEA's "State Plan for Bilingual Education." The Board decided to extend the bilingual education program through the fifth grade. All school districts were required to provide special language programs for all children identified as limited English-speaking ability (LESA) children in kindergarten through the twelfth grade. The Board nullified previous state policy, which only required the school district to take steps to implement a bilingual education program if there were 20 children or more at one grade level in grades kindergarten through three. School district teachers were required to use the criteria and procedures established by TEA to identify children for entry into and exit from the special programs. A failure to implement the mandate of the State Board would result in review of a district's accreditation status and an on-site visit by TEA officials (Texas Education Agency, June, 1978).

In September the Commission of TEA, M. L. Brockette, was informed by Joe Rich, a U.S. Department of Justice official, that the

State's plan lacked adequate enforcement provisions. On October 12, the State Board of Education held a public hearing on the state's guidelines on bilingual education before they were permanently adopted. According to most newspaper accounts of the public hearing, the majority of those who testified before the committee opposed the Board's emergency guidelines on bilingual education. Some argued that the cost of such a program would be enormous and beyond the means of many small school districts. Others stated that there simply were not enough competent bilingual teachers in the state to accomplish the goals of the program. The program's guidelines had failed to consider the priorities and needs of local school districts. Many Anglo and Mexican-American teachers and administrators voiced their belief that Mexican-American school children could learn English by the time they exited from the third grade. The English language was recognized as an international language, whose use and mastery were essential for all Mexican-American children in Texas. Hosever, those who supported the Board's June 10 policy wanted bilingual education to be mandated as were other parts of the state education curriculum, e.g., math, social studies, reading, et cetera. They argued that the admission of limited English-speaking ability (LESA) students into a bilingual program should not be left up to parental discretion.

On November 11, members of the State Board voted to rescind the June 10 emergency policy statement, replacing it with a more conservative version. The Board ruled that school districts where there were 20 or more LESA children of the same language classification at any grade level had to provide a full bilingual education program in kindergarten through the third grade. All LESA students in kindergarten through twelfth grade had to be provided an English language development program. Bilingual education could be offered in the fourth and fifth grades if students had "not progressed sufficiently in the use of the English language to participate in the regular school curriculum. Any bilingual program beyond the fifth grade was to be at the expense of the respective local school districts" (Texas Education Agency, November, 1978).

Mexican-American professionals also sought to introduce curriculum changes through the courts. On July 10, 1972, LULAC and American G.I. Forum were allowed by the presiding federal district judge, William Wayne Justice, to represent all Mexican-Americans in the State of Texas as plaintiffs-intervenors in the case of

U.S. v. Texas. The court was able to allow the intervention of the plaintiffs in the case because it had retained the power of jurisdiction to enforce and modify the court's original orders on the basis of any new allegations directly concerned with the issue of unequal educational opportunity of racial and national origin minority group children.

The suit originated as a desegregation action against the State of Texas and its agent TEA in 1970. It charged the parties with having created and maintained nine all-black school districts throughout the state, and failing to provide equal educational opportunity without regard to race (321 F. Supp. 1043). On July 13, 1971, TEA was ordered by the court to conduct a study which would detail the educational needs of minority children in the entire state. In section G of the order, entitled Curriculum and Compensatory Education, TEA was instructed to make:

(a) Recommendations of specific curricular offerings and programs which will insure equal educational opportunities for all students regardless of race, color or national origin. These curricular offerings and programs shall include specific educational programs designed to compensate minority group children for unequal educational opportunities and ethnic isolation, as well as programs and curriculum designed to meet the special educational needs of students whose primary language is other than English;

(b) Explanation of presently existing programs funded by the State of Texas or by the Federal Government which are available to local districts to meet these special educational needs and how such programs might be applied to these educational needs;

(c) Explanation of specific standards by which the defendants will determine when a local district, which has racially or ethnically isolated schools or which has students whose primary language is other than English, shall be required by the defendants to participate in the special compensatory educational programs available; and

(d) Explanation of procedures for applying these stan-

dards to local districts including appropriate
sanctions to be employed by the defendants should
a district refuse to participate in special compensatory educational programs where it has been
instructed to do so pursuant to application of
the standards developed under subsection (c) above
(U.S. v. Texas, Civil Action 5281, 1982).

On June 3, 1975, the plaintiffs asked the court to enforce the
provisions of Section G alleging that Mexican-American students had
been denied an equal educational opportunity as required by law.
They asked the court to direct TEA to provide bilingual education
instruction to all limited English proficiency students. Judge
Justice denied the plaintiff's requiest for relief because the 1971
court order had only requested TEA to write a report on how it expected to address the problems of the nine segregated school districts. At the time no evidence had been presented on the educational problems faced by Mexican-American students on the basis of
ethno-linguistic issues.

It took four years before plaintiffs were able to come to
trial on December 3, 1979 to present their case before the federal
court in Tyler, Texas. In the interim the state legislature had
amended the bilingual law in 1975, but had failed to make any further changes or increase the funding levels for bilingual education
until 1981.

THE 67th LEGISLATIVE SESSION

The 67th Legislative Session began on January 13, 1981 and
ended on June 1, 1981. Among the four thousand house and senate
bills considered by the legislature during this session were
Senate Bill 477 and the companion bill House Bill 886, both on the
subject of bilingual education. Debate on the controversial bill
lasted until the very end of the legislative session. Its passage
on June 1 represented the legislature's response to a federal court
order in mid-April which had mandated the implementation of a bilingual education program in grades K through twelve for all Mexican-American children in the state identified as LESA students.
Without the pressure of the court action, it seems doubtful that
the legislative leadership would have enacted a second amended version of the Bilingual Education and Training Act of 1973 (Summary
of Enactments, 1981).

The Federal Court Decree

Four days before the 67th Legislative Session was officially convened, Federal District Judge William Wayne Justice issued a 67 page memorandum opinion on the complaints and the suggested relief brought to the court's attention by the plaintiffs, American G.I. Forum and LULAC. The court ruled that the State of Texas had pervasively and invidiously violated the constitutional rights of Mexican-American students to equal protection under the Fourteenth Amendment. It also ruled that the State of Texas had violated the civil rights of Mexican-American students under Section 1703 (F) of the Equal Educational Opportunity Act of 1974. In the suit plaintiffs had also claimed their right to relief under Title VI of the Civil Rights Act of 1964. This was the same statute which had been successfully used by plaintiffs in the Lau v. Nichols case (414 U.S. 563; 1974). Relying on the statute, and on its interpretation by HEW, the Supreme Court in 1974 ruled that the actions of defendants, San Francisco United School District, had had the effect of discriminating against the defendants, 1800 non-English speaking Chinese students, even though no evidence had been presented to show that the behavior of school officials had been intentional. Two years later the Supreme Court in the case of Washington v. Davis (426 U.S. 229) reversed the principle of "effect," which it had set in Lau, and emphasized the principle of "intent" based on the expanded views expressed in the 1978 case of University of California Regents v. Bakke (438 U.S. 265). In this case the court decided that for most cases the protective provisions of the Fourteenth Amendment were the same as those stated in Title VI. Congress, the justices found, had not expanded "the concept of discrimination under law, but rather" had extended "the existing requirements of the Fourteenth Amendment to private programs that receive federal funds" (Civil Action Number 5281, 1981, 44). Based on the Supreme Court's new interpretation of the relationship between the Equal Protection Clause and Title VI, the court ruled that plaintiffs had not shown that the effect of defendants' actions on Mexican-American students had been the result of purposeful discrimination.

Plaintiffs and defendants in the case were ordered to meet on or before January 29 in order to develop a comprehensive plan of relief based on the evidence presented in the memorandum of the court. Parties to the case were ordered to fashion an agreed upon proposal by March 2. If no agreement could be reached by this time they were to submit their separate proposals by March 9 (Civil

Action Number 5281, 1981).

Judicial Findings and Remedies

Judge Justice ruled that the state's bilingual education program was totally inadequate. According to the evidence presented, thousands of limited English proficiency (LEP) students were not being served because of the state's poor guidelines for identifying and verifying students who could benefit from the program. The court found that there were large gaps between TEA guidelines and the implementation of programs. State education officials lacked a monitoring and enforcement capacity to insure proper program implementation. The court also accepted plaintiff's claims that TEA criteria for exiting students from the program were not valid. Another area where the court found TEA performance lacking was in the training of administrators in the theory and practice of bilingual education, and in the underutilization of certified bilingual education teachers. These serious flaws in the state's bilingual education program were exacerbating the educational problems experienced by many LEP Mexican-American students in the public schools of Texas. Past discriminatory practices and the lingering effects of these acts and attitudes demanded the fashioning of an appropriate remedy which would encompass the student's cognitive, linguistic, and cultural development. Plaintiffs in the case argued that the best pedagogical method calculated to meet the specific findings of the court was bilingual education.

The court agreed with the contentions of plaintiffs and ordered the inclusion of remedies in four areas which were identified during the course of litigation. The four areas were: (1) Program Coverage and Content, (2) Identification of Limited English Proficiency Students, (3) Exit Criteria, and (4) Monitoring and Enforcement.

Program Coverage and Content

Required:

1. Bilingual instruction for all Mexican-American students of limited English proficiency in the public schools of Texas.

2. Program to be phased in over a six year period to ensure adequate staffing and availability of learning materials.

3. TEA to devise a plan for the recruitment and training of bilingual teachers.

4. Bilingual instruction be provided in all subject areas with the exception of art, music, and physical education, and other subjects where language proficiency was not essential for effective participation.

5. That the state not set up special schools for the sole purpose of providing bilingual instruction.

6. That to the extent possible, Mexican-American students in bilingual education programs must not be isolated from the rest of the school program.

Identification of Limited English Proficiency Students

Required:

1. School officials to survey all students entering school to determine whether they spoke another language other than English.

2. The testing of students to determine language proficiency in English.

3. The use of teacher observation and the results of tests together be taken into account to determine the student's language proficiency.

4. TEA to monitor local identification procedures through on-site visits.

Exit Criteria

Required:

1. Students placed in bilingual programs to remain enrolled until it was determined by school officials that their

145

placement in an all-English curriculum would not produce any significant impairment of their learning ability or achievement.

2. Students in bilingual programs to be tested at the end of each school year to determine the extent of their progress.

3. Student evaluation to include English language tests, tests of oral proficiency, mastery of specific language skills, subjective teacher assessment, and parental viewpoint.

4. Students to be tested in Spanish and English.

5. That reliable and valid test standards be developed which would ensure confidence in entry and exiting criteria for participants in bilingual education programs.

6. Students in grades six through twelve who could not meet the exiting criteria be transferred out of the program if a parent requested.

7. TEA to monitor the exiting standards of local school programs by on-site inspections.

Monitoring and Enforcement

Required:

1. TEA to conduct on-site inspections of local school districts to monitor compliance with state regulations at least once every three years.

2. On-site evaluations to be reported to local school officials and to the accreditation division of TEA.

3. That school districts found to be in noncompliance with state regulations and with the specific orders of the court should be warned and required to take immediate corrective action. Failure to comply should result in the loss of accreditation, loss of funding in appropriate cases, and other sanctions.

The memorandum opinion was followed by another order specifying three other details in the remedy prescribed by the court. It
called for the state to require the implementation of a K-5 bilingual education program by the 1981-82 school year, adding one grade
each year until grades nine and ten were included by the 1984-85
school year. The following school year, 1985-86, grades eleven and
twelve were to be added. Each school district with a bilingual
education program was to establish Parent Advisory Committees (PAC)
and Language Proficiency Assessment Committees (LPAC). Finally,
TEA was ordered to develop a teacher recruitment and training plan
by October 1, 1981 (Bilingual Education Law in Texas, 1981; Civil
Action Number 5281; 1981).

Judicial Mandate - Legislative Reaction

Shortly after the mandate by the court was issued on January
9, state Attorney General Mark White requested a three month delay
on the March 9 deadline. He argued that the legislature should be
given an opportunity to act on the bilingual education bill which
Senator Truan had filed on February 9. The state's Board of Education and the Civil Rights Division of the Department of Justice
both favored a delay in the court order. The court, however, denied the request for a delay contending that it could not wait to
second guess the legislature's intent or its wishes.

As the deadline for a negotiated proposal drew near, both
parties to the dispute had not reached any substantive agreement.
The principal source of disagreement seems to have been the plan's
coverage. Plaintiffs supported a plan which included all grades.
The state and federal lawyers argued for a bilingual education program through the fifth grade.

One day after the March 9 deadline Governor William P. Clements, acting on the suggestion of Lieutenant Governor William P.
Hobby, issued an executive order establishing a Task Force on Bilingual Education that would study and make recommendations to the
legislature on the subject. The Task Force, consisting of 15 members, was directed:

> To examine the transition period beyond the pre-
> sent program of bilingual teaching from kinder-
> garten through the third grade with reemphasis
> on the importance of a strong and smooth transi-

tion into the area of primary English language
teaching. The Task Force is further directed to
develop a program for those students who need
extra help, from kindergarten through the 12th
grade. The Task Force shall also study the methods
to best implement a program of summer school language support classes for grades one through 12
(Task Force on Bilingual Education, Executive
Order WPC - 20, March 10, 1981).

The Task Force was directed to present its recommendations to
the legislative leadership by April 15. The first meeting was held
on March 26. After four more meetings the work of the committee
was finalized on April 14. Committee members heard from expert
witnesses in the four areas which had been mentioned in the Memorandum of Opinion of January 9. Committee members seemed to agree
on the gravity of the problem, but not on how to address it. The
committee was divided evenly on the question of the appropriate
methodology. One side argued in favor of implementing bilingual
program in all grades. The other half supported limiting bilingual
instruction to the elementary grades. In a vote on the issue the
chairman of the Task Force, Willis M. Tate, broke the deadlock,
voting against extending bilingual instruction beyond the primary
grades (Bilingual Education Law in Texas, 1981).

On April 17, Judge Justice issued the court's plan to address
the constitutional and statutory violations which had been brought
to its attention by the plaintiffs. At the center of the remedy
was the court's order to extend bilingual education to all Mexican-
American LEP students in all grades.

Prior to the ruling in April, Senator Truan's bill, S.B. 477,
had been referred to the Committee on Education and two public
hearings had been held. From March 25 until May 13 the bill was
assigned to an education subcommittee. On May 15 a substitute
bill was favorably reported and sent on to the Senate floor. On
May 21 four amendments to the bill were offered. By the 26th the
Senate passed its version of the bill and sent it to the House. In
the House two amendments were tacked on to the bill and it was returned to the Senate on May 30. The Senate refused to concur with
the House amendments. To settle the differences the bill was en-
trusted to a Conference Committee. On the very last day of the
session both houses agreed to a compromise version of the Bilingual
Education and Special Language Programs bill. The bill was signed

by Governor Clements on June 12, and became effective on September 1.

State Appeals the Court's Order

In September of 1980 the state's attorney general filed a motion which sought to nullify the statements of fact to which defendants had originally agreed during the eight day trial in December of 1979. The motion was denied by the court. In July of 1981 the state, with the assistance of an Austin law firm, sought to persuade the court that the stipulations to which assistant attorney general Susan Dasher had agreed had been done without proper authorization from her superiors. They now wanted an opportunity to file their objections to the same stipulations of fact before the court. This motion was also denied. Judge Justice observed that the motions had been filed because the defendants now felt that "the outcome of the case might have been more favorable to them had these stipulations not been entered into. If they were accorded the luxury of a second trial, they would, no doubt, employ a different strategy" (Bilingual Education Law in Texas, 1981, p. 26).

The state's attorney general received considerable criticism over the handling of the case. However, by the end of the summer of 1981 the state's new legal strategies were strengthened by the favorable decisions of the U.S. 5th Circuit Court of Appeals in two separate law suits. The Gregory-Portland case and the Castenada v. Picard case provided defendants with ample arguments with which to contest Civil Action Suit 5281 when it too was appealed to the U.S. 5th Circuit Court of Appeals.

The Gregory-Portland case was a desegregation suit charging that the minority enrollment of schools in the cities of Gregory and Portland was perpetuated by local school officials. The Anglo enrollment for elementary schools in Portland was 81%; the Mexican-American enrollment for elementary schools in Gregory was 95%. The case of Castenada v. Pickard was a discrimination suit against the Raymondville school district. The court was also asked to make a ruling over the quality of the bilingual education program.

In the case of Gregory-Portland, the Appeals court ruled that the ethnic imbalance resulted from settlement patterns and not from the deliberate actions of local school officials. The court ser-

149

iously undermined Judge Justice's complete reliance on the stipulations of fact in rendering his decisions in the case. In Castenada
v. Picard the Appeals court ruled that the program violated neither
constitutional nor statutory laws. One of the most devastating
parts of this case was the court's role in determining the efficacy
of one educational method over another.

In their appeal to the U.S. 5th Circuit, attorneys for the
State of Texas used many of the arguments and rulings handed down
in the previous two cases to successfully argue against Civil Action 5281. The state developed and modified the following arguments in its case:

1. The court erred in basing its decision on Constitutional
   issues, based on the finding of historical discrimination
   against Mexican-Americans, since Constitutional questions
   were not litigated.

2. Assuming a Constitutional issue was presented, the case
   should have been heard by a three-judge panel, since it met
   procedural prerequisites for such a panel.

3. Use of the stipulations represented a "manifest injustice"
   since counsel was not authorized by her superiors or by the
   defendants to enter them.

4. There was insufficient evidence to prove statewide discrimination against Mexican-Americans.

5. Even if there were sufficient evidence of discrimination,
   the remedy exceeds the scope of the violation.

6. Federal courts should not deprive educators of discretion
   in choosing instructional methodology.

7. The remedy is impossible since the state could not hire
   enough bilingual teachers to implement the program.

8. The order conflicts with the 5th Circuit in Castenada.

9. The order affects individual school districts that were not
   a party to the suit.

Judge Justice's final order on August 19 was held in abeyance

by the Court of Appeals while it heard arguments by defendants in
the case. On July 12 the court overturned U.S. District Judge
Justice's order. Plaintiffs in the case were disappointed with the
decision. However, in their quest for equal educational opportunity through the federal courts, they had provided the needed impetus to force the Texas legislature to enact a more comprehensive
educational program for Mexican-American students (U.S. v. Texas,
1982).

The Bilingual Educational Law - 1981

Senator Truan's original version of S.B. 477 followed the
court's orders for relief. After considerable debate the sponsors
of the bill agreed to alter some of the bill's language and provisions in line with the Task Force recommendations. The level of
funding was another major obstacle in the bill. Truan initially
requested $150 per student enrolled in a bilingual education pro-
gram. By May 27 the amount was cut to $50 per student with an al-
location of $12.50 for students receiving English-as-a-Second-Lan-
guage instruction (ESL). Based on a student count of 220,000 in
ESL and bilingual education programs during the 1982 fiscal year,
the additional cost for implementing the new provisions of the bill
was calculated to be $4,622,500. The total revenues needed for the
program were estimated to be $8,812,500. This amount included the
appropriations allocated under the 1975 bilingual education law.

The law required the establishment of bilingual education and
special language programs in school districts with an enrollment of
20 or more LEP students in any language classification in the same
grade level. Bilingual education instruction was to be provided
LEP students from kindergarten to the fifth grade. In grades six
through eight school districts were required to provide bilingual
instruction, ESL or any other approved transitional language program. Students in high school were to receive ESL instruction.
The state Board of Education was authorized to establish procedural
rules for identifying school districts where the program would be
required. School districts which chose to employ an instructional
methodology other than bilingual instruction in the primary grades
were required to file a request for an exception with TEA. The exception was valid for one year and its approval would be contingent
upon a school district's detailed documentation of its affirmative
action hiring practices and its good faith effort to rectify the
condition which contributed to the original request for an exemp-

tion.

School districts were required to establish a full-time program consisting of classes in ESL and instruction in specific subjects in the primary language of the student. The curriculum which
was implemented had to take into consideration the student's learning experiences and was supposed to include aspects of the student's culture. The ESL program was to be directed by teachers who
were trained to recognize and deal appropriately with language differences. Students in the program were not to be isolated from
other English-speaking students.

The area of student identification was a crucial issue. The
law authorized the State Board of Education to establish standardized criteria for identifying, assessing, and classifying LEP students. The assessment and classification of LEP students was to be
done by a Language Proficiency Assessment Committee in each school
district where a bilingual education and special language program
was offered. The committee was to have a bilingual teacher, an ESL
teacher, a parent with a child in the program, and a school administrator. The committee was responsible for classifying a student
based on one or more criteria. Students in grades two through
twelve who scored below the 23rd percentile in an English reading
and language arts standardized achievement test would be eligible
for the program. Those students who scored between the 23rd and
40th percentile on a written standardized test would be assessed on
the basis of other pertinent factors to determine their eligibil-
ity. Students who scored at or above the 40th percentile would not
be considered LEP or could exit from the program. Another significant part of the law was the participation of non-LEP students.
Their participation, however, could not exceed 40% of the students
enrolled in a program. Parental consent for participation in
either program was required.

The State Board of Education was also held responsible for the
recruitment and preparation of bilingual educationand ESL teachers.
It was charged to fashion a plan which would reduce the teacher
shortage for these two areas. The Board was required to submit the
plan to the 68th Legislature, which would be convened in January,
1983.

In court and in the legislature bilingual education advocates
sought to include strict enforcement and monitoring provisions.
The new law required TEA officials to conduct on-site inspections

of programs at least once every three years. The areas to be monitored included: 1) program content and design, 2) program coverage, 3) identification and classification procedures, 4) staffing,
5) testing and learning materials, 6) activities of the Language
Proficiency Assessment Committee. Thirty days after the visit the
TEA official was supposed to report his findings to the school district and to the agency's accreditation division. A school found
to be out of compliance was to be notified and ordered to take the
necessary corrective action. Failure or a refusal to comply by the
local school officials could result in the district's loss of accreditation, loss of state funds, or both (Appendix M).

Conclusions

The successful enactment of the Bilingual Education and Special Language Programs Act in 1981 represented a major political accomplishment for middle-class Mexican-American leaders, educators, and politicians who supported bilingual education. For them this instructional innovation held the greatest potential for meeting the cognitive and affective needs of linguistically and culturally different Mexican-American students in Texas. Prior to 1969 Mexican-American educators had exercised little or no significant influence on the state's educational policy-making process. With the assistance of the federal government during the decades of the 1960s and 1970s they were able to force the State Board of Education and the Texas Legislature to respond to their demands for a greater share of the state's resources.

Since 1969 the enactment of bilingual education legislation in Texas has been strongly influenced by the ethnic factor. For many Mexican-Americans the enactment of bilingual education laws represented an affirmation of their language, history, and culture. It signified a concrete admission by state elected officials of the importance of their presence in the social, economic, and political life of the State of Texas. They labored for an opportunity to develop a curriculum which incorporated their language and values. They pleaded for a chance to fashion an educational program which mirrored their reality. They argued for the right to control their own destiny free from Anglo interference.

To the supporters of bilingual instruction, emphasis on ethnic pride in the schools' curriculum was not considered incompatible or inconsistent with the political and social reality of Texan life. Experience and educational research had convincingly demonstrated the value and positive results for learning when teachers were able to use the cultural experiences of students as a vehicle to introduce new concepts and skills. Mexican-American educators argued that the development of ethnic identity was functionally related to the child's self-concept. The development of a positive self-image was a contributory factor for attaining success in school. They argued that their proposals for changing the schooling practices of the state were part of a long tradition of bilingual schooling in the United States. They did not see the maintenance of linguistic and cultural differences as being inimical to the American polity to which they had pledged their allegiance as citizens.

154

Another factor which helps to explain the enactment of bilingual education legislation in Texas was the commitment and advocacy role of many professional Mexican-American educators. They played a significantly important role in defining and writing the new components of the 1981 law. They provided a great deal of the expert testimony in the courts and in the legislature. When some of the findings in a federally sponsored 1978 study seemed to cast serious doubts on the effectiveness of bilingual education, Mexican-American professionals were able to defend their position by pointing to the serious flaws in the study's methodological and theoretical assumptions. In response they presented evidence which in their opinion demonstrated bilingual education methodology to be an effective teaching approach for meeting the educational needs of non-English and limited English-speaking students.

Mexican-American educators were able to enlist the support of the Texas State Teachers Association. Although bilingual education proponents had passed legislation without TSTA endorsement in the past, it was politically advantageous to have the public recognition and backing of the largest teacher union in the state. In 1973 the Texas Association for Bilingual Education had played no significant role in influencing the passage of bilingual education legislation. Six years later the association leadership had organized a state-wide network of legislative committees whose steadfast support contributed to the law's enactment in 1981. The work of the three member State Legislative Committee was especially important. They provided crucial expert testimony on bilingual education to the court, the legislature, and the State Board of Education. Many of the recommendations which were made by these experts were adopted by Texas legislators like Senators Brooks, Ogg, and Truan.

Court intervention in the curriculum policy-making arena has produced mixed results. In some cases the original intentions and goals of the plaintiffs have been redirected in the course of litigation. In other instances court rulings have left little room for compromise on the part of plaintiffs or defendants. Quite often favorable rulings in one court are overturned in a higher court. Evidence which is considered indisputable in a lower court may be questioned and considered moot in another. Courts have traditionally resisted efforts to make them the final arbiters on matters involving educational philosophy or teaching methods. Instead they have often chosen to leave such issues in the hands of educators and local, state elected officials. In those cases where plain-

tiffs have insisted on the court's legal opinion, or when local and
state decision-making agencies continue to ignore legal mandates or
the rightful demands of national origin minorities, the courts have
ordered sweeping educational and political changes.

During the 67th Legislative Session (1981) the federal court
order on behalf of bilingual education decisively influenced the
course and final outcome of bilingual education legislation. Supporters of the bilingual bill turned to the courts when it became
clearly evident that neither the legislature nor the State Board of
Education was going to respond to their demands for educational reform. They brought their case before a liberal and sympathetic
United States federal district judge in Tyler, Texas, who agreed
with their contentions and supported their suggestions for a remedy. State legislators, indignant over the court's usurpation of
the legislative prerogative, hastily worked out a compromise version of the original bilingual education bill. By enacting a bilingual education law which addressed all of the major issues which
had been raised by the plaintiffs, the legislature had inadver-
tantly prevented the court of appeals from rendering a judgment on
the original court ordered remedies. If the court had been forced
to make a ruling on the court ordered state-wide plan of relief,
the outcome would probably have been quite different.

The enactment of the bilingual education law was perhaps the
most comprehensive statute enacted on the subject in any state.
Its provisions carried safeguards against the future possibility of
segregating Mexican-American students from their Anglo counterparts
in the public schools. For the first time the law addressed the
problems of language minority children in grades K through 12, and
included strong enforcement measures to cajole unwilling school
districts into complying with the law. To the relief of many
legislators and educators, the law had not legalized the use of two
languages in Texas. Texan legislators finally accepted that at
least for the lower grades bilingual instruction was a feasible way
of assisting limited English proficiency students to learn English
while they acquired other learning skills in their primary language. The enhancement of the English language, however, was the
law's first concern.

A law's enactment is but the first step in addressing societal
problems. The implementation and enforcement of a law's provisions
constitutes the second step in changing behavior patterns which
will yield effective results. In the years ahead bilingual educa-

tion advocates in Texas will face several challenges. One of the problems which will seriously affect the effectiveness of bilingual instruction in the state is the lack of competently trained bilingual and English-as-a-second-language teachers. The satisfactory resolution of this problem is closely allied to another important factor, funding. Bilingual supporters must convince the governor's office and legislators to increase the level of funding in order to hire additional teachers, and allow the Texas Education Agency to monitor and enforce the new provisions in the law. In the past TEA officials have shown a traditional reluctance to enforce unpopular state or federal mandates on local school districts. The will of locally elected school board members and the authority of powerful superintendents seems to carry more weight than the laws which are enacted by the state legislature or the State Board of Education. This deeply engrained political tradition in the state will probably continue to create all kinds of obstacles for the effective implementation of bilingual education legislation.

Another closely related issue which may affect the course of bilingual education in the state in the future is the court's decision to limit future lawsuits against state educational authorities. In its ruling the appeals court placed great emphasis on the work and final authority of the local school district to educate children. The court stated that it was at this level where plaintiffs should file appropriate complaints, and not in Austin or in the federal court in Tyler. The court refused to focus on the similar problems which one state-wide court order could efficiently address. Instead it chose to dwell on the differences among school districts, and to minimize the constitutional role of the state legislature to enact educational law.

APPENDICES

APPENDIX A

SENATE BILL 46, 1969

61st LEGISLATIVE SESSION

By: Bernal, Patman, Mauzy, Snelson
    Harrington, Cole, Brooks, Kennard
    Moore, Jordan, McKool, Bates, Schwartz

S.B. No. 46

A BILL TO BE ENTITLED:
AN ACT

requiring that English shall be the basic language of instruction in all grade schools; providing the governing body of the school district or school may determine when, in which grades or classes, and circumstances instruction may be given bilingually; declaring state policy on bilingual instruction; amending subdivision 1 of Article 2893, Revised Civil Statutes, 1925; repealing Article 288, Penal Code of Texas, 1925, as amended; repealing Article 298, Penal Code of Texas, 1925; and declaring an emergency.

BE IT ENACTED BY THE LEGISLATURE OF THE STATE OF TEXAS:

Section 1. English shall be the basic language of instruction in all schools. The governing board of any school district and any private or parochial school may determine when, in which grades, and under what circumstances instruction may be given bilingually.

Sec. 2. It is the policy of this state to insure the mastery of English by all pupils in the shcools; provided that bilingual instruction may be offered or permitted in those situations when such instruction is educationally advantageous to the pupils. Such bilingual instruction may not be offered or permitted above the Sixth Grade without the express approval by the Texas Education Agency, which approval shall be granted on a three-year basis subject to reapproval at the end of that time.

Sec. 3. Subdivision 1 of Article 2893, Revised Civil Statutes, 1925 (Article 2893, subdivision 1, V.T.C.S.), is hereby amended to read as follows:

"1. Any child in attendance upon a private or parochial school which shall include in its course a study of good citizenship."

Sec. 4. Article 288, Penal Code of Texas, 1925, as amended by Chapter 125, Acts of the 43rd Legislature, Regular Session, 1933 (Article 288, V.T.P.C.), and Article 298, Penal Code of Texas, 1925 (Article 298, V.T.P.C.), are hereby repealed.

162

Sec. 5. The fact, that instruction in the earlier years which includes the use of the language the child understands makes learning easier; and the further fact, that in this highly technical and scientific world where transportation and communication have literally reduced the size of the world, knowledge of languages and understandings of other peoples and where in this hemisphere Spanish is spoken by as many people as speak English, a second language becomes vitally important, create an emergency and an imperative public necessity that the Constitutional Rule requiring bills to be read on three several days in each House be suspended, and this Rule is hereby suspended; and that this Act shall take effect and be in force from and after its passage, and it is so enacted.

APPENDIX B

HOUSE BILL 103, 1969

61st LEGISLATIVE SESSION

AN ACT

requiring that English shall be the basic language of instruction in all grade schools; providing the governing body of the school district or school may determine when, in which grades or classes, and circumstances instruction may be given bilingually; declaring state policy on bilingual instruction; requiring Texas Education Agency approval for bilingual instruction above the sixth grade; amending Subdivision 1 of Article 2893, Revised Civil Statutes of Texas, 1925; repealing Article 288, Penal Code of Texas, 1925, as amended; repealing Article 298, Penal Code of Texas, 1925, as amended; and declaring an emergency.

BE IT ENACTED BY THE LEGISLATURE OF THE STATE OF TEXAS:

Section 1. English shall be the basic language of instruction in all schools. The governing board of any school district and any private or parochial school may determine when, in which grades, and under what circumstances instruction may be given bilingually.

Sec. 2. It is the policy of this state to insure the mastery of English by all pupils in the schools; provided that bilingual instruction may be offered or permitted in those situations when such instruction is educationally advantageous to the pupils. Such bilingual instruction may not be offered or permitted above the sixth grade without the express approval by the Texas Education Agency, which approval shall be granted on a three-year basis subject to reapproval at the end of that time.

Sec. 3. Subdivision 1, Article 2893, Revised Civil Statutes of Texas, 1925, as last amended by Section 1, Chapter 504, Acts of the 59th Legislature, Regular Session, 1965, is hereby amended to read as follows:

"Article 2893. Exemptions

"The following classes of children are exempt from the requirements of this law:

"1. Any child in attendance upon a private or parochial school which shall include in its course a study of good citizenship.

"2. Any child whose bodily or mental condition is such as to render attendance inadvisable, and who holds definite certificate of a reputable physician specifying this condition and covering the period of absence.

166

"3. Any child who is blind, dumb, or feebleminded, for the instruction of whom no adequate provision had been made by the school district.

"4. Any child living more than two and one-half miles by direct and traveled road from the nearest public school supported for the children of the same race and color of such child and with no free transportation provided.

"5. Any child more than seventeen (17) years of age who has satisfactorily completed the work of the ninth grade, and whose services are needed in support of a parent or other person standing in parental relationship to the child, may, on presentation of proper evidence to the county superintendent, be exempted from further attendance at school."

Sec. 4. Article 288, Penal Code of Texas, 1925, as amended by Chapter 125, Acts of the 43rd Legislature, Regular Session, 1933, and Article 298, Penal Code of Texas, 1925, are hereby repealed.

Sec. 5. The fact that instruction in the earlier years which includes the use of language the child understands makes learning easier; and the further fact that in this highly technical and scientific world where transportation and communication have literally reduced the size of the world, knowledge of languages and understandings of other peoples and where in this hemisphere Spanish is spoken by as many people as speak English, a second language becomes vitally important, create an emergency and an imperative public necessity that the Constitutional Rule requiring bills to be read on three several days in each house be suspended, and this Rule is hereby suspended; and that this Act shall take effect and be in force from and after its passage, and it is so enacted.

Lieutenant Governor

Speaker of the House

H.B. No. 103

I hereby certify that H.B. No. 103 was passed by the House on March 10, 1969, by the following vote: Yeas 142, Nays 0; and that the House concurred in Senate amendments to H.B. No. 103 on May 7, 1969, by the following vote: Yeas 142, Nays 0.

_____
Chief Clerk of the House

I hereby certify that H.B. No. 103 was passed by the Senate, as amended, on May 7, 1969, by the following vote: Yeas 31, Nays 0.

_____
Secretary of the Senate

APPROVED: _____
Date

_____
Governor

APPENDIX C

HOUSE BILL 495, 1971

62nd LEGISLATIVE SESSION

H.B. No. 495
By: Truan
(In the House.--Filed February 10, 1971; February 11, 1971, read
first time and referred to Committee on Public Education: May 5,
1971, reported favorably, as amended, passed by unanimous voice
vote, sent to Printer.)

A BILL
TO BE ENTITLED
AN ACT relating to bilingual instruction in the public schools;
      amending Section 21.109, Texas Education Code; and
      declaring an emergency.
BE IT ENACTED BY THE LEGISLATURE OF THE STATE OF TEXAS:
  Section 1.   Section 21.109, Texas Education Code, is amended to
read as follows:
  "Section 21.109.   USE OF ENGLISH REQUIRED
Except for authorized courses in a foreign language, all courses
at all grades in the public schools shall be conducted in the
English language.
LANGUAGE OF INSTRUCTION. (a) English shall be the basic language
of instruction in all schools. The governing board of any school
district and any private or parochial school may determine when,
in which grades, and under what circumstances instruction may be
given bilingually.
  "(b) It is the policy of this state to insure the mastery of
English by all pupils in the schools; provided that where inability to speak and understand the English language excludes linguistically different children from effective participation in the
education program offered by a school district, the district may
take affirmative steps to implement a bilingual education program
in which children continue their intellectual development through
the use of their mother tongue and simultaneously develop facility
in English, thus becoming proficient in two languages.
  "(c) School districts shall not assign linguistically different
children to classes for the mentally retarded or to low tracks or
groups on the basis of criteria which essentially measure or evaluate English language skills; nor shall school districts deny
linguistically different children access to college preparatory
courses on a basis directly related to the failure of the school
system to develop academic skills. Any ability grouping or tracking system employed by the school system to deal with the special
language skill needs of linguistically different children must be
designed to meet such language skill needs as soon as possible
and must not operate as an educational dead-end or permanent
track.
  "(d) School districts shall notify adequately the parents of linguistically different children of school activities which are
called to the attention of other parents. Such notice in order to
be adequate may have to be provided in a language other than

170

English."

Sec. 2. This Act is effective September 1, 1971.

Sec. 3. The importance of this legislation and the crowded condition of the calendars in both houses create an emergency and an
imperative public necessity that the Constitutional Rule requiring bills to be read on three several days in each house be suspended, and this Rule is hereby suspended, and that this Act take
effect and be in force from and after its passage, and it is so
enacted.

COMMITTEE AMENDMENT NO. 1

Amend House Bill No. 495, First Printing, by striking the word
"shall" on line 25 and substituting the word "may".

Burgess

COMMITTEE REPORT

COMMITTEE ROOM
Austin, Texas, May 4, 1971

Hon. G. F. (Gus) Mutscher, Speaker of the House of Representatives.
SIR: We, your Committee on Public Education, to whom was referred
H. B. No 495, have had the same under consideration and beg to report with recommendation that it do pass, as amended, and be
printed.

Charles Jungmichel, Chairman

BILL ANALYSIS

Background Information:

H. B. No. 103 passed by the 61st Legislature presently permits bilingual instruction, but not above the sixth grade without
the approval of the Texas Education Agency. Tex. Educ. Code, Sec.
21.109 requires courses in public schools to be conducted in English. It is thought that this Bill will encourage linguistically
different children to remain in school and master the English language.

What the Bill Proposes to Do:

To strengthen the bilingual education programs in schools
by removing certain restrictions upon such programs in present law
and by prohibiting certain practices which retard the educational
advancement of linguistically different children.

Section by Section Analysis:

Section 1: Amends Section 21.109, Texas Education Code, as fol-
ows:

(a) The governing board of a school may provide for bilingual instruction.

(b) When linguistically different children are excluded from educational participation, school districts may implement a bilingual program whichwill develop a mastery of English.

(c) Linguistically different school children shall not be placed in classes for the mentally retarded, nor denied college preparatory courses.

(d) Parents of linguistically different children may be notified of school activities in languages other than English.

Sec. 2: Effective date: September 1, 1971.

Sec. 3: Emergency Clause.

Summary of Committee Action:

The Bill was reported out of Committee, as amended, by a unanimous voice vote.

APPENDIX D

HOUSE BILL 1024, 1971

62nd LEGISLATIVE SESSION

A BILL TO BE ENTITLED
AN ACT

relating to bilingual education training institutes, bilingual instructional materials, and salaries for bilingual education teachers; amending Subchapter A, Chapter 11, Texas Education Code, by adding Section 11.17; amending Subchapter A, Chapter 12, Texas Education Code, by adding 12.04; amending Subchapter D, Chapter 16, Texas Education Code, by adding Section 16.3061; amending Section 16.312, Texas Education Code, by adding Subsection (c-1); and declaring an emergency.

BE IT ENACTED BY THE LEGISLATURE OF THE STATE OF TEXAS:

Section 1. Subchapter A, Chapter 11, Texas Education Code, is amended by adding Section 11.17 to read as follows:

"Section 11.17 BILINGUAL EDUCATION TRAINING INSTITUTES.

(a) The Central Education Agency shall conduct bilingual education training institutes.

"(b) The agency shall make rules and regulations governing the conduct of and participation in the institutes.

"(c) Professional and paraprofessional public school personnel who participate in the bilingual education training institutes shall be reimbursed for expenses incurred as a result of their participation in accordance with rules and regulations adopted by the agency."

Sec. 2. Subchapter A, Chapter 12, Texas Education Code, is amended by adding Section 12.04 to read as follows:

"Section 12.04 BILINGUAL EDUCATION TEXTBOOKS. (a) The State Board of Education may acquire, purchase, and contract for with or without bids, subject to rules and regulations adopted by the board, textbooks and supporting media for use in bilingual education programs conducted in the public school systems of this state.

"(b) The textbooks and supporting media shall be paid for out of the textbook fund and shall be the property of the State of Texas, to be controlled, distributed, and disposed of pursuant to board regulations."

Sec. 3. Subchapter D, Chapter 16, Texas Education Code, is amended by adding Section 16.3061 to read as follows:

174

"Section 16.3061 BILINGUAL EDUCATION TEACHERS: 1970-1971.

(a) The minimum monthly base pay and increments for teaching experience for a bilingual education teacher conducting a 10, 11, or 12 months' bilingual education program approved by the state commissioner of education shall be the same as that of a classroom teacher as provided herein; provided that bilingual education teachers having qualifications approved by the State Board of Education shall be eligible for the minimum monthly base pay for a classroom teacher who holds a recognized bachelor's degree and a valid teacher's certificate.

"(b) The annual salary of bilingual education teachers shall be the monthly base salary, plus increments, multipled by 10, 11, or 12 as applicable.

"(c) The minimum salaries prescribed for bilingual education teachers mean total salaries of the teachers to be received for public school instruction, whether they are paid out of state or federal funds or both."

Sec. 4. Section 16.312, Texas Education Code, is amended by adding Subsection (c-1) to read as follows:

"(c-1) In addition to the positions described in Subsection (c), the position descriptions, required preparation and education, and number of monthly payments authorized under the Texas state public education compensation plan for bilingual education teachers are as follows:

Pay Grade	No. Mos. Paid	Class Title	Description of Positions Assigned to Class Title	Required Preparation and Education
7	10 11 12	Bilingual Education Teacher; Bachelor's Degree	Teach in a Bilingual Education Program at grade level or in teaching field for which prepared, under general supervision only.	Degree; No deficiency in professional education or in teaching field; Fully Certified; Bilingual Endorsement.
8	10 11 12	Bilingual Education Teacher; Master's Degree	Teach in a Bilingual Education Program at grade level or in teaching field for which prepared, under general supervision only.	Master's Degree; Fully certified; Bilingual Endorsement."

Sec. 5. The importance of this legislation and the crowded
condition of the calendars in both houses create an emergency and
an imperative public necessity that the Constitutional Rule requiring bills to be read on three several days in each house be
suspended, and this Rule is hereby suspended, and that this Act
take effect and be in force from and after its passage, and it is
so enacted.

APPENDIX E

HOUSE BILL 105, 1971

62nd LEGISLATIVE SESSION

By _____

A BILL TO BE ENTITLED
AN ACT

relating to the use of English as the basic language of instruction in all schools; restricting bilingual instruction beyond the third grade; making it a misdemeanor to offer bilingual instruction beyond the third grade in a public school except in certain circumstances; setting a penalty; amending Sections 1 and 2, Chapter 289, Acts of the 61st Legislature, Regular Session, 1969 (Article 2654-1d, Vernon's Texas Civil Statutes); and declaring an emergency.

BE IT ENACTED BY THE LEGISLATURE OF THE STATE OF TEXAS:

Section 1. Sections 1 and 2, Chapter 289, Acts of the 61st Legislature, Regular Session, 1969 (Article 2654-1d, Vernon's Texas Civil Statutes), are amended to read as follows:

"Section 1. It is the policy of this state to insure the mastery of English by all children, and English shall be the basic language of instruction in all schools in the state.

"Section 2. Bilingual instruction in the first through third grades may be offered or permitted by the governing board of a school district or by a private or parochial school in those situations when such instruction is educationally advantageous to the pupils. Bilingual instruction may not be offered or permitted above the third grade without the express approval of the Texas Education Agency, and approval by the agency shall be granted on a three-year basis, subject to reapproval at the end of that time. Remedial instruction in the English language shall be offered to any student above the third grade with a language deficiency which impedes his scholastic progress."

Sec. 2. Any teacher, principal, superintendent, trustee, or other school official having responsibility in the conduct of the work of any public school of this state who fails to comply with the requirement that English be used as the basic language of instruction or who offers bilingual instruction for students above the third grade without the express approval of the Texas Education Agency shall be deemed guilty of a misdemeanor and, upon conviction, shall be subject to a fine of not less than $25 nor more than $100, cancellation of his teaching certificate, or removal from office, or both fine and cancellation or fine and removal from office.

Sec. 3. The importance of this legislation and the crowded condition of the calendars in both houses create an emergency and an imperative public necessity that the Constitutional Rule requiring bills to be read on three several days in each house be suspended, and this Rule is hereby suspended, and that this Act take effect and be in force from and after its passage, and it is so enacted.

APPENDIX F

HOUSE BILL 145, 1973

63rd LEGISLATIVE SESSION

By _____

A BILL TO BE ENTITLED
AN ACT

relating to bilingual education training institutes, bilingual instructional materials, and salaries for bilingual education teachers; amending Subchapter A, Chapter 11, Texas Education Code, by adding Section 11.18; amending Subchapter A, Chapter 12, Texas Education Code, by adding Section 12.05; amending Subchapter D, Chapter 16, Texas Education Code, by adding Section 16.3061; amending Section 16.312, Texas Education Code, by adding Subsection (c-1); providing an effective date; and declaring an emergency.

BE IT ENACTED BY THE LEGISLATURE OF THE STATE OF TEXAS:

Section 1. Subchapter A, Chapter 11, Texas Education Code, is amended by adding Section 11.18 to read as follows:

"Sec. 11.18. BILINGUAL EDUCATION TRAINING INSTITUTES. (a) The Central Education Agency shall conduct bilingual education training institutes.

"(b) The agency shall make rules and regulations governing the conduct of and participation in the institutes.

"(c) Professional and paraprofessional public school personnel who participate in the bilingual education training institutes shall be reimbursed for expenses incurred as a result of their participation in accordance with rules and regulations adopted by the agency."

Sec. 2. Subchapter A, Chapter 12, Texas Education Code, is amended by adding Section 12.05 to read as follows:

"Sec. 12.05. BILINGUAL EDUCATION TEXTBOOKS. (a) The State Board of Education may acquire, purchase, and contract for, with or without bids, subject to rules and regulations adopted by the board, textbooks and supporting media for use in bilingual education programs conducted in the public school systems of this state.

"(b) The textbooks and supporting media shall be paid for out of the textbook fund and shall be the property of the State of Texas, to be controlled, distributed, and disposed of pursuant to board regulations."

Sec. 3. Subchapter D, Chapter 16, Texas Education Code, is amended by adding Section 16.3061 to read as follows:

"Sec. 16.3061. BILINGUAL EDUCATION TEACHERS (a) The minimum monthly base pay and increments for teaching experience for a bilingual education teacher ~~conducting-a-10,-11,-or-12-months~~ ~~bilingual-education-program-approved-by-the-state-commissioner-of~~ ~~education~~ shall be the same as that prescribed in this subchapter for a classroom teacher. The annual salary of bilingual education teachers shall be the monthly base salary, plus increments, multiplied by 10, 11, or 12 as applicable.

"(b) The Commissioner of Education shall develop policies, subject to approval by the State Board of Education, to determine the terms and conditions under which bilingual education teachers may be paid the monthly base salary, plus increments, multiplied by 11 or 12.

"(c) The minimum salaries prescribed for bilingual education teachers mean total salaries of the teachers to be received for public school instruction, whether they are paid out of state or federal funds or both."

Sec. 4. Section 16.312, Texas Education Code, is amended by adding Subsection (c-1) to read as follows:

"(c-1) In addition to the positions described in Subsection (c), the position descriptions, required preparation and education, and number of monthly payments authorized under the Texas state public education compensation plan for bilingual education teachers are as follows:

Pay Grade	No. Mos. Paid	Class Title	Description of Positions Assigned to Class Title	Required Preparation and Education
7	10 11 12	Bilingual Education Teacher; Bachelor's Degree	Teach in a Bilingual Education Program at grade level or in teaching field for which prepared, under general supervision only.	Degree; No deficiency in professional education or in teaching field; Fully certified; Bilingual Endorsement.
8	10 11 12	Bilingual Education Teacher; Master's Degree	Teach in a Bilingual Education Program at grade level or in teaching field for which prepared, under general supervision only.	Master's Degree; Fully certified; Bilingual Endorsement.

Sec. 5.   The effective date of this Act will be September 1, 1973.

Sec. 6.   The importance of this legislation and the crowded condition of the calendars in both houses create an emergency and an impreative public necessity that the constitutional rule requiring bills to be read on three several days in each house be suspended, and this rule is hereby suspended, and that this Act take effect and be in force from and after September 1, 1973, and it is so enacted.

APPENDIX G

HOUSE BILL 146, 1973

63rd LEGISLATIVE SESSION

By _____

A BILL TO BE ENTITLED
AN ACT

relating to bilingual instruction in the public schools; amending Section 21.109, Texas Education Code, as amended; providing an effective date, and declaring an emergency.

BE IT ENACTED BY THE LEGISLATURE OF THE STATE OF TEXAS:

Section 1. Section 21.109, Texas Education Code, as amended, is amended to read as follows:

"Section 21.109. LANGUAGE OF INSTRUCTION. (a) Since it is the policy of this state to insure the mastery of English by all pupils in the schools, English shall be the basic language of instruction. The governing board of any school district or any private or parochial school may determine in which grades instruction may be given bilingually; provided that where inability to speak and understand the English language excludes linguistically different children from effective participation in the education program offered by a school district, the district shall take affirmative steps to implement a bilingual education program in which children continue their intellectual development through the use of their mother tongue and simultaneously develop facility in English, thus becoming proficient in two languages.

"(b) School districts shall not assign linguistically different children to classes for the mentally retarded or to low tracks or groups on the basis of criteria which essentially measure or evaluate English language skills; nor shall school districts deny linguistically different children access to college preparatory courses on a basis directly related to the failure of the school system to develop academic skills. Any ability grouping or tracking system employed by the school system to deal with the special language skill needs of linguistically different children must be designed to meet such language skill needs as soon as possible and must not operate as an educational dead-end or permanent track.

"(c) School districts shall notify adequately the parents of linguistically different children of school activities which are called to the attention of other parents. Such notice in order to be adequate may have to be provided in a language other than English.

H. B. No. 146

(a)--English-shall-be-the-basic-language-of-instruction-in
all-schools.--The-governing-board-of-any-school-district-and-any
private-or-parochial-school-may-determine-when,-in-which-grades,
and-under-what-circumstances-instruction-may-be-given-bilingually.

(b)--It-is-the-policy-of-this-state-to-insure-the-mastery-of
English-by-all-pupils-in-the-schools,-provided-that-bilingual-in-
struction-may-be-offered-or-permitted-in-those-situations-when
such-instruction-is-educationally-advantageous-to-the-pupils.
Such-bilingual-instruction-may-not-be-offered-or-permitted-above
the-sixth-grade-without-the-express-approval-of-the-Texas-Educa-
tion-Agency,-which-approval-shall-be-granted-on-three-year-basis
subject-to-reapproval-at-the-end-of-that-time. "

Sec. 2. This Act is effective September 1, 1973.

Sec. 3. The importance of this legislation and the crowded
condition of the calendars in both houses create an emergency and
an imperative public necessity that the constitutional rule requiring bills to be read on three several days in each house be
suspended, and this rule is hereby suspended, and that this Act
take effect and be in force from and after September 1, 1973, and
it is so enacted.

APPENDIX H

HOUSE BILL 147, 1973

63rd LEGISLATIVE SESSION

A BILL TO BE ENTITLED
AN ACT

authorizing and providing for supplemental aid programs for adult education where provided by public educational agencies toward the education and training of certain persons not having a high school education or the educational prerequisites for developing a salable skill; providing for the financing thereof in part from state funds; providing that the Central Education Agency shall develop programs, rules, and regulations for the implementation of this Act; amending Subchapter A, Chapter 11, Texas Education Code, by adding Section 11.18; amending Section 21.902, Texas Education Code; and declaring an emergency.

BE IT ENACTED BY THE LEGISLATURE OF THE STATE OF TEXAS:

Section 1. Subchapter A, Chapter 11, Texas Education Code, is amended by adding Section 11.18, to read as follows:

"Sec. 11.18. ADULT EDUCATION. (a) As used in this section, the following words and phrases shall have the indicated meanings:

"(1) 'Adult education' means services and instruction provided by public local education agencies below the college credit level for adults.

"(2) 'Adult' means any individual who is over the age of compulsory school attendance as set forth in Section 21.032 of this code.

"(b) The Central Education Agency shall:

"(1) manage this program with adequate staffing to develop, administer, and support a comprehensive statewide adult education program and coordinate related federal and state programs for education and training of adults;

"(2) develop, implement, and regulate a comprehensive statewide program for community level education services to meet the special needs of adults;

"(3) develop the mechanism and guidelines for coordination of comprehensive adult education and related skill training services for adults with other agencies, both public and private, in planning, developing, and implementing related programs;

"(4)   administer all state and federal funds for adult education and related skill training in Texas;

"(5)   prescribe and administer standards and accrediting policies for adult education;

"(6)   prescribe and administer rules and regulations for teacher certification for adult education; and

"(7)   accept and administer grants, gifts, services, and funds from available sources for use in adult education.

"(c)   Adult education programs shall be provided by public school districts, public junior colleges, public universities, and private, non-profit, colleges and universities, approved in accordance with state statute and the regulations and standards formulated by the Central Education Agency. The programs shall be designed to meet the education and training needs of adults to the extent possible within available public and private resources. Bilingual education may be the method of instruction for students who do not function satisfactorily in English whenever it is appropriate for their optimum development.

"(d)   The State Board of Education is authorized to establish or designate an adult education advisory committee composed of no more than 21 members representing public and private education, business, labor, minority groups, and the general public for the purpose of advising the board on needs, priorities, and standards of adult education programs connected in accordance with this section of the Texas Education Code.

"(e)   Funds shall be appropriated to implement statewide adult basic education, high school equivalency, and high school credit programs to eliminate illiteracy in Texas and to implement and support a statewide program to meet the total range of adult needs for adult education and related skill training. An additional sum of money may be appropriated for the purpose of skill training in direct support of industrial expansion and start-up, in those locations, industries, and occupations designated by the Texas Industrial Commission, when such training is also in support of the basic purposes of this section."

Sec. 2.   Section 21.902, Texas Education Code, is amended to read as follows:

"Sec. 21.902.   LATE AFTERNOON AND EVENING SESSIONS. The board of trustees of any district   having-10,000-or-more-scholas-ties   may provide late afternoon and evening sessions and determine which pupils shall be admitted or assigned to such school programs. The attendance of eligible pupils as defined from time to time by the policies of the State Board of Education shall be applicable to those pupils attending late afternoon and evening sessions."

Sec. 3. The fact that 176,676 Texas adults have not completed one year of school, that 1,758,413 Texans over the age of 25 have less than a ninth grade education, and that 2,060,636 adults in this state do not have a high school diploma, and the fact that basic and continuing education is essential to both the personal development of each citizen and the economic development of the state, and the crowded condition of the calendars in both houses, create an emergency and an imperative public necessity that the consititutional rule requiring bills to be read on three several days in each house be suspended, and this rule is hereby suspended, and that this Act take effect and be in force from and after its passage, and it is so enacted.

H.B. No. 147

By: Trauan, et al.

Committee on Education

BILL ANALYSIS

Background Information:

Presently, no state funds are appropriated for adult educational programs. Limited federal funds are available under the Adult Education Act (P.L. 91-230), but this law allegedly restricts opportunities beyond the eighth grade level and limits opportunities to adults who participated in the basic education program. It is alleged that the federal program does not meet the needs of the 3,060,636 adults in this state over the age of 25 who do not have a high school diploma. (Statistic from the Texas Education Agency.)

What the Bill Proposes to Do:

To develop and fund a state-wide adult educational program.

Section by Section Analysis:

Section 1. Amends Chapter 11, Education Code, by adding a new Sec. 11.18, as follows:

Subsection (a). Definitions.

Subsection (b). Requires the Central Education Agency to develop and administer a state wide program of adult education, to coordinate with other agencies, to administer all governmental funds for adult education, to prescribe accrediting policies, to prescribe teacher certification, and to administer grants, gifts, services, and funds.

Subsection (c). Permit public school districts, junior colleges, and universities to offer adult education programs under the guidance of the C.E.A. Requires bilingual education for non-English-speaking students.

Subsection (d). Authorizes the State Board of Education to establish an adult education advisory committee to advise the Board on needs, priorities, and standards of programs.

Subsection (e). Requires appropriation of funds to implement the programs, and permits additional appropriations for skill training in direct support of industrial expansion in locations designated by the Texas Industrial Commission.

Sec. 2. Amends Sec. 21.902, Education Code, to permit late afternoon and evening sessions in any school district, instead of merely those having 10,000 or more scholastics.

Sec. 2. Emergency Clause.

Summary of Committee Action:

Public notice having been posted on February 1, 1973, the measure was considered in a public hearing on February 8, 1973. The Committee votes, by a record vote of 13 yeas and one nay, to recommend the bill back to the House favorably, as amended.

APPENDIX I

SENATE BILL 121, 1973

63rd LEGISLATIVE SESSION

AN ACT

relating to bilingual education programs in the public schools
and to bilingual training institutes for training public school
personnel; providing for funding; amending Texas Education Code
as follows: amending Chapter 21 by amending Section 21.109 and
adding a new Subchapter L; adding a new Section 11.17 to Subchapter A, Chapter 11; adding a new Subsection 12.05 to Subchapter A, Chapter 12; and declaring an emergency.

BE IT ENACTED BY THE LEGISLATURE OF THE STATE OF TEXAS:

Section 1. Chapter 21, Texas Education Code, is amended by
adding Subchapter L to read as follows:

"SUBCHAPTER L. BILINGUAL EDUCATION

"Section 21.451. STATE POLICY. The legislature finds that
there are large numbers of children in the state who come from
environments where the primary language is other than English.
Experience has shown that public school classes in which instruction is given only in English are often inadequate for the education of children whose native tongue is another language. The
legislature believes that a compensatory program of bilingual
education can meet the needs of these children and facilitate
their integration into the regular school curriculum. Therefore,
pursuant to the policy of the state to insure equal educational
opportunity to every child, and in recognition of the educational
needs of children of limited English-speaking ability, it is the
purpose of this subchapter to provide for the establishment of
bilingual education programs in the public schools and to provide
supplemental financial assistance to help local school districts
meet the extra costs of the programs.

"Section 21.452. DEFINITION. In this subchapter the following words have the indicated meanings:

"(1)   'Agency means the Central Education Agency.

"(2)   'Board' means the governing board of a school
district.

"(3)   'Children of limited English-speaking ability'
means children whose native tongue is a language other than
English and who have difficulty performing ordinary classwork in
English.

"Section 21.453. ESTABLISHMENT OF BILINGUAL PROGRAMS.

"(a) The governing board of each school district shall determine not later than the first day of March, under regulations
prescribed by the State Board of Education, the number of school-
age children of limited English-speaking ability within the district and shall classify them according to the language in which
they possess a primary speaking ability.

"(b) Beginning with the 1974-75 scholastic year, each school
district which has an enrollment of 20 or more children of limited
English-speaking ability in any language classification in the
same grade level during the preceding scholastic year, and which
does not have a program of bilingual instruction which accomplishes the state policy set out in Section 21.451 of this Act, shall
institute a program of bilingual instruction for the children in
each language classification commencing in the first grade, and
shall increase the program by one grade each year until bilingual
instruction is offered in each grade up to the sixth. The board
may establish a program with respect to a language classification
with less than 20 children.

"Section 21454. PROGRAM CONTENT: METHOD OF INSTRUCTION.

"(a) The bilingual education program established by a school
district shall be a full-time program of instruction (1) in all
subjects required by law or by the school district, which shall
be given in the native language of the children of limited English-
speaking ability who are enrolled in the program, and in the English language; (2) in the comprehension, speaking, reading and
writing of the native language of the children of limited English-
speaking ability who are enrolled in the program, and in the comprehension, speaking, reading, and writing of the English language;
and (3) in the history and culture associated with the native language of the children of limited English-speaking ability who are
enrolled in the program, and in the history and culture of the
United States.

"(b) In predominantly nonverbal subjects, such as art, music,
and physical education, children of limited English-speaking ability shall praticipate fully with their English-speaking contemporaries in regular classes provided in the subjects.

"(c) Elective courses included in the curriculum may be
taught in a language other than English.

"(d) Each school district shall insure to children enrolled in the program a meaningful opportunity to participate fully with other children in all extracurricular activities.

"Section 21.455. ENROLLMENT OF CHILDREN IN PROGRAM.

"(a) Every school-age child of limited English-speaking ability residing within a school district required to provide a bilingual program for his classification shall be enrolled in the program for a period of three years or until he achieves a level of English language proficiency which will enable him to perform successfully in classes in which instruction is given only in English, whichever first occurs.

"(b) A child of limited English-speaking ability enrolled in a program of bilingual education may continue in that program for a period longer than three years with the approval of the school district and the child's parents or legal guardian.

"(c) No school district may transfer a child of limited English-speaking ability out of a program in bilingual education prior to his third year of enrollment in the program unless the parents of the child approve the transfer in writing, and unless the child has received a score on an examination which, in the determination of the agency, reflects a level of English language skills appropriate to his or her grade level. If later evidence suggests that a child who has been transferred is still handicapped by an inadequate command of English, he may be re-enrolled in the program for a length of time equal to that which remained at the time he was transferred.

"(d) No later than 10 days after the enrollment of a child in a program in bilingual education the school district shall notify the parents or legal guardian of the child that the child has been enrolled in the program. The notice shall be in writing in English, and in the language of which the child of the parents possesses a primary speaking ability.

"Section 21.456. FACILITIES: CLASSES. (a) Programs in bilingual education, whenever possible, shall be located in the regular public schools of the district rather than in separate facilities.

"(b) Children enrolled in the program, whenever possible, shall be placed in classes with other children of approximately the same age and level of educational attainment. If children of different age groups or educational levels are combined, the school district shall insure that the instruction given each child

198

is appropriate to his or her level of educational attainment, and the district shall keep adequate records of the educational level and progress of each child enrolled in the program.

"(c) The maximum student-teacher ratio shall be set by the agency and shall reflect the special educational needs of children enrolled in programs of bilingual education.

"Section 21.457. COOPERATION AMONG DISTRICTS. (a) A school district may join with any other district or districts to provide the programs in bilingual education required or permitted by this subchapter. The availability of the programs shall be publicized throughout the affected districts.

"(b) A school district may allow a nonresident child of limited English-speaking ability to enroll in or attend its program in bilingual education, and the tuition for the child shall be paid by the district in which the child resides.

"Section 21.458. PRESCHOOL AND SUMMER SCHOOL PROGRAMS. A school district may establish on a full- or part-time basis preschool or summer school programs in bilingual education for children of limited English-speaking ability and may join with other districts in establishing the programs. The preschool or summer programs shall not be a substitute for programs required to be provided during the regular school year.

"Section 21.459. BILINGUAL EDUCATION TEACHERS. (a) The State Board of Education shall promulgate rules and regulations governing the issuance of teaching certificates with bilingual education endorsements to teachers who possess a speaking and reading ability in a language other than English in which bilingual education programs are offered and who meet the general requirements set out in Chapter 13 of this code.

"(b) The minimum monthly base pay and increments for teaching experience for a bilingual education teacher are the same as for a classroom teacher with an equivalent degree under the Texas State Public Education Compensation Plan. The minimum annual salary for a bilingual education teacher is the monthly base salary, plus increments, multiplied by 10, 11, or 12, as applicable.

"Section 12.460. ALLOTMENTS FOR OPERATIONAL EXPENSES AND TRANSPORTATION. (a) To each school district operating an approved bilingual education program there shall be allotted a special allowance in an amount to be determined by the agency for pupil evaluation, books, instructional media, and other supplies required for quality instruction.

199

"(b)   The cost of transporting bilingual education students from one campus to another within a district or from a sending district to an area vocational school or to an approved post-secondary institution under a contract for instruction approved by the Central Education Agency shall be reimbursed based on the number of actual miles traveled times the district's official extracurricular travel per mile rate as set by their local board of trustees and approved by the Central Education Agency.

"(c)   The Foundation School Fund Budget Committee shall consider all amounts required for the operation of bilingual education programs in estimating the funds needed for purposes of the Foundation School Program.

"(d)   The cost of funding this Act shall, for fiscal years 1974 and 1975, be maintained at the level contained in House Bill 139, 63rd Legislature, Regular Session, 1973."

Sec. 2.   Subchapter A, Chapter 11, Texas Education Code, is amended by adding Section 11.17 to read as follows:

"Section 11.17.   BILINGUAL EDUCATION TRAINING INSTITUTES.

"(a)   The Central Education Agency shall conduct bilingual education training institutes.

"(b)   The agency shall make rules and regulations governing the conduct of and participation in the institutes.

"(c)   Professional and paraprofessional public school personnel who participate in the bilingual education training institutes shall be reimbursed for expenses incurred as a result of their participation in accordance with rules and regulations adopted by the agency."

Sec. 3.   Subchapter A, Chapter 12, Texas Education Code, is amended by adding Section 12.04 to read as follows:

"Section 12.04.   BILINGUAL EDUCATION TEXTBOOKS.   (a)   The State Board of Education shall acquire, purchase, and contract for, with bids, subject to rules and regulations adopted by the board, free textbooks and supporting media for use in bilingual education programs conducted in the public school systems of this state.

"(b)   The textbooks and supporting media shall be paid for out of the textbook fund and shall be the property of the State of Texas, to be controlled, distributed, and disposed of pursuant

S. B. No. 121

to board regulations."

Sec. 4.   Section 21.109, Texas Education Code, is amended to read as follows:

"Section 21.109.   LANGUAGE OF INSTRUCTION.   (a)   English shall be the basic language of instruction in all schools.   ~~The governing-board-of-any-school-district-and-any-private-or-parochial-school-may-determine-when,-in-which-grades,-and-under-what circumstances-instruction-may-be-given-bilingually.~~

"(b)   It is the policy of this state to insure the mastery of English by all pupils in the schools; provided that bilingual instruction may be offered or permitted in those situations when such instruction is <u>necessary to insure their reasonable efficiency in the English langauge so as not to be educationally disadvantaged</u>.   ~~educationally-advantageous-to-the-pupils.---Such-bilingual instruction-may-not-be-offered-or-permitted-above-the-sixth-grade without-the-express-approval-of-the-Texas-Education-Agency,-which approval-shall-be-granted-on-a-three-year-basis-subject-to-reapproval-at-the-end-of-that-time.~~ "

Sec. 5.   The importance of this legislation and the crowded condition of the calendars in both houses create an emergency and an imperative public necessity that the constitutional rule requiring bills to be read on three several days in each house be suspended, and this rule is hereby suspended, and that this Act take effect and be in force from and after its passage, and it is so enacted.

201

S. B. No. 121

_____   _____
President of the Senate   Speaker of the House

    I hereby certify that S.B. No. 121 passed the senate on April 30, 1973, by a viva-voice vote; May 23, 1973, senate concurred in house amendments by a viva-voce vote.

                              _____
                              Secretary of the Senate

    I hereby certify that S.B. No. 121 passed the house, with amendments, on May 23, 1973, by the following vote: YEAS 112, Nays 21, two present not voting.

                              _____
                              Chief Clerk of the House

Approved:

_____
       Date

_____
       Governor

APPENDIX J

HOUSE BILL 289, 1975

64th LEGISLATIVE SESSION

Official House Printing, 64th Legislature

By: Truan, et al.   H.B. No. 289

A BILL TO BE ENTITLED

AN ACT

relating to bilingual education programs in public schools; amending Sections 21.451, 21.452, 21.453, 21.454, 21.455, 21.456, and
21460, Texas Education Code; amending and renumbering Section
11.17, Texas Education Code, as added by Section 2, Chapter 392,
Acts of the 63rd Legislature, 1973; and declaring an emergency.

BE IT ENACTED BY THE LEGISLATURE OF THE STATE OF TEXAS:

COMMITTEE AMENDMENT NO. 1

Amend H.B. No. 289 by striking all below the enacting
clause and substituting in lieu thereof the following:

Section1. Sections 21.451, 21.452, 21.453, 21.454, 21.455,
21.456, and 21.460, Texas Education Code, are amended to read as
follows:

"Sec. 21.451. STATE POLICY. The legislature finds that
there are large numbers of children in the state who come from
environments where the primary language is other than English and
who have a cultural heritage that differs from that of speakers
of English as a primary language. Experience has shown that a
primary means by which a child learns is through the use of his
or her language and cultural heritage and that public school
classes in which instruction is given only in English are often
inadequate for the education of children (whose-native-tonue-is
another-language). The legislature believes that large numbers
of children of limited English-speaking ability have educational
needs that are best met through bilingual instruction to (a
compensatory-program-of-bilingual-education-can-meet-the-needs
of-these-children-and) facilitate their integration into the
regular school curriculum. Therefore, pursuant to the policy of
the state to insure equal educational opportunity to every child,
and in recognition of the educational needs of children of limited
English-speaking ability, it is the purpose of this subchapter
to provide for the establishment of bilingual education programs
in the public schools and to provide supplemental financial
assistance to help local school districts meet the extra costs of
the programs.

"Sec. 21.452. DEFINITIONS. In this subchapter the follow-ing words hav the indicated meanings:

"(1)   'Agency' means the Central Education Agency.

"(2)   'Board' means the governing board of a school district.

"(3)   'Children of limited English-speaking ability' means children whose primary home (native-tongue-is-a) language is other than English (and-who-have-difficulty-performing-ordinary classwork-in-English).

"(4)   'Primary language' means the language that is most commonly used for ordinary verbal transactions.

"Sec. 21.453. ESTABLISHMENT OF BILINGUAL PROGRAMS. (a) The governing board of each school district shall determine not later than the first day of March, under regulations prescribed by the State Board of Education, the number of school-age chil-dren of limited English-speaking ability within the district and shall classify them according to the language in which they possess a primary speaking ability.

"(b)   Each (Beginning-with-the-1974-75-scholastic-year, each) school district with (which-has) an enrollment of 20 or more children of limited English-speaking ability in any language classification in the same grade level (during-the-preceding scholastic-year), and which does not have a program of bilingual instruction which accomplishes the state policy set our in Section 21.451 of this subchapter (Act), shall intitute a program of bi-lingual instruction for the children in each language classifica-tion. The district shall offer the program at the kindergarten level and first and second grade levels during the 1975-76 scho-lastic year. (commencing-in-the-first-grade,) and shall increase the program by one grade each year until bilingual instruction is offered in each grade through (up-to) the sixth. The board may establish a program with respect to a language classification with less than 20 children.

"Sec. 21.454. PROGRAM CONTENT: METHOD OF INSTRUCTION. (a) The bilingual education program established by a school district shall be a full-time program of instruction (1) in all subjects required by law or by the school district, which shall be given in the primary (native) language of the children of limited English-speaking ability who are enrolled in the program, and in the English language when the children have acquired proficiency in English; (2) in the comprehension, speaking, reading, and writing of the primary (native) language of the children of limited English-speaking ability who are enrolled in the program,

and in the comprehension, speaking, reading (~~and~~) writing, <u>and</u>
<u>continued skill development</u> of the English language; and (3) in
the history and culture associated with the primary(~~native~~) language of the children of limited English-speaking ability (~~who~~
~~are-enrolled-in-the-program~~), and in the history and culture of
the United States.

"(b) In (~~predominantly-nonverbal~~) subjects (~~,~~) such as art,
music, and physical education, children of limited English-speaking ability shall participate fully with their English-speaking
contemporaries in regular classes provided in the subjects.

"(c) Elective courses included in the curriculum may be
taught in a language other than English.

"(d) Each school district shall insure to children enrolled in the program a meaningful opportunity to participate
fully with other children in all <u>classroom and</u> extracurricular
activities.

"Sec. 21.455. ENROLLMENT OF CHILDREN IN PROGRAM. (a)
Every school-age child of limited English-speaking ability residing within a school district required to provide a bilingual program for his classification shall be enrolled in the program <u>until</u>
<u>he completes the third grade</u> (~~for-a-period-of-three-years-or-until~~
~~he-achieves-a-level-of-English-language-proficiency-which-will~~
~~which-will-enable-him-to-perform-successfully-in-classes-in-which~~
~~instruction-is-given-only-in-English,-whichever-first-occurs~~).

~~(b)--A-child-of-limited-English-speaking-ability-enrolled~~
~~in-a-program-of-bilingual-education-may-continue-in-that-program~~
~~for-a-period-longer-than-three-years-with-the-approval-of-the~~
~~school-district-and-the-child's-parents-or-legal-guardian.~~

"<u>(b)</u> ~~(c)~~ A ~~(No)~~ school district mya transfer a child of
limited English-speaking ability out of a program in bilingual
education <u>after he has completed the third grade if</u> (~~prior-to-his~~
~~third-year-of-enrollment-in-the-program-unless~~) the parents of the
child approve the transfer in writing, and <u>if</u> (~~unless~~) the child
has received a score on an examination which, in the determination
of the agency, reflects a level of English language skills appropriate to his or her grade level. If later evidence suggests
that a child who has been transferred is still handicapped by an
inadequate command of English, he may be re-enrolled in the program (~~for-a-length-of-time-equal-to-that-which-remained-at-the~~
~~time-he-was-transferred~~).

"<u>(c)</u> ~~(d)~~ No later than 10 days after the enrollment of a
child in a program in bilingual education the school district
shall notify the parents or legal guardian of the child that the

child has been enrolled in the program. The notice shall be in writing in English, and in the language of which the child of the parents possesses a primary speaking ability.

"(d) A local board shall make porvision for the voluntary enrollment into the biliingual programs of children whose primary language is English, in order that they may acquire an understanding of the language and cultural heritage of the children of limited English-speaking ability for whom the particular program is designed.

"Sec. 21.456. FACILITIES: CLASSES. (a) Programs in bilingual education (7-whenever-possible7) shall be located in the regular public schools of the district rather than in separate facilities.

"(b) Children enrolled in the program(7-whenever-possible7) shall be placed in classes with other children of approximately the same age and level of educational attainment. If children of different age groups or educational levels are combined, the school district shall insure that the instruction given each child is appropriate to his or her level of educational attainment, and the district shall keep adequate records of the educational level and progress of each child enrolled in the program.

"(c) The maximum student-teacher ratio shall be set by the agency and shall reflect the special educational needs of children enrolled in programs of bilingual education."

"Sec. 21.460. ALLOTMENTS FOR OPERATIONAL EXPENSES AND TRANSPORTATION. (a) To each school district operating an approved bilingual education program there shall be allotted a special allowance in an amount to be determined by the agency for pupil evaluation, books, instructional media, and other supplies required for quality instruction.

"(b) To the Central Education Agency there shall be allotted an allowance in an amount to be determined by the agency for research and development in the areas of curriculum, materials, and assessment and evaluation instruments.

"(c) (b) The cost of transporting bilingual education students from one campus to another within a district (or-from-a sending-district-to-an-area-vocational-school-or-to-an-approved post-secondary-institution-under-a-contract-for-instruction approved-by-the-Central-Education-Egency) sha-l be reimbursed in full based on the number of actual miles traveled times the district's official extracurricular travel per mile rate as set by their local board of trustees and approved by the Central Education Agency.

"(d) (c) The Foundation School Fund Budget Committee shall consider all amounts required for the operation of bilingual education programs in estimating the funds needed for purposes of the oundation School Program.

((d)--The-cost-of-funding-this-Act-shall,-for-fiscal-years 1974-and-1975,-be-maintained-at-the-level-contained-in-House-Bill 139,-63rd-Legislature,-Regular-Session,-1973.)"

Sec. 2. Section 11.17, Texas Education Code, as added by Section 2, Chapter 392, Acts of the 63rd Legislature, 1973, is amended and renumbered to read as follows:

"Sec. 11.19 (11.17). BILINGUAL EDUCATION TRAINING PROGRAMS (INSTITUTES). (a) The Central Education Agency shall provide for (conduct) bilingual education training programs (institutes) designed to (1) train and certify teachers, and train administrators, paraprofessionals, and parents and (2) train bilingual education personnel to teach and counsel teachers, paraprofessionals, parents, and administrators.

"(b) The agency shall make rules and regularions governing the conduct of and participation in the training programs (institutes).

"(c) Professional and paraprofessional public school personnel who participate in the bilingual education training programs (institutes) shall be reimbursed for expernses incurred as a result of their participation in accordance with rules and regulations adopted by the agency.

"(d) The Central Education Agency shall provide for the development of bilingual training education programs in higher educational institutions such as four-year universities and junior AND COMMUNITY COLLEGES, BOTH PRIVATE AND PUBLIC, IN ACCORDANCE with rules and regulations adopted by the agency."

Sec. 3. The importance of this legislation and the crowded condition of the calendars in both houses create an emergency and an imperative public necessity that the constitutional rule requiring bill to be read on three several days in each house be suspended, and this rule is herby suspended, and that this Act take effect and be in force from and after its passage, and it is so enacted.

Madla

APPENDIX K

HOUSE BILL 1640, 1975

64th LEGISLATIVE SESSION

By: Massey

A BILL TO BE ENTITLED

AN ACT

relating to bilingual educatin; amending Section 21.457, Subsection (a) of Section 21.455, Subsection (a) of Section 21.457 and Section 21.459, Texas Education Code, as amended; repealing Subsection (d) of Section 21.460.

BE IT ENACTED BY THE LEGISLATURE OF THE STATE OF TEXAS:

Section 1. Section 21.453, Texas Education Code, as amended, is amended to read as follows:

"Sec. 21.453. ESTABLISHMENT OF BILINGUAL PROGRAMS. (a) (The-governing-board-of-each-school-district-shall-determine-not later-than-the-first-day-of-March,-under-regulations-prescribed by-the-State-Board-of-Education,-the-number-of-school-age-child- dren-of-limited-English-speaking-ability-within-the-district-and shall-classify-them-according-to-the-language-in-which-they possess-a-primary-speaking-ability.)

(b) Each school district (which-has-an-enrollment-of-20 or-more-children-of-limited-English-speaking-ability-in-any-lan- guage-classification-in-the-same-grade-level-during-the-preceding scholastic-year,-and) which does not have a program of bilingual instruction which accomplishes the state policy of facilitating integration into the regular school curriculum as set out in Section 21.451 of this code, may (article,-shall) institute a pro- gram of bilingual instruction for the children in each language classification in kindergarten, first grade, (and) second grade, (by-the-1975-76-school-year) and (also-in-the) third grade (by the-1976-77-school-year). (Bilingual-instruction-may-be-offered in-the-fourth-and-fifth-grades-for-students-who-have-not-pro- gressed-sufficiently-to-participate-in-the-regular-school-curri- culum.) Any bilingual program beyond the third (fifth) grade shall be at the expense of the respective local school district. (The-board-may-establish-a-program-with-respect-to-a-language classification-with-less-than-20-children.)

"(b) A school district wich provides a program of bilin- gual instruction may discontinue the program at any time."

Sec. 2. Subsection (a), Section 21.455, Texas Education Code, is amended to read as follows:

"(a) Every school-age child of limited English-speaking ability residing within a school district which provides

210

(~~required-to-provide~~) a bilingual program for his clasification shall be enrolled in the program for a period of three years or until he achieves a level of English language proficiency which will enable him to perform successfully in classes in which instruction is given only in English, whichever, first occurs."

Sec. 3. Subsection (a), Section 21.457, Texas Education Code, is amended to read as follows:

"(a) A school district may join with any other district or districts to provide the programs in bilingual education (~~required-or~~) permitted by this subchapter. The availability of the programs shall be publicized throughout the affected districts."

Sec. 4. Section 21.458, Texas Education Code, is amended to read as follows:

"Sec. 21.458. PRESCHOOL AND SUMMER SHCOOL PROGRAMS. A school district may establish on a full- or part-time basis preschool or summer school programs in bilingual education for children of limited English-speaking ability and may join with other districts in establishing the programs. (~~The-preschool-or summer-programs-shall-not-be-a-substitute-for-programs-required to-be-provided-during-the-regular-school-year.~~)"

Sec. 6. Subsection (d), Section 21.460, Texas Education ode, is repealed.

Sec. 6. The importance of this legislation and the crowded condition of the caldars in both houses create an emergency and an imperative public necessity that the constitutional rule requiring bills to be read on three several days in each house be suspended, and this rule is hereby suspended, and that this Act take effect and be in force from and after its passage, and it is so enacted.

APPENDIX L

SENATE SUBSTITUTE SENATE BILL 195, 1979

66th LEGISLATIVE SESSION

By Truan   S.B. No. 195

Substitute the following for S.B. No. 195:

By _____   C.S.S.B. No. 195

A BILL TO BE ENTITLED

AN ACT

relating to bilingual education programs in public schools.

BE IT ENACTED BY THE LEGISLATURE OF THE STATE OF TEXAS:

SECTION 1. Sections 21.451, 21.452, 21.453, 21.454, 21.455, 21.456, 21.458, 21.459, and 21.460, Texas Education Code, as amended, are amended to read as follows:

Sec. 21.451. STATE POLICY. The legislature recognizes that the mastery of basic English skills is a prerequisite for effective participation in the state's educational program and that those who do not understand English are certain to find their classroom experiences wholly incomprehensible and in no way meaningful (finds-that-there-are-large-numbers-of-children-in-the state-who-come-from-environments-where-the-primary-language-is other-than-English). Experience has shown that the most effective means by which a student learns is through the use of his or her language and cultural heritage (public-school-classes-in-which instruction-is-given-only-in-English-are-often-inadequate-for-the education-of-children-whose-native-tongue-is-another-language). The legislature believes that large numbers of students with limited English language skills have educational needs that are best met through bilingual instruction and the fullest use of of multiple lanuage and cultural resources (a compensatory program of-bilingual-education-can-meet-the-needs-of-those-children-and and-facilitate-their-integration-into-the-regular-school-curriculum). Therefore, pursuant to the policy of the state to provide a thorough and efficient system of public education (insure-equal educational-opportunity-to-every-child), and in recognition of the educational needs of students with (children-of) limited English language skills (English-speaking-ability), it is the purpose of this subchapter to provide for the establishment of (bilingual education) programs for student with limited English language skills in the public schools and to provide supplemental financial assistance to help local school districts meet the extra costs of the programs.

Sec. 21.452. DEFINITIONS. In this subchapter the following words have the indicated meanings:

214

(1) "Agency" means the Central Education Agency.

(2) "Board" means the governing board of a school dis-
     trict.

(3) "English language skills" means the ability to understand, speak, read, and write the English language to the extent
normal for a person of the same age group ("Children-of-limited
English-speaking-ability"-means-children-whose-native-tongue-is
a-language-other-than-English-and-who-have-difficulty-perform-
ing-ordinary-classwork-in-English).

(4) "Primary language" means the language that is most
commonly used for ordinary verbal transactions.

(5) "Language response program" means a program of instruction of English language skills for students in grades
7-12 whose primary language is other than English.

(6) "Self-contained classroom" means a unit consisting
of a group of students receiving instruction in all curricular
offering from the same teacher.

(7) "Teaching team" means one certified teacher with bilingual endorsement and one or more certified teachers who may
or may not have bilingual endorsement.

Sec. 21.453. ESTABLISHMENT OF BILINGUAL EDUCATION AND
LANGUAGE RESPONSE PROGRAMS. (a) Before October 30, 1980, the
Central Education Agency shall issue a plan for the identification of children of limited English language skills in the state's
public elementary and secondary schools. The identification of
these students is to be executed by the governing board of each
school district. At a minimum the state plan shall set forth
appropriate options for school districts of varying characteristics regarding:

(1) instrumentation and procedures for the identification
of these students;

(2) the analysis and recording of student data; and

(3) procedures for reporting student data to the agency
(The-governing-board-of-each-school-district-shall-determine-not
later-than-the-first-day-of-March,-under-regulations-prescribed
by-the-State-Board-of-Education,-the-number-of-school-age-chil-
dren-of-limited-English-speaking-ability-within-the-district-and
shall-classify-them-accrding-to-the-language-in-which-they-po-
ssess-a-primary-speaking-ability).

(b) Each school district with ~~(which-has)~~ an enrollment of 20 or more students with ~~(children-of)~~ limited English language skills ~~(English-speaking-ability)~~ in any language classification in the same grade level at grades k-6 ~~(during-the-preceding-scholastic-year,-and)~~ which does not have a program of bilingual education which accomplishes the state policy ~~(of-facilitating integration-into-the-regular-school-curriculum-as)~~ set out in Section 21.451 of this code ~~(article)~~, shall institute a program of bilingual instruction for the students ~~(children)~~ in each language classification ~~(in-kindergarten,-first-grade,-and-second grade-by-the-1975-76-school-year-and-also-in-the-third-grade-by the-1976-77-school-year). (Bilingual-instruction-may-be-offered in-the-fourth-and-fifth-grades-for-students-who-have-not-progressed-sufficiently-to-participate-in-the-regular-school-curriculum.--Any-bilingual-program-beyond-the-fifth-grade-shall-be-at the-expense-of-the-respective-local-school-district.)~~ The board may establish a program with respect to a language classification with less than 20 students ~~(children)~~.

(c) Each district that identifies students who have limited English language skills at grades 7-12 shall provide a language response program designed to meet diagnosed student needs.

Sec. 21.454. PROGRAM CONTENT, PRINCIPLES, AND ~~(,)~~ METHOD OF INSTRUCTION. (a) The bilingual program in grades k-6 established by a school district shall be a full-time program of instruction (1) in all subjects required by law or by the school district, which shall be given in the primary ~~(native)~~ language of the students with ~~(children-of)~~ limited English language skills ~~(English-speaking-ability)~~ who are enrolled in the program, and in the English language when the students have acquired proficiency in English; (2) in the comprehension, speaking, reading, and writing of, and listening to, the primary ~~(native)~~ language of the students with ~~(children-of)~~ limited English language skills ~~(English-speaking-ability)~~ who are enrolled in the program, and in the comprehension, speaking, reading, and writing of, and listening to, the English language; and (3) in the history and culture associated with the primary ~~(native)~~ language of the students with ~~(children-of)~~ limited English language skills ~~(English-speaking-ability-who-are-enrolled-in-the-program)~~, and in the history and culture of the United States.

(b) In ~~(predominantly-nonverbal)~~ subjects ~~(,)~~ such as art, music, and physical education, students with ~~(children-of)~~ limited English language skills ~~(English-speaking-ability)~~ shall participate fully with their English-speaking contemporaries in regular classes provided in the subjects.

(c) Elective courses included in the curriculum may be taught in a language other than English.

216

(d)   Each school district shall insure to students (children) enrolled in the program a meaningful opportunity to participate fully with other children in all extracurricular activities.

(e)   The program shall:

(1) use a diagnostic/prescriptive approach providing for the individual assessed needs of each student;

(2) use appropriate evaluation and assignment procedures with language minority students; and

(3) provide for a variety of learning approaches.

(f)   For each student enrolled in a bilingual or language response program, the school district shall, within 30 days of the student's enrollment, assess the language proficiency in English and in the primary language.   Each student shall be instructed in all subjects required by law at a level appropriate to the assessed needs and in the language in which the student demonstrates the most skill.   Each student shall receive specialized instruction in the English language based on his assessed needs. The school district shall maintain continuous evaluation and documentation of the program of instruction and of each student's progress.

(g)   The bilingual education program in grades k-6 shall provide the sequential development of basic language arts skills in both the primary and English languages, including listening, speaking, reading, and writing.   The language response program in grades 7-12 shall provide instruction in the basic language arts skills in only the English language.

Sec. 21.455.   ENROLLMENT OF CHILDREN IN PROGRAM.   (a) Every student with (school-age-child-of) limited English language skills (English-speaking-ability) residing within a school district (required-to-provide-a-bilingual-program-for-his-classification) shall be provided an appropriate bilingual education or language response program until he or she acquires English language skills sufficient to enable him or her to perform successfully in classes in which instruction is provided in English   (enrolled-in-the-program-for-a-period-of-three-years-or-until-he-achieves-a-level-of English-language-proficiency-which-will-enable-him-to-perform successfully-in-classes-in-which-instruction-is-given-only-in English,-whichever-first-occurs).

(b)   A student with (child-of) limited English language skills (English-speaking-ability) enrolled in a language response program (of-bilingual-education) may continue in that program

217

until he or she acquires English language skills sufficient to enable him or her to perform successfully in classes in which instruction is provided in English ~~(for-a-period-longer-than-three years-with-the-approval-of-the-school-district-and-the-child's parents-or-legal-guardian)~~.

(c) No school district may transfer a student with ~~(child of)~~ limited English language skills ~~(English-speaking-ability)~~ out of a bilingual education or prescribed language response program ~~(in-bilingual-education-prior-to-his-third-year-of-enrollment-in the-program-unless-the-parents-of-the-child-approve-the-transfer in-writing,-and)~~ unless the student ~~(child)~~ has demonstrated his or her mastery of the English language through performance on a designated ~~(received-a-score-on-an)~~ examination which, in the determination of the agency, reflects a level of English language skills appropriate to his or her grade level. If later evidence suggests that a student ~~(child)~~ who has been transferred has ~~(is-still-handicapped-by-an)~~ inadequate ~~(command-of)~~ English language skills, he or she may be re-enrolled in the program ~~(for a-length-of-time-equal-to-that-which-remained-at-the-time-he-was transferred)~~.

(d) With the approval of the school district and a child's parents, students who do not have limited English language skills may also participate in programs for students with limited English language skills, provided that the number of these students does not exceed 40 percent of the students enrolled in the program ~~(No-later-than-10-days-after-the-enrollment-of-a-child-in-a-program-in-bilingual-education-the-school-district-shall-notify-the parents-or-legal-guardian-of-the-child-that-the-child-has-been enrolled-in-the-program.--The-notice-shall-be-in-writing-in English,-and-in-the-language-of-which-the-child-of-the-parents possess-a-primary-speaking-ability)~~.

Sec. 21.456.   FACILITIES: CLASSES.   (a) Bilingual (P̶r̶o̶-g̶r̶a̶m̶s̶-i̶n̶-b̶i̶l̶i̶n̶g̶u̶a̶l̶) education and language response programs (̶,̶ w̶h̶e̶n̶e̶v̶e̶r̶-p̶o̶s̶s̶i̶b̶l̶e̶,̶) shall be located in the regular public schools of the district rather than in separate facilities.

(b) Students (C̶h̶i̶l̶d̶r̶e̶n̶) enrolled in a bilingual education or language response (t̶h̶e̶) program (̶,̶-w̶h̶e̶n̶e̶v̶e̶r̶-p̶o̶s̶s̶i̶b̶l̶e̶,̶) shall be placed in classes with other students (c̶h̶i̶l̶d̶r̶e̶n̶) of approx- imately the same age and level of educational attainment. If students (c̶h̶i̶l̶d̶r̶e̶n̶) of different age groups or educational levels are combined, the school district shall insure that the instruc- tion given each student (c̶h̶i̶l̶d̶) is appropriate to his or her level of educational attainment, and the district shall keep adequate records of the educational level and progress of each student (c̶h̶i̶l̶d̶) enrolled in the program.

(c) The maximum student-teacher ratio shall be set by the agency and shall reflect the special educational needs of students (c̶h̶i̶l̶d̶r̶e̶n̶) enrolled in the programs (o̶f̶-b̶i̶l̶i̶n̶g̶u̶a̶l̶-e̶d̶u̶c̶a̶t̶i̶o̶n̶).

Sec. 21.458.   PRESCHOOLS AND SUMMER SCHOOL PROGRAMS. A school district may establish on a full- or part-time basis pre- school or summer school programs in bilingual education for students with (c̶h̶i̶l̶d̶r̶e̶n̶-o̶f̶) limited English language skills (E̶n̶g̶l̶i̶s̶h̶-s̶p̶e̶a̶k̶i̶n̶g̶-a̶b̶i̶l̶i̶t̶y̶) and may join other districts in establishing the programs. The preschool or summer programs shall not be a substitute for programs required to be provided during the regular school year.

Sec. 21.459.   BILINGUAL   EDUCATION AND LANGUAGE RESPONSE PROGRAM TEACHERS.   (a) The State Board of Education shall prom- ulgate rules and regulations governing the issuance of teaching certificates with bilingual education endorsements to teachers who possess a speaking and reading ability in a language other than English in which bilingual education programs are offered and who meet the general requirements set out in Chapter 13 of this code.

(b) The minum monthly base apy and increments for teach- ing experience for a bilingual education teacher are the same as for a classroom teacher with an equivalent degree under the Texas State Public Education Compensation Plan. The minimum annual salary for a bilingual education teacher is the monthly base salary, plus increments, multiplied by 10, 11, or 12, as applicable.

(c) A teacher assigned to self-contained classrooms in bilingual education programs in greades K-6 must have a valid Texas teacher's certificate with a bilingual education endorse- ment.

(d) A monolingual English-speaking teacher assigned to teach a bilingual education program in grades K-6 as part of a teaching team must have a valid Texas teacher's certificate and must participate in language response program training as specified by the agency.

(e) A teacher assigned to language response program classes in grades 7-12 must participate in language response program training as specified by the agency.

Sec. 21.460. ALLOTMENTS FOR OPERATIONAL EXPENSES AND TRANSPORTATION. (a) To each school district operating an approved bilingual education program there shall be allotted a special allowance in an amount to be determined by the agency for pupil evaluation, books, instructional media, and other supplies required for quality instruction.

(b) The cost of transporting bilingual education students from one campus to another within a district (or-from-a-sending district-to-an-area-vocational-school-or-to-an-approved-post secondary-institution-under-a-contract-for-instruction-approved by-the-Central-Education-Agency) shall be reimbursed based on the number of (or) actual miles traveled times the district's official extracurricular travel per mile rate as set by their local board of trustees and approved by the Central Education Agency.

(c) The Foundation School Fund Budget Committee shall consider all amounts required for the operation of bilingual education programs in estimating the funds needed for purposes of the Foundation School Program.

(fd)--The-cost-of-funding-this-Act-shall7-for-fiscal-years 1974-and-19757-be-maintained-at-the-level-contained-in-House-Bill 1397-63rd-Legislature7-Regular-Session7-1973.)

SECTION 2. Section 11.17, Texas Education Code, as added by Section 2, Chapter 392, Acts of the 635d Legislature, 1973 is amended and renumbered to read as follows:

Sec. 11.171 (11.17). BILINGUAL EDUCATION TRAINING PROGRAMS (INSTITUTES). (a) The Central Education Agency shall provide for (conduct) bilingual education training programs (institutes) designed to (1) train teachers, administrators, paraprofessionals, and parents, and (2) train bilingual education personnel to teach and counsel teachers, paraprofessionals, parents, and administrators.

(b) The agency shall make rules and regulations governing the conduct of and participation in the training programs (institutes).

220

(c) Professional and paraprofessional public school personnel who participate in the bilingual education training programs (institutes) shall be reimbursed for expenses incurred as a result of their participation in accordance with rules and regulations adopted by the agency.

(d) The Central Education Agency shall also provide for the development of bilingual training education programs leading to certification or endorsement in higher educational institutions such as four-year universities and junior and community colleges, both private and public, in accordance with rules and regulations adopted by the agency.

SECTION 3. The importance of this legislation and the crowded condition of the calendars in both houses create an emergency and an imperative public necessity that the constitutional rule requiring bills to be read on three several days in each house be suspended, and this rule is hereby suspended, and the this Act take effect and be in force from and after its passage, and it is so enacted.

APPENDIX M

SENATE BILL 477, 1981

67th LEGISLATIVE SESSION

By: Truan, et al.   S.B. No. 477

A BILL TO BE ENTITLED

AN ACT

relating to bilingual education and English as a second language
and other special language programs in public schools; amending
Subchapter L, Chapter 21, Texas Education Code, as amended.

BE IT ENACTED BY THE LEGISLATURE OF THE STATE OF TEXAS:

SECTION 1. Subchapter L, Chapter 21, Texas Education Code,
as amended, is amended to read as follows:

"SUBCHAPTER L. BILINGUAL EDUCATION AND
SPECIAL LANGUAGE PROGRAMS

"Section 21.451. STATE POLICY.

English is the basic language of the State of Texas. Public
schools are responsible for providing full opportunity for all students to become competent in speaking, reading, writing and compre-
hending the English language. The legislature finds that there are
large numbers of students in the state who come from environments
where the primary language is other than English. Experience has
shown that public school classes in which instruction is given only
in English are often inadequate for the education of these students. The legislature recognizes that the mastery of basic English language skills is a prerequisite for effective participation
in the state's educational program. The legislature believes that
bilingual education and special language programs can meet the
needs of these students and facilitate their integration into the
regular school curriculum. Therefore, pursuant to the policy of
the state to insure equal educational opportunity to every student,
and in recognition of the educational needs of students of limited
English proficiency, it is the purpose of this subchapter to provide for the establishment of bilingual education and special language programs in the public schools and to provide supplemental
financial assistance to help local school districts meet the extra
costs of the programs.

"Section 21.452. DEFINITIONS. In this subchapter the following words have the indicated meanings:

"(1) 'Agency' means the Central Education Agency.

"(2) 'Board' means the governing board of a school district.

"(3) 'Students of limited English proficiency means students whose primary language is other than English and whose English language skills are such that the students have difficulty performing ordinary classwork in English.

"(4) 'Parent' means the parent(s) or legal guardian(s) of the student.

"Section 21.453. ESTABLISHMENT OF BILINGUAL EDUCATION AND SPECIAL LANGUAGE PROGRAMS.

(a) The State Board of Education shall adopt rules establishing a procedure for identifying school districts that are required to offer bilingual education and special language programs in accordance with this subchapter.

"(b) Within the first four weeks following the first day of school, the language proficiency assessment committee established under Section 21.462 shall determine and report to the governing board of the school district the number of students of limited English proficiency on each campus and shall classify them according to the language in which they possess primary proficiency. The governing board shall report that information to the agency before the first day of November each year.

"(c) Each school district which has an enrollment of 20 or more students of limited English proficiency in any language classification in the same grade level shall offer a bilingual education or special language program.

"(d) Each district that is required to offer bilingual education and special language programs under this section shall offer the following for students of limited English proficiency:

"(1) bilingual education in kindergarten through the elementary grades;

"(2) bilingual education, instruction in English as a second

225

language, or other transitional language instruction approved by the agency in post-elementary grades through grade 8; and

"(3) instruction in English as a second language in grades 9-12.

"(e) If a program other than bilingual education must be used in kindergarten through the elementary grades, documentation for the exception must be filed with and approved by the commissioner of education, pursuant to the rules of the State Board of Education.

"(f) An application for an exception may be filed with the commissioner of education when an individual district is unable to hire a sufficient number of endorsed bilingual teachers to staff the required program. The exception must be accompanied by:

"(1) documentation showing that the district has taken all reasonable affirmative steps to secure endorsed bilingual teachers and has failed;

"(2) documentation showing that the district has affirmative hiring policies and procedures consistent with the need to serve limited English proficiency students;

"(3) documentation showing that, on the basis of district records, no teacher with a bilingual endorsement or emergency credentials has been unjustifiably denied employment by the district within the past 12 months; and

"(4) a plan detailing specific measures to be used by the district to eliminate the conditions that created the need for an exception.

"(g) An exception shall be granted under Subsection (f) of this section on an individual district basis and is valid for only one year. Application for an exception a second or succeeding year must be accompanied by the documentation set forth in Subdivisions (1), (2), (3), and (4) of Subsection (f) of this section.

"(h) During the period of time for which the school district is granted an exception under Subsection (f) of this section, it must use alternative methods approved by the commissioner of education, pursuant to the rules of the State Board of Education, to meet the needs of its students of limited English proficiency such as, but not limited to, the hiring of teaching personnel on a bilingual emergency permit.

"Section 21.454. PROGRAM CONTENT; METHOD OF INSTRUCTION.

(a) The bilingual education program established by a school district shall be a full-time program of dual-language instruction that provides for learning basic skills in the primary language of the students of limited English proficiency who are enrolled in the program, and that provides for carefully structured and sequenced mastery of English language skills. The program shall be designed to consider the students' learning experiences and shall incorporate the cultural aspects of the students' backgrounds.

"(b) The program of instruction in English as a second language established by a school district shall be a program of intensive instruction in English from teachers trained in recognizing and dealing with language differences. The program shall be designed to consider the students' learning experiences and shall incorporate the cultural aspects of the students' backgrounds.

"(c) In subjects such as art, music, and physical education, students of limited English proficiency shall participate fully with English-speaking students in regular classes provided in the subjects.

"(d) Elective courses included in the curriculum may be taught in a language other than English.

"(e) Each school district shall insure to students enrolled in the program a meaningful opportunity to participate fully with other students in all extracurricular activities.

"(f) The State Board of Education shall establish a limited number of pilot programs for the purpose of examining alternative methods of instruction in bilingual education and special language programs.

"(g) Districts approved to establish pilot programs as required by Subsection (f) of this section shall be allocated an amount per student which is equal to the amount per student allocated to districts with approved bilingual education programs as outlined in this subchapter.

"Section 21.455. ENROLLMENT OF STUDENTS IN PROGRAM.

(a) The State Board of Education by rule shall adopt standardized criteria for the identification, assessment, and classification of students of limited English proficiency eligible for entry into the program or exit from the program. The parent must be notified of a student's entry into the program, exit from the program, or placement within the program. A student's entry into the program or placement within the program must be approved by the student's parents. The local school district may appeal the decision under Section 21.463 of this code. The parent may appeal the decision under Section 21.463 of this code. The criteria may include, but are not limited to, the following:

"(1) results of a home language survey conducted within four weeks of each student's enrollment in order to determine the language normally used in the home and the language normally used by the student, conducted in English and the home language, signed by the student's parent if in kindergarten through grade 8 or by the student if in grades 9 through 12, and kept in the student's permanent folder by the language proficiency assessment committee;

"(2) the results of an agency-approved English language proficiency test administered to all students identified through the home survey as normally speaking a language other than English to determine the level of English language proficiency, with students in kindergarten or grade 1 being administered an oral English proficiency test and students in grades 2 through 12 being administered an oral and written English proficiency test; and

"(3) the results of an agency-approved proficiency test in the primary language administered to all students identified under Subdivision (2) of this subsection as being of limited English proficiency to determine the level of primary language proficiency, with students in kindergarten or grade 1 being administered an oral primary language proficiency test and students in grades 2 through 12 being administered an oral and written primary language proficiency test.

"(b) Tests under Subsection (a) of this section should be administered by professionals or paraprofessionals with the appropriate English and primary language skills and the training required by the test publisher.

"(c) The language proficiency assessment committee may classify a student as limited English proficiency if one or more of the following criteria are met:

"(1) the student's ability in English is so limited or the student is so handicapped that assessment procedures cannot be administered;

"(2) the student's score or relative degree of achievement on the agency-approved English proficiency test is below the levels established by the agency as indicative of reasonable proficiency;

"(3) the student's primary language proficiency score as measured by an agency-approved test is greater than his proficiency in English; or

"(4) the language proficiency assessment committee determines, based on other information such as (but not limited to) teacher evaluation, parental viewpoint, or student interview, that the student's primary language proficiency is greater than his proficiency in English or that the student is not reasonably proficient in English.

"(d) Within 10 days after the student's classification as limited English proficiency, the language proficiency assessment committee shall give written notice of the classification to the student's parent. The notice must be in English and the primary language. The parents of students eligible to participate in the required bilingual education program shall be informed of the benefits of the bilingual education or special language program and that it is an integral part of the school program.

"(e) All records obtained under this section may be retained by the language proficiency assessment committee for documentation purposes.

"(f) The school district may not refuse instruction in a language other than English to a student solely because the student has a handicapping condition.

"(g) With the approval of the school district and a student's parents, a student who does not have limited English proficiency may also participate in a bilingual education program. The number of participating students who do not have limited English proficiency may not exceed 40 percent of the students enrolled in the program.

"(h) A school district may transfer a student of limited English proficiency out of a bilingual education or special language program if the student is able to participate equally in an regular all-English instructional program as determined by:

"(1) tests administered at the end of each school year to determine the extent to which the student has developed oral and written language proficiency and specific language skills in both the student's primary language and English;

"(2) an achievement score at or above the 40th percentile in the reading and language arts sections of an English standardized test approved by the agency; and

"(3) other indications of a student's overall progress as determined by, but not limited to, criterion-referenced test scores, subjective teacher evaluation, and parental evaluation.

"(i) If later evidence suggests that a student who has been transferred out of a bilingual education or special language program has inadequate English proficiency and achievement, the language proficiency assessment committee may reenroll the student in the program. Classification of student for reenrollment must be based on the criteria required by this section.

"Section 21.456. FACILITIES; CLASSES.

(a) Bilingual education and special language programs shall be located in the regular public schools of the district rather than in separate facilities.

"(b) Students enrolled in bilingual education or a special language program shall be placed in classes with other students of approximately the same age and level of educational attainment. The school district shall insure that the instruction given each student is appropriate to his or her level of educational attainment, and the district shall keep adequate records of the educational level and progress of each student enrolled in the program.

"(c) The maximum student-teacher ratio shall be set by the agency and shall reflect the special educational needs of students enrolled in the programs.

230

"Section 21.457. COOPERATION AMONG DISTRICTS.

(a) A school district may join with any other district or districts to provide the bilingual education and special language programs required by this subchapter. The availability of the programs shall be publicized throughout the affected districts.

"(b) A school district may allow a nonresident student of limited English proficiency to enroll in or attend its bilingual education or special language programs if the student's district of residence provides no appropriate program. The tuition for the student shall be paid by the district in which the student resides.

"Section 21.458. PRESCHOOL, SUMMER SCHOOL, AND EXTENDED TIME PROGRAMS.

A school district may establish on a full- or part-time basis preschool, summer school, extended day, or extended week bilingual education or special language programs for students of limited English proficiency and may join with other districts in establishing the programs. The preschool or summer programs shall not be a substitute for programs required to be provided during the regular school year.

"Section 21.459. BILINGUAL EDUCATION AND SPECIAL LANGUAGE PROGRAM TEACHERS.

(a) The State Board of Education shall promulgate rules and regulations governing the issuance of teaching certificates with bilingual education endorsements to teachers who possess a speaking, reading, and writing ability in a language other than English in which bilingual education programs are offered and who meet the general requirements set out in Chapter 13 of this code. The State Board of Education shall also promulgate rules and regulations governing the issuance of teaching certificates with an endorsement for teaching English as a second language. The agency may issue emergency endorsements in bilingual education and in teaching English as a second language.

"(b) A teacher assigned to a bilingual education program must be appropriately certified by the agency for bilingual education.

"(c) A teacher assigned to an English as a second language or other special language program must be appropriately certified by the agency for English as a second language.

"(d) The minimum monthly base pay and increments for teaching experience for a bilingual education teacher or a special language program teacher are the same as for a classroom teacher with an equivalent degree under the Texas State Public Education Compensation Plan. The minimum annual salary for a bilingual education teacher or a special language program teacher is the monthly base salary, plus increments, multiplied by 10, 11, or 12, as applicable.

"(e) The district may compensate out of funds appropriated in Subsection (a) of Section 21.460 of this subchapter a bilingual education or special language teacher for participating in a continuing education program which is in addition to the teacher's regular contract. The continuing education program must be designed to gain advanced bilingual education or special language program endorsement or skills.

"(f) The agency shall be authorized to conduct or contract for teacher training for persons in the acquisition of endorsements in English as a second language. The agency shall determine the amount required for the implementation of this subsection.

"(g) The State Board of Education, through the Commission on Standards for the Teaching Profession, and the Coordinating Board, Texas College and University System, shall develop a comprehensive plan for meeting the teacher supply needs created by the programs outlined in this subchapter. The board shall submit a plan, which includes legislative recommendations, to the 68th Legislature in January, 1983.

"Section 21.460. ALLOTMENTS FOR OPERATIONAL EXPENSES AND TRANSPORTATION.

(a) Under the rules of the State Board of Education, each school district operating an approved bilingual education or special language program shall be allotted a special allowance equal to: (1) the number of limited English proficiency students enrolled in the bilingual education program multiplied by $50, or a greater amount as provided by the General Appropriations Act, and (2) the number of limited English proficiency students enrolled in the ESL or special language program multiplied by 25 percent of the bilingual education per pupil allocation. A district's bilingual education or special language allocation may be used for program and pupil evaluation and equipment, instructional materials and equipment, staff development, supplemental staff expenses, and other supplies required for quality instruction.

"(b) The cost of transporting bilingual education and special language program students from one campus to another within a district or from a sending district to an area vocational school or to an approved post-secondary institution under a contract for instruction approved by the agency shall be reimbursed based on the number of actual miles traveled times the district's official extracurricular travel per mile rate as set by their local board of trustees and approved by the agency.

"(c) The Foundation School Fund Budget Committee shall consider all amounts required for the operation of bilingual education and special language programs in estimating the funds needed for purposes of the Foundation School Program.

"Section 21.461. COMPLIANCE.

(a) The legislature recognizes that compliance with this subchapter is an imperative public necessity. Therefore, pursuant to the policy of the state, the agency shall monitor school district compliance with state rules by inspecting each school district at least every three years.

"(b) The areas to be monitored include:

"(1) program content and design;
"(2) program coverage;
"(3) identification procedures;
"(4) classification procedures;
"(5) staffing;
"(6) learning materials;
"(7) testing materials;
"(8) reclassification of students for either entry into regular classes conducted exclusively in English or for reentry into a bilingual education or special language program; and
"(9) activities of the language proficiency assessment committee.

"(c) Not later than the 30th day after the date of an on-site monitoring inspection, the agency shall report its findings to the

233

school district and to the division of accreditation.

"(d) The agency shall notify a school district found to be in noncompliance in writing not later than the 30th day after the date of the on-site monitoring. The district shall take immediate corrective action.

"(e) If a school district fails to or refuses to comply after proper notification, the agency shall apply sanctions, which may include removal of accreditation, loss of foundation school funds, or both.

"Section 21.462. LANGUAGE PROFICIENCY ASSESSMENT COMMITTEES.

(a) The State Board of Education by rule shall require districts that are required to offer bilingual education and special language programs to establish a language proficiency assessment committee.

"(b) Each committee shall be composed of members including but not limited to a professional bilingual educator, professional transitional language educator, a parent of a limited English proficiency student, and a campus administrator.

"(c) The language proficiency assessment committee shall:

"(1) review all pertinent information on limited English proficiency students, including the home language survey, the language proficiency tests in English and the primary language, each student's achievement in content areas, and each student's emotional and social attainment;

"(2) make recommendations concerning the most appropriate placement for the educational advancement of the limited English proficiency student after the elementary grades;

"(3) review each limited English proficiency student's progress at the end of the school year in order to determine future appropriate placement;

"(4) monitor the progress of students formerly classified as limited English proficiency who have exited from the bilingual education or special language program and, based on the information, designate the most appropriate placement for the student; and

234

"(5) determine the appropriateness of an extended program (beyond the regular school) depending on the needs of each limited English proficiency student.

"(d) The State Board of Education by rule may prescribe additional duties for language proficiency assessment committees.

"Section 21.463. APPEALS.

A parent of a student enrolled in a district offering bilingual education or special language programs may appeal to the commissioner of education under Section 11.13 of this code if the district fails to comply with the requirements of law or the rules of the State Board of Education. If the parent disagrees with the placement of the student in the program, he or she may appeal that decision to the local board of trustees. Appeals shall be in accordance with procedures adopted by the State Board of Education consistent with the appeal of contested cases under the Administrative Procedure and Texas Register Act, as amended (Article 6252-13a, Vernon's Texas Civil Statutes)."

SECTION 2. Bilingual education or special language programs as defined by this Act shall be taught in the public schools only for the purpose of assisting the learning ability of limited English proficiency students and to enhance the English language.

SECTION 3. This Act takes effect beginning with the 1981-1982 school year.

SECTION 4. The importance of this legislation and the crowded condition of the calendars in both houses create an emergency and an imperative public necessity that the constitutional rule requiring bills to be read on three several days in each house be suspended, and this rule is hereby suspended, and that this Act takes effect and be in force according to its terms, and it is so enacted.

SELECTED BIBLIOGRAPHY

Books and Articles

Abernathy, David, and Coombe, Trevor. "Education and Politics in Developing Countries," Harvard Educational Review, 35 (Summer 1965), 287-302.

Accomplishments of the 61st Legislature-Regular Session-January 14, 1969 to June 2, 1969. Austin: Texas Legislative Council, 1969.

Accomplishments of the 62nd Legislature-Regular and First Called Sessions-January 12, 1971 to May 31, 1971. Austin: Texas Legislative Council, 1971.

Accomplishments of the 63rd Legislature-Regular Session-January 9, 1973 to May 28, 1973. Austin: Texas Legislative Council, 1973.

Accomplishments of the 64th Legislature-Regular Session-January 14, 1975 to June 2, 1975. Austin: Texas Legislative Council, 1975.

Accomplishments of the 65th Legislature-Regular Session-January 11, 1977 to May 39, 1977. Austin: Texas Legislative Council, 1977.

Alexander, Kern; Corns, Ray; and McCann, Walter. Public School Law. St. Paul, Minnesota: West Publishing Co., 1969.

Allen, Hollis P. The Federal Government and Education. New York: McGraw-Hill, 1950.

Anderson, James E. Public Policy-making. New York: Praeger Publishers, 1975.

Andersson, Theodore. Foreign Languages in the Elementary School: A Struggle Against Mediocrity. Austin: The University of Texas Press, 1969.

Andersson, Theodore, and Boyer, Mildred. Bilingual Schooling in the United States, 2 Vols. Washington, D.C.: U.S. Government. Printing Office, 1970.

A Study of State Programs in Bilingual Education. "A Final Report on Their Status." Supporting Volumes I-IV. Washington, D.C.: Development Associates, Inc., 1521 New Hampshire Avenue, N.W. (20036), March, 1977.

Atkin, J. Myron. "On Looking Gift Horses in the Mouth," Educational Forum, 34 (November 1969), 9-20.

Babbidge, Homer D., Jr., and Rosenzweig, Robert M. The Federal Interest in Higher Education. New York: McGraw-Hill, 1962.

Bailey, Harry A., and Katz, Ellis, eds. Ethnic Group Politics. Columbus, Ohio: Charles E. Merrill Publishing Company, 1969.

Bailey, Stephen K. "The Office of Education and the Education Act of 1965." In The Politics of Education at the Local, State, and Federal Levels, pp. 357-383. Edited by Michael W. Kirst. Berkeley, California: McCutchan Publishing Corporation, 1970.

Bailey, Stephen K., and Mosher, Edith K. The Office of Education Administers a Law. Syracuse, New York: Syracuse University Press, 1968.

Bailey, Stephen K., et al. Schoolmen and Politics: A Study of State Aid to Education in the Northeast. Syracuse, New York: Syracuse University Press, 1962.

Banfield, Edward C., and Wilson, James Q. City Politics. Cambridge, Massachusetts: Harvard University Press, 1963.

Barkin, David, and Hettich, Walter. The Elementary and Secondary Educational Act: A Distributional Analysis. St. Louis, Missouri: Washington University Press, 1968.

Bauer, Raymond A.; Pool, Ithiel de Sola; and Dexter, Lewis Anthony. American Business and Public Policy. New York: Atherton Press, 1968.

Benton, Wilbourn, E. Texas: Its Government and Politics. 2nd ed. Englewood Cliffs, New Jersey: Prentice-Hall, Inc., 1966.

Berke, Joel S., and Kirst, Michael W. Federal Aid to Education: Who Benefits? Who Governs? Lexington, Kentucky: D. C. Heath and Company, 1972.

Bernal, Joe Juarez. Legislative Action Network Manual. Texas Association for Bilingual Education: San Antonio, Texas, 1981-82.

Bernal, Joe Juarez. "A Study of Bilingual Bicultural Education: Contrasting Influences on Texas Legislators With Results of an Attitudinal Survey of the Members of the 64th Legislature." Ph.D. dissertation. The University of Texas at Austin, 1978.

Bernal, Joseph J. "The Role of the State." In *Educating the Mexican-American*. Eds., Henry Sioux Johnson and William J. Hernandez, pp. 363-368. Valley Forge, Pennsylvania: Judson Press, 1970.

Bilingual-Bicultural Education: A Handbook for Attorneys and Community Workers. Cambridge, Massachusetts: Center for Law and Education, 1975.

Bilingual Education in Texas. House Study Group. Special Legislative Report Number 78. Texas House of Representatives, Austin, Texas, 1981.

Borg, Walter R., and Gall, Meredith D. *Educational Research*. 2nd ed. New York: David Mckay Company, 1971.

Bowhay, James H., and Thrall, Virginia D. *State Legislative Appropriations Process*. Lexington, Kentucky: Council of State Governments and National Conference of State Legislatures, 1975.

Boyd, William Lowe. "The Changing Politics of Curriculum Policy-Making for American Schools," *Review of Educational Research*, 48, No. 4 (Fall 1978), 577-628.

Callahan, Raymond E. *Education and the Cult of Efficiency*. Chicago: The University of Chicago Press, 1962.

Cardenas, Jose A.; Bernal, Joe J.; and Kean, William. *Bilingual Education Cost Analysis*. San Antonio, Texas: Intercultural Development Research Association, 1976.

Carter, Thomas P. *Mexican Americans in School: A History of Educational Neglect*. New York: College Entrance Examination Board, 1970.

Casso, Henry J. *Bilingual-Bicultural Education and Teacher Training*. Washington, D.C.: National Education Association, 1976.

Castro, Tony. "A Third Party Is Born," *Race Relations Reporter*, 4 (January 1973), 13-17.

The Challenge and the Chance (Research Report Volume II, Public Education in Texas--Program Evaluation, 1969). Austin, Texas: Governor's Committee on Public School Education, 1968.

Clinchy, Jr., Everett Ross. *Equality of Opportunity for Latin-Americans in Texas*. New York: Arno Press, 1974.

Curtis, Tom. "Raza Desunida." In Texas Monthly's Political Leader, 1st ed., pp. 38-42. Austin, Texas: Sterling Swift Publishing Company, 1978.

Deaton, Charles. The Year They Threw the Rascals Out. Austin, Texas: Shoal Creek Publishers, Inc., 1973.

Dinnerstein, Leonard, and Reimers, David M. Ethnic Americans. New York: Dodd, Mead and Company, 1975.

Dror, Yehezkel. Public Policymaking Reexamined. San Francisco: Chandler Publishing Company, 1968.

Dye, Thomas R. Policy Analysis. University, Alabama: The University of Alabama Press, 1976.

Dye, Thomas R. Politics in States and Communities, 3rd ed. Englewood Cliffs, New Jersey: Prentice-Hall, Inc., 1977.

Dye, Thomas R. Understanding Public Policy. Englewood Cliffs, New Jersey: Prentice-Hall, Inc., 1978.

Easton, David. "An Approach to the Analysis of Political Systems," World Politics, IX (April 1957), 383-400.

Easton, David. A Framework for Political Analysis. Englewood Cliffs, New Jersey: Prentice-Hall, Inc., 1965.

Easton, David. A Systems Analysis of Political Life. New York: John Wiley and Sons, Inc., 1965.

Eckstein, Harry, and Apter, David E. Comparative Politics. New York: The Free Press of Glencoe, 1963.

Education in the States: Historical Development and Outlook. Washington, D.C.: National Education Association, 1969.

Eidenberg, Eugene, and Morey, Roy D. An Act of Congress: The Legislative Process in the Making of Educational Policy. New York: W. W. Norton, 1969.

Elazar, Daniel. American Federalism: A View from the States. New York: T. Y. Crowell Company, 1966.

Eliot, Thomas H. "Toward an Understanding of Public School Politics," American Political Science Review, 53 (December 1959), 1032-1051.

Epstein, Noel. Language, Ethnicity, and the Schools. The George Washington University: Institute for Educational Leadership, 1977.

240

Fishman, Joshua A. Language Loyalty in the United States. The
     Hague: Mouton and Company, 1966.

Fishman, Joshua A. "Bilingual Education in a Sociolinguistic
     Perspective." In The Language Education of Minority Chil-
     dren, pp. 83-93. Edited by Bernard Spolsky. Rowley: New-
     bury House, 1972.

Fishman, Joshua A. "The Social Science Perspective." In Bilin-
     gual Education: Current Perspectives Volume I. Arlington,
     Virginia: Center for Applied Linguistics, 1977.

Gambone, James V. "Bilingual-Bicultural Educational Civil Rights:
     The May 25th Memorandum and Oppressive School Practices."
     Ph.D. dissertation, University of New Mexico, 1973.

Garcia, Chris. Political Socialization of Chicano Children. New
     York: Praeger, 1973.

Garcia, F. C. ed. Chicano Politics. New York: M.S.S. Informa-
     tion Corp., 1973.

Gerry, Martin H. "Cultural Freedom in the Schools: The Right of
     Mexican American Children to Succeed." In Mexican-Americans
     and Educational Change, pp. 226-254. Eds. Alfredo Castaneda,
     et al. New York: Arno Press, 1974.

Geske, Terry G. "The Politics of Reforming School Finance in Wis-
     consin." Ph.D. dissertation, University of Wisconsin, 1975.

General Laws of the State of Texas, Regular Session, 29th Legis-
     lature, 1905.

General and Special Laws of the State of Texas, Fourth Called
     Session, 35th Legislature, 1918.

General and Special Laws of the State of Texas, Regular Session,
     40th Legislature, 1927.

General and Special Laws of Texas, Regular Session, 63rd Legisla-
     ture, 1973.

General and Special Laws of the State of Texas, Regular Session,
     64th Legislature, 1975.

Glazer, Nathan, and Moynihan, Daniel Patrick. Beyond the Melting
     Pot, 2nd ed. Cambridge, Massachusetts: The M.I.T. Press,
     1970.

241

Gordon, Milton M. <u>Assimilation in American Life</u>. New York: Oxford University Press, 1964.

Gordy, Margaret S. "The Massachusetts Story," <u>Today's Education</u>, January-February 1975, pp. 79-80.

Grebler, Leo; Moore, Joan W.; and Guzman, Ralph C. <u>The Mexican-American People</u>. New York: The Free Press, 1970.

Handlin, Oscar. "The Immigrant and American Politics." In <u>Foreign Influences in American Life</u>. Edited by David F. Bowers. Princeton, New Jersey: Princeton University Press, 1944.

Hardgrave, Jr., Robert L., and Hinojosa, Santiago. <u>The Politics of Bilingual Education: A Study of Four Southwest Texas Communities</u>. Manchaca, Texas: Sterling Swift Publishing Company, 1975.

Harman, G. S. <u>The Politics of Education</u>. St. Lucia, Australia: University of Queensland Press, 1974.

Hawkins, Brett W., and Lorinskas, Robert A. <u>The Ethnic Factor in American Politics</u>. Columbus, Ohio: Merrill, 1970.

Hays, Samuel P. "The Politics of Reform in Municipal Government in the Progressive Era," <u>Pacific Northwest Quarterly</u>, 55 (Octover 1964), 157-169.

Hofstadter, Richard. <u>The Age of Reform</u>. New York: Alfred A. Knopf, 1955.

Hurwitz, Jr., Emanuel, and Tesconi, Jr., Charles A. <u>Challenges to Education</u>. New York: Dodd, Mead and Company, 1972.

Iannaccone, Laurence. <u>Politics of Education</u>. New York: Center for Applied Research in Education, Inc., 1967.

Iannaccone, Laurence, and Lutz, Frank W. <u>Politics, Power, and Policy</u>. Columbus, Ohio: Charles E. Merrill Publishing Company, 1970.

James, Tom. "Teachers, State Politics, and the Making of Educational Policy," <u>Phi Delta Kappan</u>, 58 (October 1976), 165-168.

Johnson, Henry Sioux, and Hernandez, William J. eds. <u>Educating the Mexican American</u>. Valley Forge: Judson Press, 1970.

Katz, Harvey. <u>Shadow on the Alamo</u>. Garden City, New York: Doubleday & Company, 1971.

Kerlinger, Fred N. Foundations of Behavioral Research, 2nd ed. New York: Holt, Rinehart and Winston, Inc., 1973.

Key, Jr., V. O. Public Opinion and American Democracy. New York: Alfred A. Knopf, 1961.

Key, Jr., V. O. Southern Politics in State and Nation. New York: Alfred A. Knopf, 1949.

Kinch, Jr., Sam, and Proctor, Ben. Texas Under a Cloud: Story of the Texas Stock Fraud Scandal. Austin, Texas: Jenkins Publishing Co., 1972.

Kirp, David L. "Law, Politics, and Equal Educational Opportunity: The Limits of Judicial Involvement," Harvard Educational Review, 47 (May 1977), 117-137.

Kirst, Michael W., and Mosher, Edith K. "Politics of Education," Review of Educational Research, 39 (December 1969), 623-639.

Kirst, Michael W. State, School, and Politics. Lexington, Kentucky: D. C. Heath and Company, 1972.

Kirst, Michael W. "The Politics of Federal Aid to Education in Texas." In Federal Aid to Education: Who Benefits? Who Governs? pp. 235-275. Edited by Joel S. Berke and Michael W. Kirst. Lexington, Kentucky: D. C. Heath and Company, 1972.

Kloss, Heinz. The American Bilingual Tradition. Rowley: Newbury House Publishers, Inc., 1977.

Krug, Mark. The Melting of the Ethnics. Bloomington, Indiana: Phi Delta Kappa, 1976.

Leibowitz, Arnold H. Educational Policy and Political Acceptance: The Imposition of English as the Language of Instruction in American Schools. Washington, D.C.: Center for Applied Linguistics, 1971.

Levy, Mark R., and Kramer, Michael S. The Ethnic Factor: How America's Minorities Decide Elections. New York: Simon and Shuster, 1972.

Lindblom, Charles E. The Policy-making Process. Englewood Cliffs, New Jersey: Prentice-Hall, Inc., 1968.

Litt, Edgar. Ethnic Politics in American Life. Glenview, Illinois: Scott, Foresman, 1970.

243

Lockard, Duane. _New England State Politics_. Princeton, New Jersey: Princeton University Press, 1959.

Lockard, Duane. _The Politics of State and Local Government_, 2nd ed. New York: The Macmillan Company, 1969.

Mackey, William Francis, and Beebe, Von Nieda. _Bilingual Schools for a Bicultural Community_. Rowley, Massachusetts: Newbury House Publishers, Inc., 1977.

Mann, Dale. _Policy Decision-making in Education_. New York: Teachers College Press, 1975.

Masters, Nicholas A.; Salisbury, Robert H.; and Eliot, Thomas H. _State Politics and the Public Schools_. New York: Alfred A. Knopf, 1964.

Maxwell, Jane Carlisle. _Litigation of Texas Election Laws: Toward Democratization of the Political Process_. Austin, Texas: The University of Texas at Austin, 1972.

McClesky, Clifton. _The Government and Politics of Texas_, 2nd ed. Boston: Little, Brown and Company, 1966.

McClesky, Clifton, and Merrill, Bruce. "Mexican American Political Behavior in Texas," _Social Science Quarterly_, 51 (September 1970), 785-797.

McLaughlin, Milbrey Wallin. _Evaluation and Reform: The Elementary and Secondary Education Act of 1965, Title I_. Cambridge, Massachusetts: Ballinger Publishing Company, 1975.

McWilliams, Carey. _North from Mexico_. New York: Greenwood Press, 1968.

Meranto, Philip. _The Politics of Federal Aid to Education in 1965: A Study in Political Innovation_. Syracuse, New York: Syracuse University Press, 1967.

Milstein, Mike M. "The Roles of the States and the Federal Government in Metropolitan Educational Organization," _Urban Education_, 5 (July 1970), 179-198.

Milstein, Mike M., and Jennings, Robert E. _Educational Policy-making and the State Legislature_. New York: Praeger Publishers, 1973.

Montoya, Honorable Joseph M. "Bilingual-Bicultural Education: Making Equal Educational Opportunities Available to National Origin Minority Students," _The Georgetown Law Journal_, 61 (March 1973), 990-1007.

Mosher, Edith K., and Wagoner, Jr., Jennings L. eds. The Changing Politics of Education. Berkeley, California: McCutchan Publishing Corporation, 1978.

Moya, Frank. "Bilingual Battling," Nuestro, October 1977, p. 52.

Murphy, Jerome T. "Title I of ESEA: The Politics of Implementing Federal Education Reform," Harvard Educational Review, 41 (February 1971), 64-92.

Nimmo, Dan, and Oden, William. The Texas Political System. Englewood Cliffs, New Jersey: Prentice-Hall, Inc., 1971.

Navarro, Armando. "The Evolution of Chicano Politics," Aztlan, 5 (Spring and Fall 1974), 57-83.

Nelson, Eugene. "Huelga: New Goals for Labor," The Nation, June 1967, pp. 724-725.

Ogletree, Earl J., and Garcia, David, eds. Education of the Spanish-Speaking Urban Child. Springfield, Illinois: Charles C. Thomas, 1975.

Orfield, Gary. Must We Bus? Segregated Schools and National Policy. Washington, D.C.: The Brookings Institution, 1978.

Ortego, Philip. "The Minority on the Border-Cabinet Meeting in El Paso," The Nation, December 1967, pp. 624-627.

Parenti, Michael. "Ethnic Politics and the Persistence of Ethnic Identity," American Political Social Science Review, 61 (September 1967), 717-726.

Pettit, Lawrence K. "The Policy Process in Congress: Passing the Higher Education Academic Facilities Act of 1963." Ph.D. dissertation, University of Wisconsin, 1965.

Pettus, Beryl E., and Bland, Randall W. Texas Government Today. Homewood, Illinois: The Dorsey Press, 1976.

Phillips, Bernard S. Social Research. New York: The Macmillan Company, 1966.

Rangel, Jorge C., and Alcala, Carlos M. "Project Report: De Jure Segregation of Chicanos in Texas," Harvard Civil Rights-Civil Liberties Law Review, 7 (March 1972), 307-391.

Recommendations for Legislative Consideration on Public Education in Texas. Austin: Texas Education Agency, 1968, 1970, 1972.

Recommendations for Legislative Consideration in Texas. Austin, Texas: Texas Education Agency, 1974, 1976, 1978.

Reform Legislation: Text, Analysis, and Forms. Austin: Texas Legislative Council, November, 1973.

Reveles, Robert A. "Biculturalism and the United States Congress: The Dynamics of Political Change." In Mexican-Americans and Educational Change, pp. 205-225. Eds. Alfredo Castaneda, et al. New York: Arno Press, 1974.

Rogler, Lloyd. "The Changing Role of a Political Boss in a Puerto Rican Community," American Sociological Review, 39 (February 1974), 57-67.

Rosenbaum, Robert J. "History: Hindrance to Unity," Race Relations Reporter, 4 (July 1973), 29-33.

Rosenthal, Alan. Legislative Performance in the States. Explorations of Committee Behavior. New York: The Free Press, 1974.

Ross, Robert S. Public Choice and Public Policy. Chicago: Markham Publishing Company, 1971.

Salisbury, Robert H. "State Politics and Education." In Politics in the American States, pp. 331-369. Edited by Herbert Jacob and Kenneth N. Vines. Boston: Little, Brown and Company, 1965.

Sanchez, George I. "History, Culture, and Education." In The Changing Mexican-American, pp. 24-52. Edited by Rudolph Gomez. El Paso, Texas: University of El Paso, 1972.

Sanchez, Gilbert. "An Analysis of the Bilingual Education Act." Ed.D. dissertation, University of Massachusetts, 1973.

Schneider, Susan Gilbert. Revolution, Reaction or Reform: The 1974 Bilingual Education Act. New York: Las Americas, 1976.

Shelton, Edgar Greer. "Political Conditions Among Texas Mexicans Along the Rio Grande." Thesis, University of Texas, Austin, 1946.

Sixty-fifth Legislature (Regular Session). House Bill No. 510. General Appropriations Bill for 1978-79 Fiscal Years, Beginning September 1, 1977.

Smith, Timothy L. "Immigrant Social Aspirations and American Education, 1880-1930," American Quarterly, 21 (Fall 1969), 523-543.

Summary of Enactments. 66th Legislature Regular Session-January 9, 1979 to May 28, 1979. Austin, Texas: Texas Legislative Council, 1979.

Summary of Enactments. 67th Legislature Regular and First Called Sessions. January 13, 1981 to June 1, 1981. Austin, Texas: Texas Legislative Council, 1981.

Sundquist, James L. "For the Young, Schools." In The Politics of Education at the Local, State and Federal Levels, pp. 326-356. Edited by Michael W. Kirst. Berkeley, California: McCutchan Publishing Corporation, 1970.

Task Force on Bilinugal Education. Executive Order WPC-20. The State of Texas Executive Department, Office of the Governor: Austin, Texas, March 10, 1981.

Teitelbaum, Herbert, and Hiller, Richard J. "Bilingual Education: The Legal Mandate," Harvard Educational Review, 47 (May 1977), 138-170.

Texas Education Agency. A Guide for Implementing International Education Programs. Austin, Texas, 1970.

Texas Education Agency. Forty-sixth Biennial Report to the Governor and Legislature, 1968-1970: Commitment to Education, Bulletin No. 705, Austin, Texas, 1970.

Texas Education Agency. Forty-seventh Biennial Report to the Governor and Legislature, 1970-72: Years of Transition. Austin, Texas, 1972.

Texas Education Agency. Forty-eighth Biennial Report to the Governor and Legislature, 1972-74: Public School Education in Texas, Bulletin No. 751. Austin, Texas, 1974.

Texas Education Agency. Official Agenda of State Board of Education. Austin, Texas, 1968-1970.

Texas Education Agency. State Board of Education Action. Policy 3252, Bilingual Education. Austin, Texas: November 28, 1978.

Texas Education Agency. State Board of Education Action. Proposed Amendment to Policy 3252, Bilingual Education. Austin, Texas: June 10, 1978.

Texas Education Agency. <u>Tentative Course of Study for the Teaching of Spanish in Grades 3 to 8 Inclusive.</u> Austin, Texas: State Superintendent of Public Instruction, #426, February 1, 1943.

Texas, <u>Executive Budget for 1974-1975 Biennium.</u> Submitted to the Sixty-Third Legislature. Austin, Texas: Legislative Budget Board, 1973.

Texas, House of Representatives. <u>Journal of the House of Representatives of the Regular Session of the Sixtieth Legislature</u> (Volumes I & II). Austin, Texas, 1967.

Texas, House of Representatives. <u>Journal of the House of Representatives of the Regular Session of the Sixty-First Legislature</u> (Volumes I & II). Austin, Texas, 1969.

Texas, House of Representatives. <u>Journal of the House of Representatives of the Regular Session of the Sixty-Second Legislature</u> (Volumes I, II, III and IV). Austin, Texas, 1971.

Texas, House of Representatives. <u>Journal of the House of Representatives of the Regular Session of the Sixty-Third Legislature</u> (Volumes I, II, & III). Austin, Texas, 1973.

Texas, House of Representatives. <u>Journal of the House of Representatives of the Regular Session of the Sixty-fourth Legislature</u> (Volumes I, II, III). Austin, Texas, 1975.

Texas, House of Representatives. <u>Journal of the Regular Session of the Sixty-fifth Legislature</u> (Volumes I, II, III). Austin, Texas, 1977.

<u>Texas Legislative Manual.</u> Austin, Texas: Legislative Council, 1971.

<u>Texas Outlook.</u> "Another Lanugage (Bilingualism)." November, 1976, pp. 31-36.

<u>Texas Public Schools 1854-1954: Centennial Handbook.</u> Austin, Texas Education Agency, 1954.

Texas, Senate. <u>Journal of the Senate of the State of Texas Sixty-First Legislature Regular Session</u> (Volumes I & II). Austin, Texas: Von Boeckman-Jones Co., 1971.

Texas, Senate. <u>Journal of the Senate of the State of Texas Third Called Session of the Sixty-Second Legislature.</u> Austin, Texas: Von Boeckman-Jones Co., 1971.

Texas, Senate. Journal of the Senate of the State of Texas Sixty-Third Legislature Regular Session (Volumes I & II). Austin, Texas: Texas State Senate, 1973.

Texas, Senate. Journal of the State of Texas Sixty-Fourth Legislature Regular Session (Volumes I & II). Austin, Texas: Texas State Senate, 1975.

Texas, Senate. Journal of the State of Texas Sixty-Fifth Legislature Regular Session (Volumes I & II). Austin, Texas: Texas State Senate, 1977.

Texas, Senate. Journal of the State of Texas Sixty-Sixth Legislature Regular Session (Volumes I, II & III). Austin, Texas: Texas State Senate, 1979.

Tiedt, Sidney W. The Role of the Federal Government in Education. New York: Oxford University Press, 1966.

Truan, Carlos F. "Community Action Programs." In The Mexican American: A New Focus on Opportunity, pp. 199-202. Washington, D.C.: Inter-Agency Committee on Mexican American Affairs, 1967.

Truan, Carlos F. "Legislation and Bilingual Education." In Proceedings: National Conference on Bilingual Education-April 14-15, 1972, pp. 235-239. Austin, Taxas: Dissemination Center for Bilingual Bicultural Education, 1972.

Tyack, David B. The One Best System. Cambridge, Massachusetts; Harvard University Press, 1974.

Ukeles, Jacob B. "Policy Analysis: Myth or Reality," Public Administration Review, 37 (May-June 1977), 223-228.

United States Commission on Civil Rights, Mexican American Education Study, 6 volumes. Washington, D.C.: Government Printing Office, 1971-1974.

United States Congress, 91st, 2nd session, Senate Select Committee on Equal Educational Opportunity, Equal Educational Opportunity: Hearings Part 4, Mexican American Education. Washington, D.C.: Government Printing Office, 1967.

United States Congress, 90th, 1st session, Senate Committee on Labor and Public Welfare, Special Subcommittee on Bilingual Education, Bilingual Education Hearings: Part I & II. Washington, D.C.: Government Printing Office, 1975.

United States Commission on Civil Rights. _A Better Chance to Learn: Bilingual-Bicultural Education_. Publication Number 51. Washington, D.C.: Government Printing Office, 1968.

United States Commission on Civil Rights. _Hearings Held in San Antonio, December 9-14, 1968_. Washington, D.C.: Government Printing Office, 1968.

United States Commission on Civil Rights. _Mexican American Education in Texas: A Function of Wealth_. Report IV of the Mexican American Study. Washington, D.C.: Government Printing Office, 1972.

Untermeyer, Chase. "The Politics of Outsiders." In _Texas Monthly's Political Reader_, 1st ed., pp. 43-46. Austin, Texas: Sterling Swift Publishing Company, 1978.

Usdan, Michael D. _The Political Power of Education in New York State_. New York: Teachers College, 1963.

Usdan, Michael D., et al. _Education and State Politics_. New York: Teachers College Press, 1969.

Weeks, O. Douglas. "The League of United Laint-American Citizens: A Texas-Mexican Civic Organization," _The Southwestern Political and Social Science Quarterly_, 10 (December 1929), 257-278.

Weinberg, Meyer. _A Chance to Learn_. Cambridge, Massachusetts: Cambridge University Press, 1977.

Welch, Susan; Comer, John; and Steinman, Michael. "Political Participation Among Mexican Americans: An Exploratory Examination," _Social Science Quarterly_, 51 (September 1970), 799-813.

Wirt, Frederick M. "Reassessment Needs in the Study of the Politics of Education," _Teachers College Record_, 78 (May 1977), 401-412.

Wirt, Frederick M., and Kirst, Michael A., eds. _Political and Social Foundations of Education_. Berkeley, California: McCutchan Publishing Corporation, 1975.

Wirth, Louis. _The Ghetto_. Chicago: Chicago University Press, 1928.

Zamora, Jesus Ernesto. "A Survey of Texas' Bilingual-Bicultural Education Programs." Ph.D. dissertation, the University of Texas at Austin, 1977.

Periodicals

"Bilingual Education Push Gains," San Antonio Light, 16 April 1972, p. 5.

"An Appalling Waste," The Texas Observer, 23 August 1963, p. 1.

"Children Show Results of Bilingual Ed," The Texas Outlook, 7 July 1971, p. 19.
"Boost for Adult Education," The Texas Outlook, January 1973, p. 46.

"Bilingual Education," The New Republic, October 1967, pp. 9-10.

"LULAC's Approve Valley Strike Aid," San Antonio News, 18 July 1966, p. 10.

"Cities Vie for New Schools," The Texas Observer, 10 January 1969, p. 11.

"Migrant Students Display Skills in Two Languages," San Antonio Express, 7 April 1971, p. 10.

"Mr. Speaker Daniel," The Texas Observer, 2 February 1973, p. 1.

"New Leaders of TACE Named at Fall Conference," The Texas Outlook, January 1972, p. 43.

"Truan Endorses Plea for More Bilingual Education Funds," San Antonio Express, 17 June 1972, p. 13.

"The New Establishment," The Texas Observer, 10 January 1968, p. 7.

"Trying Again on Bilingual Ed.," The Texas Observer, 30 March 1973, p. 10.

"U.S. Court Revises Texas Districts," New York Times, 23 January 1972, p. 30.

"Voting Residency Rule Cut to 30 Days in Texas," New York Times, 1 April 1972, p. 8.

Court Cases

Aspira of New York, Inc., et al. v. Board of Education. Consent
Decree (S.D.N.Y. August 29, 1974).

Brown v. Board of Education of Topeka, Kansas, 347 U.S. 483, 74
S.Ct. 686 (1954).

Brown v. Board of Education of Topeka, Kansas, 349 U.S. 294, 75
S.Ct. 753 (1977).

Castaneda v. Pickard, (648 F. 2d. 989, 5th Cir. 1981).

Farrington v. Tokushige, 273 U.S. 284 (1927).

Lau v. Nichols, 414 U.S. 563, 94 S.Ct. 786 (1974).

Meyer v. Nebraska, 262 U.S. 390 (1923).

Mo Hock Ke Lok Po v. Stainback, District Court Hawaii, 74 F. Supp.
852 (1944).

Serrano v. Priest, 5 Cal. 3d 584, 96 Cal.Rptr. 601, 487 P2d 1241
(1971).

United States v. Gregory Portland Independent School District,
'498 F. Supp. 1356; E.D. Tex. 1980; Rev'd, 654 F. 2nd. 989
(5th Cir. 1981).

United States v. State of Texas, (Nos. 81-2196, 81-2310, and
81-2330. 5th Cir., July 12, 1982).

United States v. State of Texas, (Civil Action Suit Number 5281
Bilingual Education. January 9, 1981.)

United States v. Texas, (321 F. Supplement 1043).

University of California Regents v. Bakke, (438 U.S. 265).

Wasington v. Davis, (426 U.S. 229).

Yu Cong Eng v. Trinidad, 271 U.S. 500 (1925).